名著名译英汉对照读本

AN IDEAL HUSBAND
理想丈夫

〔英〕奥斯卡·王尔德 著
文心 译

商务印书馆
The Commercial Press

2016年·北京

图书在版编目(CIP)数据

理想丈夫:英汉对照/(英)王尔德(Wilde, O.)著;
文心译.—北京:商务印书馆,2012(2016.3重印)
(名著名译英汉对照读本丛书)
ISBN 978-7-100-07593-0

Ⅰ.①理… Ⅱ.①王…②文… Ⅲ.①英语—汉语—
对照读物②戏剧—剧本—英国—近代 Ⅳ.①H319.4:I

中国版本图书馆 CIP 数据核字(2010)第 250231 号

所有权利保留。
未经许可,不得以任何方式使用。

名著名译英汉对照读本
理 想 丈 夫
〔英〕奥斯卡·王尔德 著
文心 译

商 务 印 书 馆 出 版
(北京王府井大街36号 邮政编码 100710)
商 务 印 书 馆 发 行
北 京 冠 中 印 刷 厂 印 刷
ISBN 978-7-100-07593-0

2012年10月第1版 开本 850×1168 1/32
2016年3月北京第2次印刷 印张 8⅛
定价:28.00元

前　　言

　　这套丛书的名字比较长：名著名译英汉对照读本。还应该长一点儿才更准确，比如叫做"名著名译英汉对照翻译教程读本"，因为这更接近我们费尽周折编出这套书的全部用意和目的。下面简单地说明一下。

　　名著。外国文学名著成千上万，按说选出十种八种，做成英汉对照读物，奉献给读者，不应该是难事。但凡事怕讲条件。英汉对照读物不宜太长，最好在八九万字的篇幅；体裁要丰富，至少戏剧、长篇和短篇小说要照顾到；英语难易要兼顾，各个时期尽量不漏，写作风格多样化；译文优秀，确实可以作为翻译教程式的读本……这么多条件相加，名著挑选起来就有相当难度了。多亏了各家老字号出版社几十年来出版的外国文化和文学翻译作品十分丰厚，虽然花费了不少力气，但结果相当令人满意。且看我们所选作品的书目：剧本有《哈姆莱特》、《凯撒和克莉奥佩特拉》和《理想丈夫》；长篇小说有《名利场》和《简·爱》；中篇小说有《伊坦·弗洛美》和《黑暗的心》；随笔有《一间自己的房间》；短篇小说有《马克·吐温短篇小说选》和《欧·亨利短篇小说选》。

　　三个戏剧。流传下来的优秀戏剧作品是西方文学的重要组成部分。阅读西方文学作品，必须阅读优秀的戏剧作品。另外，戏剧是西方文学的重要形式之一。在小说形式没有出现之前，戏剧是文艺创作中最具包容量的形式。小

I

说出现后，戏剧除了不断丰富自己，仍然保持着所有文艺创作形式所无法取代的优势，那就是舞台演出。小说可以朗读，但是无法在舞台上演出。要想登台演出，还得改编成剧本。因此，戏剧仍然是阅读的主要对象。《哈姆莱特》不仅是莎士比亚的扛鼎之作，也是所有剧本中公认的代表之作，其深度、广度和厚度，只有亲自阅读才能领会。莎士比亚是戏剧发展史上的一座山，后来者只有仰望的，没有叫板的，偏偏出了个萧伯纳要与他试比高低。萧伯纳发愤读书（包括不列颠百科全书的全部），勤奋写作（共写了五十余部），还创办"费边社"。莎士比亚有个名剧叫《安东尼与克莉奥佩特拉》，写古罗马人的人性和爱情。萧伯纳说，不，古人更喜欢政治，不信你看我写的《凯撒和克莉奥佩特拉》。后者也成了名剧，还拍成了电影，成为电影经典。才子作家奥斯卡·王尔德却说，爱情和政治都重要，唯美主义更重要，我来写一出唯美剧本《理想丈夫》让你们看看。于是，《理想丈夫》集爱情、政治讽刺与社会风俗于一体，上演时轰动一时，也成了名剧。

　　长篇。为了适合英汉对照，我们只能选长篇小说名著的若干章节。萨克雷的《名利场》和夏洛特·勃朗特的《简·爱》我们各选了其中的八九万字，首先是因为这两部作品在西方文学史上具有独一无二的地位，其次是因为这个译本已经成了翻译外国文学作品的范本。所选的几章当然是其中最精彩的，完全可以当做短篇小说看，却又大体上窥见了全书中的几个主人公。萨克雷生前十分走红，许多后起作家都对他十分仰慕，夏洛特·勃朗特就是他的追星族，醉心文学，终写出一部《简·爱》献给他，勃朗特也从此成名。

　　两个中篇。实际上，英语文学里没有中篇小说这个明确概念。三四万字的短篇仍视为短篇,五六万字的作品就可以算作小长篇了。这里所选的两个中篇分别在八九万字,已经是名副其实的长篇了。康拉德的《黑暗的心》是公认的二十世纪文学经典,剥葱皮一样把殖民主义者的心态一层层刻画得淋漓尽致,其影响之大,先是在二十世纪三四十年代直接触动著名诗人托马斯·艾略特写出了《荒原》,后又在八十年代造就了轰动全球的电影大片《现代启示录》。美国心理派女作家伊迪丝·华顿以特有的细腻和力量,在她的最负盛名的《伊坦·弗洛美》里,写出了当初美国从农业国转向工业国时产生的物质问题和道德问题。

一则随笔。随笔是英语文学中非常重要的部分,但译得好的很少,只选了一篇。《一间自己的房间》,是英国女作家弗吉尼亚·吴尔夫的著名随笔,从一个思想相对开明的知识女性角度,把女性在社会上的地位问题进行了令人信服的阐述,被后来者誉为女性解放的宣言书。

最后是两位在中国读者群里最有声望的美国作家——马克·吐温和欧·亨利——的短篇小说选。马克·吐温的幽默讽刺和欧·亨利的巧妙构思,使他们跻身于世界文坛。我们选收时尽量照顾他们的创作特色,例如马克·吐温的《一张百万英镑钞票》和《腐蚀了哈德利堡镇居民的人》,欧·亨利的《麦琪的礼物》、《最后的常春藤叶》和《警察和赞美诗》,等等。

名译。"名译"的基点是译作出版后,经过一段时间考验,已经得到读者和专家的认可。大部分名译出自名家之手,如朱生豪、吕叔湘、杨宪益、杨必、黄雨石,自然算得上"名译"了。不过,这套丛书还特别强调了新中国成立以后文学翻译的历史与传统,变化与取向。新中国成立前的文学翻译是八仙过海各显神通，虽然不乏优秀的翻译作品，但是自由发挥随意删改的译风也确实存在，甚至在一些翻译作品中相当厉害。近几十年来，经过几代编辑的编辑和修订，共同努力，留住了一批新中国成立前的翻译作品，如朱生豪的《莎士比亚戏剧集》，吕叔湘的《伊坦·弗洛美》，徐霞村的《鲁滨孙飘流记》，等等。更重要的是通过淘汰、修改和碰撞，翻译界渐渐产生共识，形成了一种认真、严谨、准确、精当的译文标准取向，与当代白话文更加接轨了。读者通过每一种书的千把字的"翻译谈"，完全可以体会到这种变化和历史。

在这十种翻译作品里，《哈姆莱特》、《伊坦·弗洛美》、《名利场》可归为一类。它们更注重段落的信息，有时不惜打乱一点儿句序，力求更传神，更口语化，更接近白话文小说的味道与表达。译者能做到这点，靠的是雄厚的英文和汉语底子，尤其汉语。《凯撒和克莉奥佩特拉》是一种游刃有余的翻译，两种文字都照顾得很好；杨宪益、朱光潜、杨周翰、潘家洵，都算得上这种优秀的翻译的代表。《马克·吐温短篇小说选》的翻译，是一种更容易反映作者写作风格的译文。《简·爱》是目前英语作品之中汉译版本最多的。吴钧燮的译本是较早的，超过了过去的译本，后来的译本又无一可及，从此不难看出翻译不是谁都能做好的。《欧·亨利短篇小说选》、《一间自己的房间》、《黑暗的心》和《理想丈夫》的译文简朴、清顺，更贴近原文的原貌，代表了今后译文的走向。

英汉对照。译家和编辑有一句大白话：译文和原文对不上（或对得上）。这话往往代表一种翻译的优劣标准。这个系列的所有翻译都是"对得上的"，尽管程度上会出现差别。但是读者在对照英文和中文的时候，一定要琢磨一下，消化一下，发现有"对不上的"也切不要立即下结论，最好回头看看书前的那篇千把字的"翻译谈"，然后再下结论。你这样做了，无论发现什么结果，都会产生一种意想不到的飞跃，英文的和中文的。

读本。既然是读本，首先考虑的是为读者服务。无论英文中文，均有难易之分。按我们的设想，先读短篇，而后中篇，然后长篇，最后是戏剧。但是如果你只读英语，参考译文，那么先读戏剧中的对话倒是一个提高英语理解的有效捷径。

另外，前边说过，我们的这套书应该叫做"翻译教程读本"才更尽其意。我们知道，许多优秀的译家都承认他们从优秀的译本中获益颇多，翻译的经验和感受很重要，例如，"关键是'信''达'"，"务使作者之命意豁然呈露"，"一仆二主"，"五点谈"，"首要原则是忠实，并力求神似"，"学会表达"，"拉住两个朋友的手"，等等，都在每一读本的前面作了具体而珍贵的详述。如果有什么东西可以称为翻译教程的话，这些类似"翻译谈"的东西才当之无愧。

苏福忠

《理想丈夫》翻译谈

学 会 表 达

　　写作也好,翻译也罢,作家和译家都要学会表达。表达必须具备一定条件。比如译者,一是外文好,二是中文好。二者具备,只要想做翻译,没有做不成译家的。

　　其实,中国人学外语,从一开始就存在翻译的问题。你学了一个单词 room,老师或者字典,都会告诉你它的意思是"房间"。随后学会一句英语:I have a room. 你脑子里就出现了"我有一间房间。"的中文。再后来,有人问你"There is no room for him."怎么讲,你就牛哄哄地说:"没有他的房间了。"其实,大错特错,贻笑大方!

　　大学就要毕业了,系里组织我们翻译联合国文件。三个人一组,翻译一样的内容。译完了,由一个老师和我们坐在一起,选择最好的译文。我们组是一位年近花甲的姓李的女教师带领。她曾在美国学习多年体育,讲一口流利的美国口语,一开口能让我们羡慕死。我们每人说出自己的译文,集体讨论,最后由她点头拍板。有时候遇上一个难办的句子,我们怎么也理不顺,就请李老师说一句算了。但李老师总是痛苦地摇着头说:"我的中文不行,说不出来啊!"她看见我们都一脸迷惑,又找补一句说:"心里明白,就是想不出合适的话来。"当时我以为她怕闹出"没有他的房间了"之类的错误,后来的工作实践才意识到"说不出来啊"就是表达不行。这样的表达不行一定与中文不行有关系。

　　看别人的稿子,自己也做点翻译,掐指算来二十多年过

i

去了,这两件事情我始终忘不了:一个人不能按自己的愿望进行正确的表达,是再可悲不过的事情。语言是人类的专利,表达是语言的升华,而精彩的表达则是一个有心人的一生追求。一个人的母语最容易被自己不当回事,尤其笔头表达,因为提高母语水平实在是一件痛苦而漫长的过程。可以说,作为一个最终靠方块字征服读者的译家(我想也包括写家吧),解放后的中文教育只是一个不同程度的扫盲过程。要想让自己的表达更正确,更精彩,更艺术,必须进行艰苦的修炼和阅读。

当然,做翻译还要把外语学好,学精,学懂。具备这两个重要条件,一个译家好比拿着两个等圆圈往一起摞。译家认真,严谨,又注重不断打磨,两个圆圈吻合到了多半甚至更多,就算合格译家了。两个等圆圈一丝不爽的吻合是没有的,因此"等效翻译"之说本不存在。但是,两个等圆圈不断地追求吻合,是译家一辈子的追求。

换句话说,译家的路,是一辈子孜孜以求的路。

文　心

CONTENTS 目录

Act One ·· 4
　第一幕 ··· 5
Act Two ·· 76
　第二幕 ··· 77
Act Three ·· 142
　第三幕 ··· 143
Act Four ··· 196
　第四幕 ··· 197

AN IDEAL HUSBAND
理 想 丈 夫

THE PERSONS OF THE PLAY

THE EARL of CAVERSHAM. K. G.
VISCOUNT GORING, his son
SIR ROBERT CHILTERN, Bart.,
    Under-Secretary for Foreign Affairs
VICOMTE DE NANJAC, Attaché at
    French Embassy in London
MR. MONTFORD
MASON, Butler to Sir Robert Chiltern
PHIPPS, Lord Goring's servant
JAMES and HAROLD, Footmen
LADY CHILTERN
LADY MARKBY
THE COUNTESS OF BASILDON
MRS. MARCHMONT
MISS MABEL CHILTERN,
    Sir Robert Chiltern's sister
MRS. CHEVELEY

剧 中 人 物

卡弗沙姆伯爵　嘉德勋爵

戈林子爵　其子

罗伯特·奇尔顿　准男爵，副外交大臣

德·南加克子爵　伦敦法国使馆使节

蒙特福德先生

梅森　罗伯特·奇尔顿爵士的管家

菲普斯　戈林子爵的仆人

詹姆斯和哈罗德　男仆

奇尔顿夫人

马克比夫人

巴西尔顿伯爵夫人

马奇蒙特太太

梅布尔·奇尔顿小姐　罗伯特·奇尔顿爵士的妹妹

谢弗利太太

ACT ONE

SCENE: The octagon room at Sir Robert Chiltern's house in Grosvenor Square, London. The action of the play is completed within twenty-four hours.

TIME: The present. The room is brilliantly lighted and full of guests.

> At the top of the staircase stands LADY CHILTERN, *a woman of grave Greek beauty, about twenty-seven years of age. She receives the guests as they come up. Over the well of the staircase hangs a great chandelier with wax lights, which illumine a large eighteenth-century French tapestry—representing the Triumph of Love, from a design by Boucher—that is stretched on the staircase wall. On the right is the entrance to the music-room. The sound of a string quartette is faintly heard. The entrance on the left leads to other reception-rooms.* MRS. MARCHMONT *and* LADY BASILDON, *two very pretty women, are seated together on a Louis Seize sofa. They are types of exquisite fragility. Their affectation of manner has a delicate charm. Watteau would have loved to paint them.*

MRS. MARCHMONT: Going on to the Hartlocks' tonight, Margaret?

LADY BASILDON: I suppose so. Are you?

MRS. MARCHMONT: Yes. Horribly tedious parties they give, don't they?

第 一 幕

场景：伦敦格罗夫纳广场罗伯特·奇尔顿府上的八角形房间。本剧的活动全部在二十四小时内完成。

时间：现在。

房间里灯火辉煌，宾客如云。

〔楼梯顶上站着奇尔顿夫人，一位具有浓厚希腊美的女人，约二十七岁的样子。客人上来楼梯均受到她的接待。楼梯凹顶的上方挂着一盏枝形吊灯，蜡烛点燃，照亮了一幅巨大的十八世纪法国挂毯——画面是《维纳斯的胜利》，按布歇①的名作设计——装点着楼梯上方的墙壁。右边是通向音乐室的出入口。一支弹弦四重唱隐约可辨。出入口往左通着其他会客室。马奇蒙特太太和巴西尔顿夫人，两位非常标致的女人，坐在一张路易十六时代风格的沙发上。她们天生丽质，娇态百种。她们做张做智的样子别有韵味。华托②应该乐意为她们作画。

马奇蒙特太太　今晚去哈特洛克斯家吗，玛格丽特？
巴西尔顿夫人　我想会去吧。你呢？
马奇蒙特太太　我去。他们举办的晚宴乏味死了，不是吗？

---

① 布歇(Boucher, 1703—1770)，法国洛可可风格代表画家。
② 华托(Watteau, 1684—1721)，法国画家。

LADY BASILDON: Horribly tedious! Never know why I go. Never know why I go anywhere.

MRS. MARCHMONT: I come here to be educated.

LADY BASILDON: Ah! I hate being educated!

MRS. MARCHMONT: So do I. It puts one almost on a level with the commercial classes, doesn't it? But dear Gertrude Chiltern is always telling me that I should have some serious purpose in life. So I come here to try to find one.

LADY BASILDON (*looking round through her lorgnette*): I don't see anybody here to-night whom one could possibly call a serious purpose. The man who took me in to dinner talked to me about his wife the whole time.

MRS. MARCHMONT: How very trivial of him!

LADY BASILDON: Terribly trivial! What did your man talk about?

MRS. MARCHMONT: About myself.

LADY BASILDON (*languidly*): And were you interested?

MRS. MARCHMONT (*shaking her head*): Not in the smallest degree.

LADY BASILDON: What martyrs we are, dear Margaret!

MRS. MARCHMONT (*rising*): And how well it becomes us, Olivia!

They rise and go towards the music-room. The VICOMTE DE NANJAC, *a young attaché known for his neckties and his Anglomania, approaches with a low bow, and enters into conversation.*

MASON (*announcing guests from the top of the staircase*): Mr. and Lady Jane Barford. Lord Caversham.

巴西尔顿夫人　可不是乏味死了嘛！从来不明白我为什么要去参加。从来不明白我为什么会到处参加晚宴。

马奇蒙特太太　我是到这里来受教育了。

巴西尔顿夫人　啊！我厌恶别人教育我！

马奇蒙特太太　我也是。那简直是让人接受商务课程，对不？不过亲爱的格特鲁德·奇尔顿老是说我应该生活得有什么正经的目的。所以我就来这里试着找到一个。

巴西尔顿夫人　(从她的长柄眼镜四下搜寻)我看今天晚上来这里的人，谁都不可能有什么目的。那位带我去用餐的男人始终在喋喋不休地谈论他的妻子。

马奇蒙特太太　那他可够碎嘴子的！

巴西尔顿夫人　碎嘴得厉害！你家老公爱说些什么？

马奇蒙特太太　关于我自己呗。

巴西尔顿夫人　(没精打采地)你有兴趣吗？

马奇蒙特太太　(摇摇头)一点兴趣也没有。

巴西尔顿夫人　亲爱的玛格丽特，我们可真是苦难多多啊！

马奇蒙特太太　(起立)不过我们也幸运多多啊，奥利维亚！

〔她们站起来朝音乐室走去。德·南加克子爵，一个年轻的使节，以讲究领带出名，酷爱英国的一切，这时走过来深鞠一躬，加入了谈话。

梅森　(从楼梯顶部为客人点到)简·巴福德先生和简·巴福德夫人到。卡弗沙姆伯爵到。

Enter LORD CAVERSHAM, *an old gentleman of seventy, wearing the riband and star of the Garter. A fine Whig type. Rather like a portrait by Lawrence.*

LORD CAVERSHAM: Good-evening, Lady Chiltern! Has my good-for-nothing young son been here?

LADY CHILTERN(*smiling*): I don't think Lord Goring has arrived yet.

MABEL CHILTERN(*coming up to* LORD CAVERSHAM): Why do you call Lord Goring good-for-nothing?

MABEL CHILTERN *is a perfect example of the English type of prettiness, the apple-blossom type. She has all the fragrance and freedom of a flower. There is ripple after ripple of sunlight in her hair, and the little mouth, with its parted lips, is expectant, like the mouth of a child. She has the fascinating tyranny of youth, and the astonishing courage of innocence. To sane people she is not reminiscent of any work of art. But she is really like a Tanagra statuette, and would be rather annoyed if she were told so.*

LORD CAVERSHAM: Because he leads such an idle life.

MABEL CHILTERN: How can you say such a thing? Why, he rides in the Row at ten o'clock in the morning, goes to the Opera three times a week, changes his clothes at least five times a day, and dines out every night of the season. You don't call that leading an idle life, do you?

LORD CAVERSHAM(*looking at her with a kindly twinkle in his eyes*): You are a very charming young lady!

MABEL CHILTERN: How sweet of you to say that, Lord Caversham! Do come to us more often. You know we are always at home on Wednesdays, and you look so

〔卡弗沙姆伯爵上场，一位年逾古稀的老绅士，戴着绶带和嘉德勋章。一个优秀的辉格派。很像劳伦斯①笔下的肖像。

卡弗沙姆伯爵　晚安，奇尔顿夫人！我那现世宝儿子在这里吗？

奇尔顿夫人　（莞尔一笑）戈林子爵还没有到吧。

梅布尔·奇尔顿　（走到卡弗沙姆伯爵跟前）您为什么叫戈林子爵现世宝呢？

〔梅布尔·奇尔顿是一个十全十美的英国美人胚子，像朵盛开的苹果花儿。她集一朵花儿的芳香和自由于一身。她的秀发闪耀着日光的粼粼波纹，纤巧的小嘴微微张开，若有所期，像一张孩子的嘴。她身上有股青春的霸气和令人惊诧的天真朝气。在常人看来，她简直就是活生生的艺术品。不过她的确像塔纳格拉小塑像，只是她听人这样说她，她准会十分生气的。

卡弗沙姆伯爵　因为他过着无所事事的生活。

梅布尔·奇尔顿　你怎么能这样讲话呢？嚯，他上午十点钟就到跑马场去骑马，一星期到歌剧院看三次歌剧，一天至少换五次衣服，社交季节每天晚上都去参加宴会。你难道称这是过着无所事事的生活，对吗？

卡弗沙姆伯爵　（他眨着和善的眼睛看着她）你是一个很可爱的小姑娘啊！

奇尔顿夫人　您说这话是多么悦耳啊，卡弗沙姆伯爵！千万多到我们家来作客。你知道我们星期三总是在家

---

① 劳伦斯（Thomas Lawrence，1769—1830），英国肖像画家，曾任皇家学院院长，代表作有《乔治四世和卡罗琳公主》等。

well with your star!

LORD CAVERSHAM: Never go anywhere now. Sick of London Society. Shouldn't mind being introduced to my own tailor; he always votes on the right side. But object strongly to being sent down to dinner with my wife's milliner. Never could stand Lady Caversham's bonnets.

MABEL CHILTERN: Oh, I love London Society! I think it has immensely improved. It is entirely composed now of beautiful idiots and brilliant lunatics. Just what Society should be.

LORD CAVERSHAM: Hum! Which is Goring? Beautiful idiot, or the other thing?

MABEL CHILTERN (*gravely*): I have been obliged for the present to put Lord Goring into a class quite by himself. But he is developing charmingly!

LORD CAVERSHAM: Into what?

MABEL CHILTERN (*with a little curtsey*): I hope to let you know very soon, Lord Caversham!

MASON (*announcing guests*): Lady Markby. Mrs. Cheveley.

Enter LADY MARKBY *and* MRS. CHEVELEY. LADY MARKBY *is a pleasant, kindly, popular woman, with gray hair à la marquise and good lace. *MRS. CHEVELEY, *who accompanies her, is tall and rather slight. Lips very thin and highly-coloured, a line of scarlet on a pallid face. Venetian red hair, aquiline nose, and long throat. Rouge accentuates the natural paleness of her complexion. Gray-green eyes that move restlessly. She is in heliotrope, with diamonds. She looks rather like an orchid, and makes great demands on one's curiosity. In all her movements she is extremely graceful. A work of art, on the*

的,你戴上嘉德勋章看上去特别精神!

卡弗沙姆伯爵　现在哪里都懒得去了。伦敦的上流社会让人腻烦。倒是不反对让人领着去见我自己的裁缝;他总是站在正确的一边发表意见。可是决难同意让人叫到餐桌旁看着我妻子的头饰用餐。怎么都看不惯卡弗沙姆夫人的帽子。

梅布尔·奇尔顿　噢,我喜爱伦敦的上流社会!我认为伦敦上流社会大有改进。圈子里现在全是美丽的傻子和杰出的狂人。上流社会就应该是这个样子。

卡弗沙姆伯爵　哼!戈林算什么?美丽的傻子呢,还是别的什么?

梅布尔·奇尔顿　(庄重地)我眼下心存感激,看看戈林子爵往一类人里靠得多带劲。不过他还在成长,样子让人着迷!

卡弗沙姆伯爵　往哪类人里靠?

梅布尔·奇尔顿　(行小礼)但愿我能尽快地告诉您,卡弗沙姆伯爵!

梅森　(通报客人)马克比夫人到。谢弗利太太到。

〔马克比夫人和谢弗利太太上。马克比夫人是一位喜兴、和善、讨人喜欢的女人,灰发上戴着一枚卵形宝石和优质花边。与之相随的谢弗利太太高高的个儿,相当瘦弱。嘴唇精薄,抹得血红,苍白的脸上就显出一绺红线似的。棕色的头发,鹰钩鼻子,长长的脖子。口红更加突出了她脸上自然的苍白。淡蓝的眼睛不停地转动。她身着紫红服装,珠光宝气。她看上去宛若一朵兰花,由不得让人发生好奇。她一举一动都异常庄重。

whole, but showing the influence of too many schools.

LADY MARKBY: Good-evening, dear Gertrude! So kind of you to let me bring my friend, Mrs. Cheveley. Two such charming women should know each other!

LADY CHILTERN (*advances towards* MRS. CHEVELEY *with a sweet smile. Then suddenly stops, and bows rather distantly*): I think Mrs. Cheveley and I have met before. I did not know she had married a second time.

LADY MARKBY (*genially*): Ah, nowadays people marry as often as they can, don't they? It is most fashionable. (*To* DUCHESS OF MARYBOROUGH): Dear Duchess, and how is the Duke? Brain still weak, I suppose? Well, that is only to be expected, is it not? His good father was just the same. There is nothing like race, is there?

MRS. CHEVELEY (*playing with her fan*): But have we really met before, Lady Chiltern? I can't remember where. I have been out of England for so long.

LADY CHILTERN: We were at school together, Mrs. Cheveley.

MRS. CHEVELEY (*superciliously*): Indeed? I have forgotten all about my schooldays. I have a vague impression that they were detestable.

LADY CHILTERN (*coldly*): I am not surprised!

MRS. CHEVELEY (*in her sweetest manner*): Do you know, I am quite looking forward to meeting your clever husband, Lady Chiltern. Since he has been at the Foreign Office, he has been so much talked of in Vienna. They actually succeed in spelling his name right in the newspapers. That in itself is fame, on the continent.

LADY CHILTERN: I hardly think there will be much in common between you and my husband, Mrs. Cheveley!

第一幕

乍看是一件艺术品,细细看去却显得五花八门。

马克比夫人　晚安,亲爱的格特鲁德!感谢你让我带来我的朋友,谢弗利太太。这样两位迷人的女人当然应该互相认识认识了。

奇尔顿夫人　(面带微笑走向谢弗利太太。随后突然站住,远远点了一下头)我想谢弗利太太和我过去见过面的。我不知道她又嫁人了。

马克比夫人　(可亲地)啊,时下人们娶嫁成了家常便饭,不是吗?这可是最时髦不过的。(对玛丽巴勒公爵夫人)亲爱的公爵夫人,公爵怎么样呵?头还很虚,是吗?哦,这也不足为奇,不是吗?他的好父亲就是那个样子。再没有什么比家传更厉害了,是吧?

谢弗利太太　(不停摇扇子)不过我们过去真的见过面吗,奇尔顿夫人?我记不得在哪里了。我离开英格兰很长一段时间呢。

奇尔顿夫人　我们一起上过学,谢弗利太太。

谢弗利太太　(目中无人地)当真?我早把学校生活忘到脑后了。我模模糊糊记得学校的生活很令人讨厌。

奇尔顿夫人　(冷冷地)我一点不感到奇怪!

谢弗利太太　(作出一副甜蜜无比的样子)你知道吧,我就在等着和你能干的丈夫见面呢,奇尔顿夫人。由于他在外交部工作,在维也纳他可是人们经常谈到的人物。实际上他的名字还在报纸上频频出现呢。它在欧洲大陆可是响当当的名字。

奇尔顿夫人　我认为你和我丈夫根本没有什么共同之处,

(*Moves away.*)

VICOMTE DE NANJAC: Ah, chère Madame, quelle surprise! I have not seen you since Berlin!

MRS. CHEVELEY: Not since Berlin, Vicomte. Five years ago!

VICOMTE DE NANJAC: And you are younger and more beautiful than ever. How do you manage it?

MRS. CHEVELEY: By making it a rule only to talk to perfectly charming people like yourself.

VICOMTE DE NANJAC: Ah! you flatter me. You butter me, as they say here.

MRS. CHEVELEY: Do they say that here? How dreadful of them!

VICOMTE DE NANJAC: Yes, they have a wonderful language. It should be more widely known.

   SIR ROBERT CHILTERN *enters. A man of forty, but looking somewhat younger. Clean-shaven, with finely-cut features, dark-haired and dark-eyed. A personality of mark. Not popular—few personalities are. But intensely admired by the few, and deeply respected by the many. The note of his manner is that of perfect distinction, with a slight touch of pride. One feels that he is conscious of the success he has made in life. A nervous temperament, with a tired look. The firmly-chiselled mouth and chin contrast strikingly with the romantic expression in the deep-set eyes. The variance is suggestive of an almost complete separation of passion and intellect, as though thought and emotion were each isolated in its own sphere through some violence of will-power. There is nervousness in the nostrils, and in the pale, thin, pointed hands. It would be inaccurate to call him*

第 一 幕

谢弗利太太！（走开。）

德·南加克子爵　呵，是夫人，少见少见！柏林见面后我还没有看见你呢！

谢弗利太太　柏林以后是没有见过面，子爵。五年前的事了！

德·南加克子爵　你比过去更加年轻，更加漂亮了。你过得怎么样？

谢弗利太太　只有一条规矩，那就是只和你这样十全十美的人交谈。

德·南加克子爵　啊！你在恭维我。像这里的人爱说的，你在巴结我。

谢弗利太太　这里的人说这种话吗？这些人多么讨厌呀！

德·南加克子爵　不，他们的语言很传神。这样的话应该传播得更广泛。

〔罗伯特·奇尔顿爵士上。一位四十岁的男子，但是看上去还要年轻。脸刮得干净，五官清晰端庄。黑头发，黑眼睛。个性突出。不同一般——属于为数不多的那种个性。少数人十分喜欢，多数人深为尊敬。他的形容举止清楚地体现着个性，其中也不乏几分傲慢。旁观者只能感觉到他心下明白他是生活的佼佼者。神经质，面色憔悴。轮廓清晰的嘴唇和下巴，和深眼窝的眼睛里透出的浪漫情调形成鲜明的对照。这种不一致让人看得出激情和理智简直水火不容，仿佛思想和情感通过某种强烈的意志被隔离在了各自的范围里。他的鼻孔和他那双白皙、瘦细的手表露着几分紧张。说他有画感那是言过其实了。有画感的人在下议院里是没

picturesque. Picturesqueness cannot survive the House of Commons. But Vandyck would have liked to have painted his head.

SIR ROBERT CHILTERN: Good-evening, Lady Markby. I hope you have brought Sir John with you?

LADY MARKBY: Oh! I have brought a much more charming person than Sir John. Sir John's temper since he has taken seriously to politics has become quite unbearable. Really, now that the House of Commons is trying to become useful, it does a great deal of harm.

SIR ROBERT CHILTERN: I hope not, Lady Markby. At any rate we do our best to waste the public time, don't we? But who is this charming person you have been kind enough to bring to us?

LADY MARKBY: Her name is Mrs. Cheveley! One of the Dorsetshire Cheveleys, I suppose. But I really don't know. Families are so mixed nowadays. Indeed, as a rule, everybody turns out to be somebody else.

SIR ROBERT CHILTERN: Mrs. Cheveley? I seem to know the name.

LADY MARKBY: She has just arrived from Vienna.

SIR ROBERT CHILTERN: Ah! yes. I think I know whom you mean.

LADY MARKBY: Oh! she goes everywhere there, and has such pleasant scandals about all her friends. I really must go to Vienna next winter. I hope there is a good chef at the Embassy.

SIR ROBERT CHILTERN: If there is not, the Ambassador will certainly have to be recalled. Pray point out Mrs. Cheveley to me. I should like to see her.

LADY MARKBY: Let me introduce you. (*To* MRS. CHEVELEY): My dear, Sir Robert Chiltern is dying to

第 一 幕

法存在下来的。不过凡·戴克①倒也愿意为他的头作幅画儿。

罗伯特·奇尔顿爵士　晚安,马克比夫人。您要是把约翰爵士一起带来多好?

马克比夫人　喔!我带来的人可比约翰爵士让人喜欢。自从约翰爵士认真地从事政治,他变得简直让人受不了。真的,既然这下议院变得越来越有作用,它的害处也就大起来了。

罗伯特·奇尔顿爵士　我看不至于,马克比夫人。不管怎样,我们尽心尽力浪费掉了公众的时间,对不?不过你费心给我们带来的那个迷人的人是谁呢?

马克比夫人　她就是谢弗利太太!我想是多塞特郡谢弗利家族的人吧。不过我还真的不是很清楚。时下家族混杂得厉害。结果呢,人人都能证明自己出身什么名门贵族。

罗伯特·奇尔顿爵士　谢弗利太太?我好像听说过这个名字。

马克比夫人　她刚刚从维也纳来。

罗伯特·奇尔顿爵士　呵!知道了。我想我明白你说的是谁了。

马克比夫人　喔!她在伦敦到处走动,把她所有的朋友的丑闻都弄到了手,听来有趣。下个冬季我真的一定要到维也纳去。我希望那里的使馆有个好厨子。

罗伯特·奇尔顿爵士　如果没有,大使一定会被召回了。请把谢弗利太太指给我。我想见见她。

马克比夫人　让我来给你介绍一下。(对谢弗利太太)我亲爱

---

① 凡·戴克(Vandyck,1599—1641),弗兰德斯画家,主要画作有《红衣主教宾提沃利奥》、《穿猎装的查理一世》等。

know you!

SIR ROBERT CHILTERN (*bowing*): Every one is dying to know the brilliant Mrs. Cheveley. Our attachés at Vienna write to us about nothing else.

MRS. CHEVELEY: Thank you, Sir Robert. An acquaintance that begins with a compliment is sure to develop into a real friendship. It starts in the right manner. And I find that I know Lady Chiltern already.

SIR ROBERT CHILTERN: Really?

MRS. CHEVELEY: Yes. She has just reminded me that we were at school together. I remember it perfectly now. She always got the good conduct prize. I have a distinct recollection of Lady Chiltern always getting the good conduct prize!

SIR ROBERT CHILTERN (*smiling*): And what prizes did you get, Mrs. Cheveley?

MRS. CHEVELEY: My prizes came a little later on in life. I don't think any of them were for good conduct. I forget!

SIR ROBERT CHILTERN: I am sure they were for something charming!

MRS. CHEVELEY: I don't know that women are always rewarded for being charming. I think they are usually punished for it! Certainly, more women grow old nowadays through the faithfulness of their admirers than through anything else! At least that is the only way I can account for the terribly haggard look of most of your pretty women in London!

SIR ROBERT CHILTERN: What an appalling philosophy that sounds! To attempt to classify you, Mrs. Cheveley, would be an impertinence. But may I ask, at heart, are you an optimist or a pessimist? Those seem to be the

的,罗伯特·奇尔顿爵士着急想认识你呢!

罗伯特·奇尔顿爵士 (鞠躬)人人都着急认识大名鼎鼎的谢弗利太太呀。我们驻维也纳的使节给我们写信不谈别的,专说谢弗利太太。

谢弗利太太 谢谢,罗伯特爵士。熟人开始就说恭维话,准会成为真正的朋友。开头首先就开对了。我现在才明白我跟奇尔顿夫人是熟人。

罗伯特·奇尔顿爵士 是吗?

谢弗利太太 是啊。她刚刚提醒我,我们俩过去是同学。我现在完全记起来了。她当时总是得到优秀品德奖。我清清楚楚记得奇尔顿夫人总是获得优秀品德奖!

罗伯特·奇尔顿爵士 (微笑)那你得到过什么奖?

谢弗利太太 我的奖品是在稍后的生活中获得的。我想它们都不是优秀品德奖。我早忘了!

罗伯特·奇尔顿爵士 我看准它们是奖赏什么撩拨人的东西吧。

谢弗利太太 我认为女人不总是因为迷人才获得奖状的!我倒认为她们往往因为惹人瞩目遭受惩罚!真的,如今多数女人变老了,都是因为她们的崇拜者忠心耿耿崇拜的结果!你们伦敦的漂亮女人多数都看上去憔悴不堪,我看就是因为这个原因!

罗伯特·奇尔顿爵士 这话听起来深奥得很,富有哲理啊!谢弗利太太,想给你归归类可得加倍小心呢。不过我可以问一声,真心问一问,你是乐观主义者呢,还是悲

only two fashionable religions left to us nowadays.

MRS. CHEVELEY: Oh, I'm neither. Optimism begins in a broad grin, and Pessimism ends with blue spectacles. Besides, they are both of them merely poses.

SIR ROBERT CHILTERN: You prefer to be natural?

MRS. CHEVELEY: Sometimes. But it is such a very difficult pose to keep up.

SIR ROBERT CHILTERN: What would those modern psychological novelists, of whom we hear so much, say to such a theory as that?

MRS. CHEVELEY: Ah! the strength of women comes from the fact that psychology cannot explain us. Men can be analysed, women... merely adored.

SIR ROBERT CHILTERN: You think science cannot grapple with the problem of women?

MRS. CHEVELEY: Science can never grapple with the irrational. That is why it has no future before it, in this world.

SIR ROBERT CHILTERN: And women represent the irrational.

MRS. CHEVELEY: Well-dressed women do.

SIR ROBERT CHILTERN (*with a polite bow*): I fear I could hardly agree with you there. But do sit down. And now tell me, what makes you leave your brilliant Vienna for our gloomy London—or perhaps the question is indiscreet?

MRS. CHEVELEY: Questions are never indiscreet. Answers sometimes are.

SIR ROBERT CHILTERN: Well, at any rate, may I know if it is politics or pleasure?

MRS. CHEVELEY: Politics are my only pleasure. You see, nowadays it is not fashionable to flirt till one is forty,

观主义者？我们今天好像只有这两派时髦的宗教了。

谢弗利太太　喔，我什么都不是。乐观主义开始露齿一笑，悲观主义结果眼前一片暗淡。再说，它们无一不是做做姿势而已。

罗伯特·奇尔顿爵士　那么说你更喜欢自然了。

谢弗利太太　有时喜欢。不过那也是非常难摆的一种姿势。

罗伯特·奇尔顿爵士　我们经常听说现代心理描写小说家，他们对这样的理论有什么高论？

谢弗利太太　啊！女人的力量来自心理学无法解释的事实。男人能够被分析，女人呢……只受人宠爱。

罗伯特·奇尔顿爵士　你认为科学能解决女人的问题吗？

谢弗利太太　科学永远没法和没有理性的人打交道。科学在这个世界上没有前途，原因也正在这里。

罗伯特·奇尔顿爵士　那么说，女人就代表没有理性的人啰。

谢弗利太太　讲究穿戴的女人是这样的。

罗伯特·奇尔顿爵士　（客气地鞠躬）恐怕我很难同意你的说法。不过请坐下吧。现在请告诉我，你离开漂亮的维也纳，来到我们阴沉沉的伦敦，有什么要事——或许这是个唐突的问题？

谢弗利太太　问题从来没有唐突的。回答倒是有时难免唐突。

罗伯特·奇尔顿爵士　说得好，不过我还是想知道是为政治呢还是为快活？

谢弗利太太　政治就是我唯一的快活。你看，当今时兴四十岁才调情，四十五岁才讲究浪漫，所以，我们这些不

21

or to be romantic till one is forty-five, so we poor women who are under thirty, or say we are, have nothing open to us but politics or philanthropy. And philanthropy seems to me to have become simply the refuge of people who wish to annoy their fellow-creatures. I prefer politics. I think they are more... becoming!

SIR ROBERT CHILTERN: A political life is a noble career!

MRS. CHEVELEY: Sometimes. And sometimes it is a clever game, Sir Robert. And sometimes it is a great nuisance.

SIR ROBERT CHILTERN: Which do you find it?

MRS. CHEVELEY: A combination of all three. (*Drops her fan.*)

SIR ROBERT CHILTERN (*picks up fan*): Allow me!

MRS. CHEVELEY: Thanks.

SIR ROBERT CHILTERN: But you have not told me yet what makes you honour London so suddenly. Our season is almost over.

MRS. CHEVELEY: Oh! I don't care about the London season! It is too matrimonial. People are either hunting for husbands, or hiding from them. I wanted to meet you. It is quite true. You know what a woman's curiosity is. Almost as great as a man's! I wanted immensely to meet you, and... to ask you to do something for me.

SIR ROBERT CHILTERN: I hope it is not a little thing, Mrs. Cheveley. I find that little things are so very difficult to do.

MRS. CHEVELEY: (*after a moment's reflection*): No, I don't think it is quite a little thing.

SIR ROBERT CHILTERN: I am so glad. Do tell me what it is.

满三十岁或自称三十岁的女人，只好玩玩政治或慈善了。可慈善在我看来好像只是那些想给同类寻找烦恼的人的庇护所。我更喜欢政治。我认为政治更……合适！

罗伯特·奇尔顿爵士　政治活动是一种高贵的职业！

谢弗利太太　有时是的。有时它只是一种更精明的游戏，罗伯特爵士。有时它却是一种大麻烦啊。

罗伯特·奇尔顿爵士　你看上了哪一种？

谢弗利太太　三者兼而有之。(扇子掉在地上。)

罗伯特·奇尔顿爵士　(捡起扇子)我来捡好了！

谢弗利太太　多谢。

罗伯特·奇尔顿爵士　可是你还没有告诉我，你突然来到伦敦的原因呢。我们的社交季节就要结束了。

谢弗利太太　噢！我不在乎伦敦的社交季节！这里的社交活动就知道围着婚姻转。人们要么寻找丈夫，要么躲避丈夫。我只想跟你见面。这是真的。你知道女人的好奇心是怎么回事，和男人的好奇心不相上下！我想马上见到你，是……想让你为我做点事。

罗伯特·奇尔顿爵士　我希望那不会是一点点小事，谢弗利太太。我发现小事情往往十分难办。

谢弗利太太　(沉思稍许)不是的，我认为那不是区区小事一件。

罗伯特·奇尔顿爵士　那我就太高兴了。请告诉我是什么吧。

MRS. CHEVELEY: Later on. (*Rises*) And now may I walk through your beautiful house? I hear your pictures are charming. Poor Baron Arnheim—you remember the Baron? —used to tell me you had some wonderful Corots.

SIR ROBERT CHILTERN (*with an almost imperceptible start*): Did you know Baron Arnheim well?

MRS. CHEVELEY (*smiling*): Intimately. Did you?

SIR ROBERT CHILTERN: At one time.

MRS. CHEVELEY: Wonderful man, wasn't he?

SIR ROBERT CHILTERN (*after a pause*): He was very remarkable, in many ways.

MRS. CHEVELEY: I often think it such a pity he never wrote his memoirs. They would have been most interesting.

SIR ROBERT CHILTERN: Yes: he knew men and cities well, like the old Greek.

MRS. CHEVELEY: Without the dreadful disadvantage of having a Penelope waiting at home for him.

MASON: Lord Goring.

Enter LORD GORING. *Thirty-four, but always says he is younger. A well-bred, expressionless face. He is clever, but would not like to be thought so. A flawless dandy, he would be annoyed if he were considered romantic. He plays with life, and is on perfectly good terms with the world. He is fond of being misunderstood. It gives him a post of vantage.*

SIR ROBERT CHILTERN: Good-evening, my dear Arthur! Mrs. Cheveley, allow me to introduce to you Lord Goring, the idlest man in London.

第 一 幕

谢弗利太太　过一会儿再说吧(起身)现在我可以穿过你们这漂亮的宅第吗？我听说你家的画儿很好看。可怜的安海姆男爵——你还记得那位男爵吗？——常跟我说你家有一些难得的柯罗①的画作。

罗伯特·奇尔顿爵士　(稍露不易察觉的惊讶之色)你也认识安海姆男爵吗？

谢弗利太太　(莞尔一笑)老朋友了。你呢？

罗伯特·奇尔顿爵士　曾经认识。

谢弗利太太　难得的人，不是吗？

罗伯特·奇尔顿爵士　(停顿)他在不少方面都很了不起。

谢弗利太太　我常常为他没有写他的回忆录感到遗憾不已。他要是写出来，那一定引人入胜。

罗伯特·奇尔顿爵士　是的。像那位古希腊人，他对人和城市了如指掌。

谢弗利太太　可惜没有一位珀涅罗珀②为他守候家门，这对他是一大缺陷。

梅森　戈林子爵到。

〔戈林子爵上。三十四岁，但是他总是把自己的岁数报得更小一点。一张典雅却不生动的脸。他极聪明，但又不喜欢人们看出这点。一位十足的纨绔，却反感别人说他浪漫。他游戏人生。和这个世界左右逢源。他喜欢别人误解他。那样他才显得有优势。

罗伯特·奇尔顿爵士　晚安，我亲爱的亚瑟！谢弗利太太，请允许我把你介绍给戈林子爵，伦敦城的大闲人。

---

① 柯罗(Corot,1796—1875)，法国画家，在风景画上贡献卓著，代表画作有《沙特尔大教堂》、《阵风》等。

② 珀涅罗珀(Penelope)希腊神话中人物，奥德修斯的妻子，一贞妇形象。

MRS. CHEVELEY: I have met Lord Goring before.

LORD GORING (*bowing*): I did not think you would remember me, Mrs. Cheveley.

MRS. CHEVELEY: My memory is under admirable control. And are you still a bachelor?

LORD GORING: I...believe so.

MRS. CHEVELEY: How very romantic.

LORD GORING: Oh! I am not at all romantic. I am not old enough. I leave romance to my seniors.

SIR ROBERT CHILTERN: Lord Goring is the result of Boodle's Club, Mrs. Cheveley.

MRS. CHEVELEY: He reflects every credit on the institution.

LORD GORING: May I ask are you staying in London long?

MRS. CHEVELEY: That depends partly on the weather, partly on the cooking, and partly on Sir Robert.

SIR ROBERT CHILTERN: You are not going to plunge us into a European war, I hope?

MRS. CHEVELEY: There is no danger, at present!

She nods to LORD GORING, *with a look of amusement in her eyes, and goes out with* SIR ROBERT CHILTERN. LORD GORING *saunters over to* MABEL CHILTERN.

MABEL CHILTERN: You are very late!

LORD GORING: Have you missed me?

MABEL CHILTERN: Awfully!

LORD GORING: Then I am sorry I did not stay away longer. I like being missed.

MABEL CHILTERN: How very selfish of you!

LORD GORING: I am very selfish.

MABEL CHILTERN: You are always telling me of your

谢弗利太太　我跟戈林子爵过去见过面。

戈林子爵　（鞠躬）我还以为你记不得我了。谢弗利太太。

谢弗利太太　我的记忆掌握得令人佩服。你还是单身一人吗？

戈林子爵　我……想是的。

谢弗利太太　活得真叫浪漫。

戈林子爵　哦！我才一点都不浪漫呢。我还不算太老。我还是把浪漫留给比我老的人吧。

罗伯特·奇尔顿爵士　戈林子爵不愧为群体俱乐部的成员，谢弗利太太。

谢弗利太太　他给那个组织增光不少。

戈林子爵　我不妨问一下，你在伦敦会呆很久吗？

谢弗利太太　这一方面要看天气的情况，一方面要看烹调的情况，还要看罗伯特爵士的情况。

罗伯特·奇尔顿爵士　但愿你不是要把我们拖进一场欧洲战争吧。

谢弗利太太　目前还不至于吧。

〔她向戈林子爵点点头，眼睛里露出调皮的目光，和罗伯特·奇尔顿爵士走出去。戈林子爵晃晃荡荡向梅布尔·奇尔顿走去。

梅布尔·奇尔顿　你来晚了！

戈林子爵　你想我了？

梅布尔·奇尔顿　想得厉害！

戈林子爵　那我很遗憾没有多耽搁一会儿。我喜欢让人想我。

梅布尔·奇尔顿　你真够自私的！

戈林子爵　我是很自私。

梅布尔·奇尔顿　你总是把你的坏品质告诉我，戈林子爵。

bad qualities, Lord Goring.

LORD GORING: I have only told you half of them as yet, Miss Mabel!

MABEL CHILTERN: Are the others very bad?

LORD GORING: Quite dreadful! When I think of them at night I go to sleep at once.

MABEL CHILTERN: Well, I delight in your bad qualities. I wouldn't have you part with one of them.

LORD GORING: How very nice of you! But then you are always nice. By the way, I want to ask you a question, Miss Mabel. Who brought Mrs. Cheveley here? That woman in heliotrope, who has just gone out of the room with your brother?

MABEL CHILTERN: Oh, I think Lady Markby brought her. Why do you ask?

LORD GORING: I haven't seen her for years, that is all.

MABEL CHILTERN: What an absurd reason!

LORD GORING: All reasons are absurd.

MABEL CHILTERN: What sort of a woman is she?

LORD GORING: Oh! a genius in the daytime and a beauty at night!

MABEL CHILTERN: I dislike her already.

LORD GORING: That shows your admirable good taste.

VICOMTE DE NANJAC (*approaching*): Ah, the English young lady is the dragon of good taste, is she not? Quite the dragon of good taste.

LORD GORING: So the newspapers are always telling us.

VICOMTE DE NANJAC: I read all your English newspapers. I find them so amusing.

戈林子爵　我才跟你说了一半,梅布尔小姐!

梅布尔·奇尔顿　另一半也很坏吗?

戈林子爵　坏透了!每当我夜里想起它们,马上就入睡了。

梅布尔·奇尔顿　噢,我倒很喜欢你的坏毛病。但愿你不要丢掉这些坏毛病。

戈林子爵　你真是太好了!不过你这人一贯都很好。喂,我想问你一个问题,梅布尔小姐。是谁把谢弗利太太带来的?就是穿得大红大紫的那个女人,她刚刚和你哥哥离开这间屋子。

梅布尔·奇尔顿　哦,我想是马克比夫人带她来的。你问这干什么?

戈林子爵　没什么,只是我多年没有看见她了。

梅布尔·奇尔顿　这理由多可笑啊!

戈林子爵　理由都是可笑的。

梅布尔·奇尔顿　她是哪种女人?

戈林子爵　喔!白天是一位天才,夜里是一个美人儿!

梅布尔·奇尔顿　我已经讨厌她了。

戈林子爵　这表明你的趣味不同一般。

德·南加克子爵　(走过来)呵,英国的年轻女士是高雅趣味的警惕的守护神,不是吗?完全是高雅趣味的警惕的守护神。

戈林子爵　报纸总是这样跟我们讲的。

德·南加克子爵　我读遍了你们的报纸。我发现你们的报纸很有意思。

LORD GORING: Then, my dear Nanjac, you must certainly read between the lines.

VICOMTE DE NANJAC: I should like to, but my professor objects. (*To* MABEL CHILTERN): May I have the pleasure of escorting you to the music-room, Mademoiselle?

MABEL CHILTERN (*looking very disappointed*): Delighted, Vicomte, quite delighted! (*Turning to* LORD GORING): Aren't you coming to the music-room?

LORD GORING: Not if there is any music going on, Miss Mabel.

MABEL CHILTERN (*severely*): The music is in German. You would not understand it.

Goes out with the VICOMTE DE NANJAC. LORD CAVERSHAM *comes up to his son.*

LORD CAVERSHAM: Well, sir! what are you doing here? Wasting your life as usual! You should be in bed, sir. You keep too late hours! I heard of you the other night at Lady Rufford's dancing till four o'clock in the morning!

LORD GORING: Only a quarter to four, father.

LORD CAVERSHAM: Can't make out how you stand London Society. The thing has gone to the dogs, a lot of damned nobodies talking about nothing.

LORD GORING: I love talking about nothing, father. It is the only thing I know anything about.

LORD CAVERSHAM: You seem to me to be living entirely for pleasure.

LORD GORING: What else is there to live for, father? Nothing ages like happiness.

LORD CAVERSHAM: You are heartless, sir, very heartless.

戈林子爵　那么,我亲爱的南加克,你毫无疑问是字里行间浏览的吧。

德·南加克子爵　我倒愿意,可是我的教授反对。(对梅布尔·奇尔顿)我可以荣幸地陪你去音乐室吗,小姐?

梅布尔·奇尔顿　(一脸失望的神色)很高兴,子爵,当然高兴!(转向戈林子爵)你到音乐室去吗?

戈林子爵　只要音乐在响,我就不想去,梅布尔小姐。

梅布尔·奇尔顿　(严肃地)音乐是德国的。你又听不懂。

〔同德·南加克子爵出去。卡弗沙姆伯爵向自己的儿子走过来。

卡弗沙姆伯爵　喔,先生!你在这里干什么?像往常一样浪费你的生命啊!你应该躺在床上睡觉,先生,你在外面呆得时间太长了!我听说你前天夜里在拉福德夫人家里跳舞一直跳到凌晨四点钟!

戈林子爵　只呆到了差一刻四点,老爸。

卡弗沙姆伯爵　怎么都不明白你怎么能受得了伦敦的上流社会。完全是在混日子,一大群什么都不是的人,在谈论什么都不是的话题。

戈林子爵　我就喜欢谈论什么都不是的话题,老爸。要说我知道点什么,我就知道什么都不是的话题。

卡弗沙姆伯爵　我觉得你活着就完全为了找快活。

戈林子爵　活着还会为了什么呢,父亲?什么都不像幸福那样命长呵。

卡弗沙姆伯爵　你无情无义,先生,真的是一点情意也没有啊!

31

LORD GORING: I hope not, father. Good-evening, Lady Basildon!

LADY BASILDON (*arching two pretty eyebrows*): Are you here? I had no idea you ever came to political parties.

LORD GORING: I adore political parties. They are the only place left to us where people don't talk politics.

LADY BASILDON: I delight in talking politics. I talk them all day long. But I can't bear listening to them. I don't know how the unfortunate men in the House stand these long debates.

LORD GORING: By never listening.

LADY BASILDON: Really?

LORD GORING (*in his most serious manner*): Of course. You see, it is a very dangerous thing to listen. If one listens one may be convinced; and a man who allows himself to be convinced by an argument is a thoroughly unreasonable person.

LADY BASILDON: Ah! that accounts for so much in men that I have never understood, and so much in women that their husbands never appreciate in them!

MRS. MARCHMONT (*with a sigh*): Our husbands never appreciate anything in us. We have to go to others for that!

LADY BASILDON (*emphatically*): Yes, always to others, have we not?

LORD GORING (*smiling*): And those are the views of the two ladies who are known to have the most admirable husbands in London.

MRS. MARCHMONT: That is exactly what we can't stand. My Reginald is quite hopelessly faultless. He is really unendurably so, at times! There is not the smallest

第 一 幕

戈林子爵　不至于吧,老爸。晚安,巴西尔顿夫人!

巴西尔顿夫人　(挑起两条漂亮的眉毛)你在这里吗?我过去记得你不曾参加过政治宴会。

戈林子爵　我很喜欢政治宴会。它们是留给我们唯一人们不谈政治的地方。

巴西尔顿夫人　我喜欢谈论政治。我整天都谈论政治。可是我就是受不了听别人谈论政治。我不知道那些不幸的人在议会里,怎么受得了那些长篇辩论。

戈林子爵　充耳不闻就是了。

巴西尔顿夫人　真的吗?

戈林子爵　(做一本正经的样子)当然。你看呀,辩论是听来非常危险的东西。你要是听了,你就会被说服;一个会被辩论说服的人,则是完全没有理智的人。

巴西尔顿夫人　啊!这话很能说明什么是男人,我过去却一点也不明白;这话也很能说明女人,她们的丈夫又欣赏不了!

马奇蒙特太太　(叹口气)我们的丈夫压根就不欣赏我们。我们只得求助别人了!

巴西尔顿夫人　(用加强的口气)是的,只好经常求助别人,不是吗?

戈林子爵　(微笑)这话可是出自两位伦敦城谁都知道嫁了最令人羡慕的丈夫的女士啊!

马奇蒙特太太　这正是我们最受不了的。我的雷金纳德完美无缺得让人绝望。有时他真的让人受不了!在他身

element of excitement in knowing him.

LORD GORING: How terrible! Really, the thing should be more widely known!

LADY BASILDON: Basildon is quite as bad; he is as domestic as if he was a bachelor.

MRS. MARCHMONT(*pressing* LADY BASILDON'S *hand*): My poor Olivia! We have married perfect husbands, and we are well punished for it.

LORD GORING: I should have thought it was the husbands who were punished.

MRS. MARCHMONT(*drawing herself up*): Oh, dear no! They are as happy as possible! And as for trusting us, it is tragic how much they trust us.

LADY BASILDON: Perfectly tragic!

LORD GORING: Or comic, Lady Basildon?

LADY BASILDON: Certainly not comic, Lord Goring. How unkind of you to suggest such a thing!

MRS. MARCHMONT: I am afraid Lord Goring is in the camp of the enemy, as usual, I saw him talking to that Mrs. Cheveley when he came in.

LORD GORING: Handsome woman, Mrs. Cheveley!

LADY BASILDON (*stiffly*): Please don't praise other women in our presence. You might wait for us to do that!

LORD GORING: I did wait.

MRS. MARCHMONT: Well, we are not going to praise her. I hear she went to the Opera on Monday night, and told Tommy Rufford at supper that, as far as she could see, London Society was entirely made up of dowdies and dandies.

LORD GORING: She is quite right, too. The men are all dowdies and the women are all dandies, aren't they?

上简直找不到一点让人激动的东西。

戈林子爵　多么可怕呀！这事真应该让更多的人知道知道！

巴西尔顿夫人　巴西尔顿就够糟糕的；他满脑子家务事，好像他还是个单身汉。

马奇蒙特太太　（按了按巴西尔顿夫人的手）我好可怜的奥利维亚！我们都嫁了十全十美的丈夫，我们为此吃尽了苦头。

戈林子爵　我倒认为吃了苦头的是丈夫们。

马奇蒙特太太　（抖抖精神）噢，天哪，不！他们享尽了幸福！说到信赖我们呢，究竟依赖到了什么地步，悲剧。

巴西尔顿夫人　不折不扣的悲剧！

戈林子爵　或者是喜剧吧，巴西尔顿夫人？

巴西尔顿夫人　当然不是喜剧，戈林子爵。你提出这样的东西简直不怀好意！

马奇蒙特太太　恐怕戈林像往常一样，又站到敌人的阵营里去了，我看见他跟那个谢弗利太太说了半天话才进来了。

戈林子爵　谢弗利太太是漂亮女人嘛！

巴西尔顿夫人　（生硬地）请别当着我们的面夸奖别的女人。你应该等着我们来夸！

戈林子爵　我是在等着的。

马奇蒙特太太　哦，我们是不会夸奖她的。我听说她星期一晚上到歌剧院，在晚宴上跟汤米·拉福德说，就她所看到的，伦敦上流社会全是些邋遢女人和花花公子。

戈林子爵　她说的完全正确。男人全是些邋遢鬼，女人都不务正业。不是吗？

MRS. MARCHMONT (*after a pause*): Oh! do you really think that is what Mrs. Cheveley meant?

LORD GORING: Of course. And a very sensible remark for Mrs. Cheveley to make, too.

Enter MABEL CHILTERN. *She joins the group.*

MABEL CHILTERN: Why are you talking about Mrs. Cheveley? Everybody is talking about Mrs. Cheveley! Lord Goring says—what did you say, Lord Goring, about Mrs. Cheveley? Oh! I remember, that she was a genius in the daytime and a beauty at night.

LADY BASILDON: What a horrid combination! So very unnatural!

MRS. MARCHMONT (*in her most dreamy manner*): I like looking at geniuses, and listening to beautiful people!

LORD GORING: Ah! that is morbid of you, Mrs. Marchmont!

MRS. MARCHMONT (*brightening to a look of real pleasure*): I am so glad to hear you say that. Marchmont and I have been married for seven years, and he has never once told me that I was morbid. Men are so painfully unobservant.

LADY BASILDON (*turning to her*): I have always said, dear Margaret, that you were the most morbid person in London.

MRS. MARCHMONT: Ah! but you are always sympathetic, Olivia!

MABEL CHILTERN: Is it morbid to have a desire for food? I have a great desire for food. Lord Goring, will you give me some supper?

LORD GORING: With pleasure, Miss Mabel. (*Moves away with her.*)

马奇蒙特太太 （稍加停顿）噢！你真的认为这就是谢弗利太太的意思吗？

戈林子爵 当然。谢弗利太太的这番话非常精彩。

〔梅布尔·奇尔顿上。她加入人群。

梅布尔·奇尔顿 为什么你们要谈论谢弗利太太呢？谁都在谈论谢弗利太太！戈林子爵说——你说谢弗利太太什么话来着，戈林子爵？噢！我想起来了，你说她白天是一个天才，夜里是个美人。

巴西尔顿夫人 多么可怕的结合体啊！太怪异了！

马奇蒙特太太 （故作一副睡眼蒙眬的样子）我喜欢看天才，喜欢听美人！

戈林子爵 啊！你这是病态，马奇蒙特太太！

马奇蒙特太太 （脸上一亮，面露喜色）你这话我听了太高兴了。马奇蒙特和我结婚七年了，他从来没有告诉我是病态的。男人简直是有眼无珠。

巴西尔顿夫人 （向她转过身去）我早就说过，亲爱的玛格丽特，你是伦敦最有病态的人物。

马奇蒙特太太 呵！不过你总是讨人喜欢的，奥利维亚！

梅布尔·奇尔顿 食欲很强是不是病态呢？我整天就想着吃。戈林子爵，你愿意给我找些晚餐吗？

戈林子爵 不胜荣幸，梅布尔小姐。（和她离去。）

37

MABEL CHILTERN: How horrid you have been! You have never talked to me the whole evening!

LORD GORING: How could I? You went away with the child-diplomatist.

MABEL CHILTERN: You might have followed us. Pursuit would have been only polite. I don't think I like you at all this evening!

LORD GORING: I like you immensely.

MABEL CHILTERN: Well, I wish you'd show it in a more marked way!

They go downstairs.

MRS. MARCHMONT: Olivia, I have a curious feeling of absolute faintness. I think I should like some supper very much. I know I should like some supper.

LADY BASILDON: I am positively dying for supper, Margaret!

MRS. MARCHMONT: Men are so horribly selfish, they never think of these things.

LADY BASILDON: Men are grossly material, grossly material!

The VICOMTE DE NANJAC *enters from the music-room with some other guests. After having carefully examined all the people present, he approaches* LADY BASILDON.

VICOMTE DE NANJAC: May I have the honour of taking you down to supper, Countess?

LADY BASILDON (*coldly*): I never take supper, thank you, Vicomte. (*The* VICOMTE *is about to retire.* LADY BASILDON, *seeing this, rises at once and takes his arm.*) But I will come down with you with pleasure.

VICOMTE DE NANJAC: I am so fond of eating! I am very English in all my tastes.

梅布尔·奇尔顿 你真够狠心的!你整个晚上都不想着跟我说说话呀!

戈林子爵 怎么会呢?你和那位儿童外交家离去了。

梅布尔·奇尔顿 你可以跟着去嘛。紧随其后本来就是一种礼貌。我想我今晚是不怎么喜欢你了!

戈林子爵 我可喜欢得你不得了。

梅布尔·奇尔顿 哦,我希望你把这种喜欢表现得更突出些!

〔他们走下楼去。

马奇蒙特太太 奥利维亚,我有一种莫名其妙的眩晕感觉。我想我一定应该吃些晚餐了。我知道我应该吃些晚餐了。

巴西尔顿夫人 我想晚餐都快想死了,玛格丽特!

马奇蒙特太太 男人都自私得要命,他们从来想不到别的事情。

巴西尔顿夫人 男人全是粗糙的材料,粗糙的材料啊!

〔德·南加克子爵和别的一些客人从音乐室上。仔细审视所有在场的人后,他走近了巴西尔顿夫人。

德·南加克子爵 我带你们到楼下用晚餐好吗,伯爵夫人?

巴西尔顿夫人 (冷冷地)我从来不用晚餐,谢谢,子爵。(子爵打算离去。巴西尔顿夫人见了马上站起来,挽住了他的臂。)不过我很高兴和你下楼去。

德·南加克子爵 我特别喜欢吃!我的胃口完全英国化了。

LADY BASILDON: You look quite English, Vicomte, quite English.

They pass out. MR. MONTFORD, a perfectly groomed young dandy, approaches MRS. MARCHMONT.

MR. MONTFORD: Like some supper, Mrs. Marchmont?

MRS. MARCHMONT (*languidly*): Thank you, Mr. Montford, I never touch supper. (*Rises hastily and takes his arm.*) But I will sit beside you, and watch you.

MR. MONTFORD: I don't know that I like being watched when I am eating!

MRS. MARCHMONT: Then I will watch some one else.

MR. MONTFORD: I don't know that I should like that either.

MRS. MARCHMONT(*severely*): Pray, Mr. Montford, do not make these painful scenes of jealousy in public!

They go downstairs with the other guests, passing SIR ROBERT CHILTERN *and* MRS. CHEVELEY, *who now enter.*

SIR ROBERT CHILTERN: And are you going to any of our country houses before you leave England, Mrs. Cheveley?

MRS. CHEVELEY: Oh, no! I can't stand your English house-parties. In England people actually try to be brilliant at breakfast. That is dreadul of them! Only dull people are brilliant at breakfast. And then the family skeleton is always reading family prayers. My stay in England really depends on you, Sir Robert. (*Sits down on the sofa.*)

SIR ROBERT CHILTERN(*taking a seat beside her*): Seriously?

MRS. CHEVELEY: Quite seriously. I want to talk to

巴西尔顿夫人　你的样子也特别英国化,子爵,特别英国化。

〔他们走出去。蒙特福德先生,一位西装革履的年轻纨绔,走近马奇蒙特太太。

蒙特福德先生　去用点晚餐吗,马奇蒙特太太?

马奇蒙特太太　(无精打采地)谢谢,蒙特福德先生,我从来不动晚餐。(立即站起,挽住他的臂。)不过我坐在你身边,看着你吃好了。

蒙特福德先生　恐怕我不喜欢一边吃饭,一边让人看着。

马奇蒙特太太　那么我看别人好了。

蒙特福德先生　恐怕我也不喜欢这种做派。

马奇蒙特太太　(严厉地)蒙特福德先生,请别当着众人的面弄出这些个讨厌的小肚子鸡肠!

〔他们和别的客人一起走下楼梯,从罗伯特·奇尔顿爵士和谢弗利太太身边走过,见他们正在用餐。

罗伯特·奇尔顿爵士　谢弗利太太,你离开英格兰之前,还会到我们的乡间宅第去做客吗?

谢弗利太太　哦!不!我可受不了你们英格兰的家宴。在英格兰,人们实际上在早餐就跃跃欲试,表现不凡。那情境实在是可怕!只有无趣之人才在早餐桌上出风头。还有,一家之主总是念家庭祷告。我在英格兰呆多久真得看你了,罗伯特。(坐在沙发上。)

罗伯特·奇尔顿爵士　(在她身边坐下)是认真的吗?

谢弗利太太　非常认真。我想和你谈一个重大的政治和经

41

you about a great political and financial scheme, about this Argentine Canal Company, in fact.

SIR ROBERT CHILTERN: What a tedious, practical subject for you to talk about, Mrs. Cheveley!

MRS. CHEVELEY: Oh, I like tedious, practical subjects. What I don't like are tedious, practical people. There is a wide difference. Besides, you are interested, I know, in International Canal schemes. You were Lord Radley's secretary, weren't you, when the Government bought the Suez Canal shares?

SIR ROBERT CHILTERN: Yes. But the Suez Canal was a very great and splendid undertaking. It gave us our direct route to India. It had imperial value. It was necessary that we should have control. This Argentine scheme is a commonplace Stock Exchange swindle.

MRS. CHEVELEY: A speculation, Sir Robert! A brilliant, daring speculation.

SIR ROBERT CHILTERN: Believe me, Mrs. Cheveley, it is a swindle. Let us call things by their proper names. It makes matters simpler. We have all the information about it at the Foreign Office. In fact, I sent out a special Commission to inquire into the matter privately, and they report that the works are hardly begun, and as for the money already subscribed, no one seems to know what has become of it. The whole thing is a second Panama, and with not a quarter of the chance of success that miserable affair ever had. I hope you have not invested in it. I am sure you are far too clever to have done that.

MRS. CHEVELEY: I have invested very largely in it.

SIR ROBERT CHILTERN: Who could have advised you to do such a foolish thing?

MRS. CHEVELEY: Your old friend—and mine.

济计划,实际上是关于阿根廷运河公司的事。

罗伯特·奇尔顿爵士　你谈这问题未免太无聊、太实际了点吧,谢弗利太太!

谢弗利太太　噢,我就喜欢又无聊又实际的问题。我所不喜欢的是又无聊又实际的人。这中间的区别可大了去了。再说,我知道你对国际运河计划也有兴趣。政府购买苏伊士运河的股票时,你是拉德利勋爵的秘书,不是吗?

罗伯特·奇尔顿爵士　是的。可是苏伊士运河是一个非常有前途的大工程。它是我们去印度非走不可的航道。它的价值无可估量。我们控制它是很有必要的。这个阿根廷计划却是一个平常的股票交易骗局。

谢弗利太太　一桩投机生意,罗伯特爵士!一桩很有潜力、很大胆的投机生意。

罗伯特·奇尔顿爵士　相信我,谢弗利太太,那是个骗局。让我们按事情本来的名字叫它吧。这样事情就简单明了多了。我们外交部收集到了关于它的全部情况。事实上,我还派了一个专门的委员会前去私下调查,他们报告说那些工作难以开始,至于已经收集到的钱,鬼知道都哪里去了。这整个事情就是第二个巴拿马,成功的可能不大,麻烦倒是不小。但愿你没有往里投资吧。我知道你这人精明过人,不会干这样的事情。

谢弗利太太　可我已经往里面投资了。

罗伯特·奇尔顿爵士　谁让你干这样的傻事情的?

谢弗利太太　你的老朋友——也是我的朋友。

SIR ROBERT CHILTERN: Who?

MRS. CHEVELEY: Baron Arnbeim.

SIR ROBERT CHILTERN (*frowning*): Ah! yes. I remember hearing, at the time of his death, that he had been mixed up in the whole affair.

MRS. CHEVELEY: It was his last romance. His last but one, to do him justice.

SIR ROBERT CHILTERN (*rising*): But you have not seen my Corots yet. They are in the music-room. Corots seem to go with music, don't they? May I show them to you?

MRS. CHEVELEY (*shaking her head*): I am not in a mood to-night for silver twilights, or rose-pink dawns. I want to talk business. (*Motions to him with her fan to sit down again beside her.*)

SIR ROBERT CHILTERN: I fear I have no advice to give you, Mrs. Cheveley, except to interest yourself in something less dangerous. The success of the Canal depends, of course, on the attitude of England, and I am going to lay the report of the Commissioners before the House to-morrow night.

MRS. CHEVELEY: That you must not do. In your own interests, Sir Robert, to say nothing of mine, you must not do that.

SIR ROBERT CHILTERN (*looking at her in wonder*): In my own interests? My dear Mrs. Cheveley, what do you mean? (*Sits down beside her.*)

MRS. CHEVELEY: Sir Robert, I will be quite frank with you. I want you to withdraw the report that you had intended to lay before the House, on the ground that you have reasons to believe that the Commissioners have been prejudiced or misinformed, or something. Then I

罗伯特·奇尔顿爵士 谁？

谢弗利太太 安海姆男爵。

罗伯特·奇尔顿爵士 （皱眉）啊？是这样。我记得在他去世时听说他参与了整个事情。

谢弗利太太 这是他的最后一次冒险。他的最后一次，也是唯一一次，公道地说。

罗伯特·奇尔顿爵士 （站起）不过你还没有看见我那些柯罗的画吧。它们在音乐室里挂着。柯罗的画好像应该和音乐在一起，对不？我可以领你去看看它们吗？

谢弗利太太 （摇摇头）今天晚上我没有心情欣赏银光点点的黄昏，也没有心情观看朝霞满天的黎明。我只想谈生意。（她用扇子示意他重新坐到她身边来。）

罗伯特·奇尔顿爵士 恐怕我给你出不了什么好主意，谢弗利太太，我只可告诉你以后干些没有多大风险的事情。这条运河的成功的确要看英国的态度，明天晚上我就要把那个调查小组的报告提交给议院了。

谢弗利太太 你千万别那样做。且别说我的什么，仅从你自己的利益着想，你也一定不要那样干。

罗伯特·奇尔顿爵士 （不解地看着她）为了我自己的利益？我亲爱的谢弗利太太，你这是什么意思？（在她身边坐下。）

谢弗利太太 罗伯特爵士，我就跟你打开天窗说亮话吧。我想要你撤回你早已打算提交议院的那份报告，借口是你有种种理由相信调查委员会抱有偏见，或者调查不够，或者别的什么。然后我想要你说几句话，起到让

45

want you to say a few words to the effect that the Government is going to reconsider the question, and that you have reason to believe that the Canal, if completed, will be of great international value. You know the sort of things ministers say in cases of this kind. A few ordinary platitudes will do. In modern life nothing produces such an effect as a good platitude. It makes the whole world kin. Will you do that for me?

SIR ROBERT CHILTERN: Mrs. Cheveley, you cannot be serious in making me such a proposition!

MRS. CHEVELEY: I am quite serious.

SIR ROBERT CHILTERN(*coldly*): Pray allow me to believe that you are not.

MRS. CHEVELEY(*speaking with great deliberation and emphasis*): Ah! but I am. And if you do what I ask you. I... will pay you very handsomely!

SIR ROBERT CHILTERN: Pay me!

MRS. CHEVELEY: Yes.

SIR ROBERT CHILTERN: I am afraid I don't quite understand what you mean.

MRS. CHEVELEY(*leaning back on the sofa and looking at him*): How very disappointing! And I have come all the way from Vienna in order that you should thoroughly understand me.

SIR ROBERT CHILTERN: I fear I don't.

MRS. CHEVELEY(*in her most nonchalant manner*): My dear Sir Robert, you are a man of the world, and you have your price, I suppose. Everybody has nowadays. The drawback is that most people are so dreadfully expensive. I know I am. I hope you will be more reasonable in your terms.

SIR ROBERT CHILTERN(*rises indignantly*): If you will

政府重新考虑这个问题的作用,而你有理由相信这条运河一旦竣工,将会带来国际价值。你知道在这种情况下内阁大臣们会说的那些话。几句再平常不过的陈词滥调就把问题解决了。在现代生活里,什么话都不如陈词滥调会有这样的效果。这种话能让全世界亲如一家。你愿意为我做这件事吗?

罗伯特·奇尔顿爵士　谢弗利太太,你向我提出这样一种要求,一定不能是严肃的吧!

谢弗利太太　我是非常严肃的。

罗伯特·奇尔顿爵士　(冷冷地)还是让我相信你是不严肃的好。

谢弗利太太　(用非常慎重和强调的口气说)呵!可我的确是严肃的。如果你按我所要求的做了,我会……会付给你非常大的一笔款子!

罗伯特·奇尔顿爵士　付给我钱!

谢弗利太太　是的。

罗伯特·奇尔顿爵士　我担心我压根没有听懂你的意思。

谢弗利太太　(背靠在沙发上看着他)多么让人失望啊!我老远从维也纳来,为的就是让你完全理解我。

罗伯特·奇尔顿爵士　恐怕我理解不了啊。

谢弗利太太　(完全一副漠然的样子)我亲爱的罗伯特爵士,你可是世界级人物,有你自身的价值,我认为。当今之日,谁都有自己的价值。退却就意味着大多数人身价百倍了。我知道我是的。我希望你说话更加理智一点儿。

罗伯特·奇尔顿爵士　(生气地站起来)你要是允许我,我这

47

allow me, I will call your carriage for you. You have lived so long abroad, Mrs. Cheveley, that you seem to be unable to realise that you are talking to an English gentleman.

MRS. CHEVELEY (*detains him by touching his arm with her fan, and keeping it there while she is talking*): I realise that I am talking to a man who laid the foundation of his fortune by selling to a Stock Exchange speculator a Cabinet secret.

SIR ROBERT CHILTERN (*biting his lip*): What do you mean?

MRS. CHEVELEY (*rising and facing him*): I mean that I know the real origin of your wealth and your career, and I have got your letter, too.

SIR ROBERT CHILTERN: What letter?

MRS. CHEVELEY (*contemptuously*): The letter you wrote to Baron Arnheim, when you were Lord Radley's secretary, telling the Baron to buy Suez Canal shares—a letter written three days before the Government announced its own purchase.

SIR ROBERT CHILTERN (*hoarsely*): It is not true.

MRS. CHEVELEY: You thought that letter had been destroyed. How foolish of you! It is in my possession.

SIR ROBERT CHILTERN: The affair to which you allude was no more than a speculation. The House of Commons had not yet passed the bill; it might have been rejected.

MRS. CHEVELEY: It was a swindle, Sir Robert. Let us call things by their proper names. It makes everything simpler. And now I am going to sell you that letter, and the price I ask for it is your public support of the Argentine scheme. You made your own fortune out of one

第 一 幕

就给你叫马车。你在国外生活得时间太长了,谢弗利太太,你好像没有明白你是在和一位英国绅士讲话吧。

谢弗利太太 (用她的扇子点住他的臂,说话时一直用扇子顶在那里)我明白我在和一个通过向股票投机商出卖内阁秘密而平步青云的人讲话。

罗伯特·奇尔顿爵士 (咬着嘴唇)你这话什么意思?

谢弗利太太 (站起面对着他)我的意思是说我知道你发家致富和飞黄腾达的真正根源,我手里还拿着你的那封信呢。

罗伯特·奇尔顿爵士 什么信?

谢弗利太太 (傲慢地)你写给安海姆男爵的那封信,那时你还是拉德利勋爵的秘书,告诉安海姆男爵购买苏伊士运河的股票——一封在政府宣布自己购买股票三天前发出去的信。

罗伯特·奇尔顿爵士 (嗓子嘶哑地)根本不是事实。

谢弗利太太 你满以为那封信毁掉了。你多么傻呀!它现在在我的手里呢。

罗伯特·奇尔顿爵士 你提到的那件事当时不过是一种投机。下议院还没有通过那个提案;它还可能被否决。

谢弗利太太 它是一个骗局,罗伯特爵士。让我们按事情的正确名字叫它们好了。这样一切都简单多了。现在我要把这封信卖给你,我所要的价钱就是你公开支持

49

canal. You must help me and my friends to make our fortunes out of another!

SIR ROBERT CHILTERN: It is infamous, what you propose—infamous!

MRS. CHEVELEY: Oh, no! This is the game of life as we all have to play it, Sir Robert, sooner or later!

SIR ROBERT CHILTERN: I cannot do what you ask me.

MRS. CHEVELEY: You mean you cannot help doing it. You know you are standing on the edge of a precipice. And it is not for you to make terms. It is for you to accept them. Supposing you refuse—

SIR ROBERT CHILTERN: What then?

MRS. CHEVELEY: My dear Sir Robert, what then? You are ruined, that is all! Remember to what a point your Puritanism in England has brought you. In old days nobody pretended to be a bit better than his neighbours. In fact, to be a bit better than one's neighbour was considered excessively vulgar and middle-class. Nowadays, with our modern mania for morality, every one has to pose as a paragon of purity, incorruptibility, and all the other seven deadly virtues—and what is the result? You all go over like ninepins—one after the other. Not a year passes in England without somebody disappearing. Scandals used to lend charm, or at least interest, to a man— now they crush him. And yours is a very nasty scandal. You couldn't survive it. If it were known that as a young man, secretary to a great and important minister, you sold a Cabinet secret for a large sum of money, and that was the origin of your wealth and career, you would be hounded out of public life, you would disappear completely. And after all, Sir Robert, why should you sacrifice your entire future rather than deal diplomatically

那个阿根廷计划。你从一条运河里发了家。你一定要帮助我和我的朋友从另一条运河里交交好运！

罗伯特·奇尔顿爵士 那是无耻之举,你所提议的——是无耻之举！

谢弗利太太 哦,不！这是我们大家迟早都要玩的游戏,罗伯特！

罗伯特·奇尔顿爵士 我不能按你所要求的做。

谢弗利太太 你是说你非做不可吧。你知道你站在了悬崖边上了。这不是你讲条件的时候。这是你接受条件的时候。假如你拒绝的话——

罗伯特·奇尔顿爵士 那又怎么样呢？

谢弗利太太 我亲爱的罗伯特爵士,那又怎么样吗？你就全毁掉了,就这个！请记住你们英国的清教徒主义把你带到了什么地步了。在过去的岁月里,谁都不想装得比自己的邻居富裕。事实上,生活得比邻居富裕会被认为是极为庸俗的,是中产阶级。当今之日呢,我们有现代道德的狂热,大家都不得不争做廉洁奉公的完人,拒腐蚀的完人,七条美德的完人——可结果怎么样呢？你们都哗啦啦倒下了——一个接一个。一年还没过到头,英国总是有某个人会销声匿迹。丑闻过去让人有吸引力,或者至少让人产生兴趣——现在却把他碾碎了。你的丑闻是臭不可闻的那种。你躲不了这一劫。如果世人都知道,你年纪轻轻给一位举足轻重的内阁大臣当秘书时,把一桩内阁秘密卖了一大笔钱,那就是你发家致富和平步青云的本钱,那么你就会被逐出公众生活,你就会彻底销声匿迹的。说到底,罗伯特爵士,你为什么要牺牲你的全部前程,而不和你的敌人

with your enemy? For the moment I am your enemy. I admit it! And I am much stronger than you are. The big battalions are on my side. You have a splendid position, but it is your splendid position that makes you so vulnerable. You can't defend it! And I am in attack. Of course I have not talked morality to you. You must admit in fairness that I have spared you that. Years ago you did a clever, unscrupulous thing; it turned out a great success. You owe to it your fortune and position. And now you have got to pay for it. Sooner or later we have all to pay for what we do. You have to pay now. Before I leave you to-night, you have got to promise me to suppress your report, and to speak in the House in favour of this scheme.

SIR ROBERT CHILTERN: What you ask is impossible.

MRS. CHEVELEY: You must make it possible. You are going to make it possible. Sir Robert, you know what your English newspapers are like. Suppose that when I leave this house I drive down to some newspaper office, and give them this scandal and the proofs of it. Think of their loathsome joy, of the delight they would have in dragging you down, of the mud and mire they would plunge you in. Think of the hypocrite with his greasy smile penning his leading article, and arranging the foulness of the public placard.

SIR ROBERT CHILTERN: Stop! You want me to withdraw the report and to make a short speech stating that I believe there are possibilities in the scheme?

MRS. CHEVELEY (*sitting down on the sofa*): Those are my terms.

SIR ROBERT CHILTERN (*in a low voice*): I will give you any sum of money you want.

MRS. CHEVELEY: Even you are not rich enough, Sir

外交谈判呢？此时此刻我就是你的敌人。我承认这个！我比你强大得多。强大的军团在我这一边。你占据了一个显要位置，可正是你的显要位置让你容易受到攻击啊。你没有办法防卫！我在攻击。当然我不是在跟你谈道德。你必须公道地承认我让你绕过了道德问题。多年前，你干了一件精明却粗心的事情；结果它证明是了不起的成功。你的运气和地位多亏了它。现在你得为它还债了。或迟或早，我们都得为我们的所作所为还债。你现在就得还债了。今晚我离开你之前，你务必答应我收回你的报告，在议院里说些对这个项目有利的话。

罗伯特·奇尔顿爵士　你的要求是不可能的。

谢弗利太太　你必须使我的要求成为可能。你要去把我的要求变成可能。罗伯特爵士，你清楚英国报纸是什么样子。假如我离开这里坐上马车到某家报纸的编辑部去，把这件丑闻和证据捅给他们，那会是什么结果。想想他们那种令人恶心的欣喜，想想他们把你拉下台的高兴劲儿，想想他们会把你推进什么泥坑。想想那个伪君子脸上带着油腻腻的笑容，写出他的大文章，在公众布告栏里精心安排这件臭事。

罗伯特·奇尔顿爵士　住口吧！你不就是想要我撤销那份报告，简单明了地声明我相信那个项目具有种种可能吗？

谢弗利太太　（坐在了沙发上）这些正是我的条件。

罗伯特·奇尔顿爵士　（低声地）我给你钱，你要多少都行。

谢弗利太太　就是你也没有富到买回自己的过去的那一

Robert, to buy back your past. No man is.

SIR ROBERT CHILTERN: I will not do what you ask me. I will not.

MRS. CHEVELEY: You have to. If you don't.... (*Rises from the sofa.*)

SIR ROBERT CHILTERN (*bewildered and unnerved*): Wait a moment! What did you propose? You said that you would give me back my letter, didn't you?

MRS. CHEVELEY: Yes. That is agreed. I will be in the Ladies' Gallery to-morrow night at half-past eleven. If by that time—and you will have had heaps of opportunity—you have made an announcement to the House in the terms I wish, I shall hand you back your letter with the prettiest thanks, and the best, or at any rate the most suitable, compliment I can think of. I intend to play quite fairly with you. One should always play fairly... when one has the winning cards. The Baron taught me that... amongst other things.

SIR ROBERT CHILTERN: You must let me have time to consider your proposal.

MRS. CHEVELEY: No; you must settle now!

SIR ROBERT CHILTERN: Give me a week—three days!

MRS. CHEVELEY: Impossible! I have got to telegraph to Vienna to-night.

SIR ROBERT CHILTERN: My God! what brought you into my life?

MRS. CHEVELEY: Circumstances. (*Moves towards the door.*)

SIR ROBERT CHILTERN: Don't go. I consent. The report shall be withdrawn. I will arrange for a question to be put to me on the subject.

MRS. CHEVELEY: Thank you. I knew we should come

步。谁都不行。

罗伯特·奇尔顿爵士　我不会按你的要求去做。我不会的。

谢弗利太太　你不得已啊。如果你不照办……(从沙发上站起来。)

罗伯特·奇尔顿爵士　(为难和妥协状)等一会儿！你提出什么条件？你说你会把我的信还给我，是吗？

谢弗利太太　是的。正是这样。我明天晚上十一点半到议院的女士听众席去。如果到了那时——这之前你还有大量的机会呢——你按我的条件在议院发表讲话，那我会把你的信还给你，还少不了最悦耳的感谢话，少不了我能想得出来的最好或最得体的恭维话。我要跟你买卖公平。人做事总是要讲公平的……尤其你稳操胜券的话。男爵告诉我的……包括别的事情。

罗伯特·奇尔顿爵士　你务必留给我时间考虑你的建议。

谢弗利太太　不；你必须现在就定下来！

罗伯特·奇尔顿爵士　给我一星期——三天！

谢弗利太太　不行！我今天晚上就要给维也纳发电报。

罗伯特·奇尔顿爵士　天哪！什么让你闯进我的生活里来了？

谢弗利太太　种种因素。(朝门口走去。)

罗伯特·奇尔顿爵士　别走。我同意了。那份报告将撤去。我会在这个计划上三思而行的。

谢弗利太太　谢谢你。我早知道我们会达成愉快的协议

55

to an amicable agreement. I understood your nature from the first. I analysed you, though you did not adore me. And now you can get my carriage for me, Sir Robert. I see the people coming up from supper, and Englishmen always get romantic after a meal, and that bores me dreadfully. (*Exit* SIR ROBERT CHILTERN.)

Enter Guests, LADY CHILTERN, LADY MARKBY, LORD CAVERSHAM, LADY BASILDON, MRS. MARCHMONT, VICOMTE DE NANJAC, MR. MONTFORD.

LADY MARKBY: Well, dear Mrs. Cheveley, I hope you have enjoyed yourself. Sir Robert is very entertaining, is he not?

MRS. CHEVELEY: Most entertaining! I have enjoyed my talk with him immensely.

LADY MARKBY: He has had a very interesting and brilliant career. And he has married a most admirable wife. Lady Chiltern is a woman of the very highest principles, I am glad to say. I am a little too old now, myself, to trouble about setting a good example, but I always admire people who do. And Lady Chiltern has a very ennobling effect on life, though her dinner-parties are rather dull sometimes. But one can't have everything, can one? And now I must go, dear. Shall I call for you to-morrow?

MRS. CHEVELEY: Thanks.

LADY MARKBY: We might drive in the Park at five. Everything looks so fresh in the Park now!

MRS. CHEVELEY: Except the people!

LADY MARKBY: Perhaps the people are a little jaded. I have often observed that the Season as it goes on produces a kind of softening of the brain. However, I think anything is better than high intellectual pressure. That is the most unbecoming thing there is. It makes the noses of

的。从一开始我就知道你的本质。我分析过你,尽管你看不起我。现在你可以给我叫马车了,罗伯特爵士。我看人们吃过晚餐上楼来了;英国人饭后总是变得很浪漫,可我就受不了这个。(罗伯特·奇尔顿爵士下。)

〔客人们上,有奇尔顿夫人、马克比夫人、卡弗沙姆伯爵、巴西尔顿夫人、马奇蒙特太太、德·南加克子爵和蒙特福德先生。

马克比夫人　哦,亲爱的谢弗利太太,我想你很快活吧。罗伯特爵士很会应酬,不是吗?

谢弗利太太　简直左右逢源!我和他谈话愉快极了。

马克比夫人　他前程远大,令人眼馋啊。他娶了一个人见人夸的好妻子。奇尔顿夫人是一个非常循规蹈矩的女人,我很高兴说这话。我现在有点老了,没有精神头给人家树立好榜样了,可是我对能当榜样的人从心里佩服。奇尔顿夫人能使生活显得高雅尊贵,尽管有时候她的家宴很是乏味。不过人不能面面俱到,是吧?我现在得赶紧走了,亲爱的。我明天去拜访你吧?

谢弗利太太　谢谢。

马克比夫人　我们五点钟可以在那个公园坐坐马车。公园里现在处处透着新鲜!

谢弗利太太　人群在外!

马克比夫人　人们也许有点疲劳了。我经常看出来,社交季节一边进行,一边让人脑子疲软。不管如何,我认为什么都比高级智力压迫强。那才是最让人倒胃口的东西。那东西让年轻的姑娘鼻子都长得过分大了。鼻子

the young girls so particularly large. And there is nothing so difficult to marry as a large nose; men don't like them. Good-night, dear! (*To* LADY CHILTERN): Goodnight, Gertrude! (*Goes out on* LORD CAVERSHAM'S *arm*.)

MRS. CHEVELEY: What a charming house you have, Lady Chiltern! I have spent a delightful evening. It has been so interesting getting to know your husband.

LADY CHILTERN: Why did you wish to meet my husband, Mrs. Cheveley?

MRS. CHEVELEY: Oh, I will tell you. I wanted to interest him in this Argentine Canal scheme, of which I dare say you have heard. And I found him most susceptible—susceptible to reason, I mean. A rare thing in a man. I converted him in ten minutes. He is going to make a speech in the House to-morrow night in favour of the idea. We must go to the Ladies' Gallery and hear him! It will be a great occasion!

LADY CHILTERN: There must be some mistake. That scheme could never have my husband's support.

MRS. CHEVELEY: Oh, I assure you it's all settled. I don't regret my tedious journey from Vienna now. It has been a great success. But, of course, for the next twenty-four hours the whole thing is a dead secret.

LADY CHILTERN(*gently*): A secret? Between whom?

MRS. CHEVELEY (*with a flash of amusement in her eyes*): Between your husband and myself.

SIR ROBERT CHILTERN (*entering*): Your carriage is here, Mrs. Cheveley!

MRS. CHEVELEY: Thanks! Good-evening, Lady Chiltern! Goodnight, Lord Goring! I am at Claridge's. Don't you think you might leave a card?

第 一 幕

  大了可就很难嫁出去了。男人可不喜欢她们。晚安，亲爱的！（对奇尔顿夫人）晚安，格特鲁德！（挽着卡弗沙姆勋爵的臂下。）

谢弗利太太　奇尔顿夫人，你的家多么阔气啊！我今晚过得很开心。认识你的丈夫真是太妙了。

奇尔顿夫人　为什么你非要见我丈夫呢，谢弗利太太？

谢弗利太太　噢，我会告诉你的。我想要他对阿根廷河计划产生兴趣，我敢说你对这个计划已经听说了。我知道他最容易受影响——最容易受理智影响，我是说。这可是人身上难得的东西。我用了十分钟就让他改变了信仰。他明天晚上要在议院发表赞成这个主意的讲话。我们一定去女士旁听席听他讲演！这可是个重大时刻！

奇尔顿夫人　这里一定发生了什么误解。那个计划永远得不到我丈夫的支持。

谢弗利太太　哦，我向你保证，这事已经说定了。我不辞路途劳累从维也纳来，现在总算不后悔了。这次是大获全胜了。不过，当然，在二十四小时内这整件事情还是一件绝密呢。

奇尔顿夫人　（温和地）一个绝密？谁和谁之间的绝密？

谢弗利太太　（眼中得意地一亮）你丈夫和我本人之间。

罗伯特·奇尔顿爵士　（上场）你的马车到了，谢弗利太太！

谢弗利太太　谢谢！晚安，奇尔顿夫人！晚安，戈林子爵！我住在柯拉里奇旅馆。你认为你不应该留一张名片吗？

理想丈夫

LORD GORING: If you wish it, Mrs. Cheveley!

MRS. CHEVELEY: Oh, don't be so solemn about it, or I shall be obliged to leave a card on you. In England I suppose that would hardly be considered *en règle*. Abroad, we are more civilised. Will you see me down, Sir Robert? Now that we have both the same interests at heart we shall be great friends, I hope!

Sails out on SIR ROBERT CHILTERN'S *arm.* LADY CHILTERN *goes to the top of the staircase and looks down at them as they descend. Her expression is troubled. After a little time she is joined by some of the guests, and passes with them into another reception room.*

MABEL CHILTERN: What a horrid woman!

LORD GORING: You should go to bed, Miss Mabel.

MABEL CHILTERN: Lord Goring!

LORD GORING: My father told me to go to bed an hour ago. I don't see why I shouldn't give you the same advice. I always pass on good advice. It is the only thing to do with it. It is never of any use to oneself.

MABEL CHILTERN: Lord Goring, you are always ordering me out of the room. I think it most courageous of you. Especially as I am not going to bed for hours. (*Goes over to the sofa.*) You can come and sit down if you like, and talk about anything in the world, except the Royal Academy, Mrs. Cheveley, or novels in Scotch dialect. They are not improving subjects. (*Catches sight of something that is lying on the sofa half-hidden by the cushion.*) What is this? Some one has dropped a diamond brooch! Quite beautiful, isn't it? (*Shows it to him.*) I wish it was mine, but Gertrude won't let me wear anything but pearls, and I am thoroughly sick of pearls. They

第 一 幕

戈林子爵　只要你希望,谢弗利太太!

谢弗利太太　哦,别对一张名片也一本正经的,要不我就得给你留下一张名片了。可这在英国几乎没有人认为是得体的。在国外,我们都学得更开放一些。你送我下楼行吗,罗伯特爵士?我希望,既然我们心里有了共同的利益,你我就应该是好朋友!

〔挽着罗伯特爵士的臂飘然而去。奇尔顿夫人走到楼梯顶上往下看他们下楼。她一脸不高兴。过了一会儿,一些客人来到她身边,她就和客人们到另一间客厅去了。

梅布尔·奇尔顿　多么可怕的女人啊!

戈林子爵　你该睡觉去了,梅布尔小姐。

梅布尔·奇尔顿　戈林子爵!

戈林子爵　我父亲一个小时前就跟我说该睡觉了。我想我当然也可以给你提同样的建议了。我总是把好建议转达给别人。这是对好建议唯一可以做的事情。好建议对自己一个人是没有什么大用处的。

梅布尔·奇尔顿　戈林子爵,你总是命令我离开这间房间。我看你也太放肆了。尤其现在还不是我睡觉的时间。(走到沙发前)你要是喜欢,你可以坐下来,谈谈世界上的任何事情,只是不要谈皇家艺术学院,不要谈谢弗利太太,不要谈用苏格兰方言写的小说。它们净是些没劲的话题。(看见什么东西半掩半露在沙发垫子下面。)这是什么?有人把钻石胸针丢了!非常美丽吧,对不?(拿给他看。)多么希望它是我的呀,可是格特鲁德只让我戴珍珠,别的什么都不让我戴,可我又烦透了珍珠。戴上

61

make one look so plain, so good and so intellectual. I wonder whom the brooch belongs to.

LORD GORING: I wonder who dropped it.

MABEL CHILTERN: It is a beautiful brooch.

LORD GORING: It is a handsome bracelet.

MABEL CHILTERN: It isn't a bracelet. It's a brooch.

LORD GORING: It can be used as a bracelet. (*Takes it from her, and, pulling out a green letter-case, puts the ornament carefully in it, and replaces the whole thing in his breast-pocket with the most perfect sang froid.*)

MABEL CHILTERN: What are you doing?

LORD GORING: Miss Mabel, I am going to make a rather strange request to you.

MABEL CHILTERN (*eagerly*): Oh, pray do! I have been waiting for it all the evening.

LORD GORING (*is a little taken aback, but recovers himself*): Don't mention to anybody that I have taken charge of this brooch. Should any one write and claim it, let me know at once.

MABEL CHILTERN: That is a strange request.

LORD GORING: Well, you see I gave this brooch to somebody once, years ago.

MABEL CHILTERN: You did?

LORD GORING: Yes.

LADY CHILTERN *enters alone. The other guests have gone.*

MABEL CHILTERN: Then I shall certainly bid you good-night. Good-night, Gertrude! (*Exit.*)

LADY CHILTERN: Good-night, dear! (*To* LORD GORING): You saw whom Lady Markby brought here to night?

LORD GORING: Yes. It was an unpleasant surprise.

珍珠让人看上去太平常,太端庄,太理智。也不知道这胸针是谁的。

戈林子爵　我也不知道谁丢的。

梅布尔·奇尔顿　这是一枚很美丽的胸针吧。

戈林子爵　这是一个很美的手镯。

梅布尔·奇尔顿　这不是手镯。这是胸针。

戈林子爵　这可以当手镯戴。(从她手里接过来,拿出一个绿色信夹,细心地把胸针装进去,然后把整件东西异常冷静地放在了胸兜里。)

梅布尔·奇尔顿　你在做什么?

戈林子爵　梅布尔小姐,我要向你提出一个很奇怪的要求。

梅布尔·奇尔顿　(急切地)哦,请说吧!我都等了一晚上了。

戈林子爵　(有点吃惊,但马上稳住自己)别向任何人说我把这枚胸针收起了。要是有人写信来要,立即告诉我。

梅布尔·奇尔顿　这还真是一个奇怪的要求。

戈林子爵　哦,你看,这胸针是我多年前送给一个人的。

梅布尔·奇尔顿　你送人的?

戈林子爵　是的。

〔奇尔顿夫人一人上。其他客人离去了。

梅布尔·奇尔顿　那我一定得向你道晚安了。晚安,格特鲁德!(下。)

奇尔顿夫人　晚安,亲爱的!(对戈林子爵)你看马克比太太今晚把谁带这里来了?

戈林子爵　是啊。这是个令人不快的意外。她来这里干什

What did she come here for?

LADY CHILTERN: Apparently to try and lure Robert to uphold some fraudulent scheme in which she is interested. The Argentine Canal, in fact.

LORD GORING: She has mistaken her man, hasn't she?

LADY CHILTERN: She is incapable of understanding an upright nature like my husband's!

LORD GORING: Yes. I should fancy she came to grief if she tried to get Robert into her toils. It is extraordinary what astounding mistakes clever women make.

LADY CHILTERN: I don't call women of that kind clever. I call them stupid!

LORD GORING: Same thing often. Good-night, Lady Chiltern!

LADY CHILTERN: Good-night!

Enter SIR ROBERT CHILTERN.

SIR ROBERT CHILTERN: My dear Arthur, you are not going? Do stop a little!

LORD GORING: Afraid I can't, thanks. I have promised to look in at the Hartlocks'. I believe they have got a mauve Hungarian band that plays mauve Hungarian music. See you soon. Good-bye! (*Exit*.)

SIR ROBERT CHILTERN: How beautiful you look tonight, Gertrude!

LADY CHILTERN: Robert, it is not true, is it? You are not going to lend your support to this Argentine speculation? You couldn't!

SIR ROBERT CHILTERN(*starting*): Who told you I intended to do so?

LADY CHILTERN: That woman who has just gone out, Mrs. Cheveley, as she calls herself now. She seemed to

么来了？

奇尔顿夫人　明摆着是来试图说服罗伯特支持某个与她利益相关的骗局的。事实上就是阿根廷运河。

戈林子爵　她把她打交道的人看错了，不是吗？

奇尔顿夫人　她对像我丈夫这样的正直品质哪能理解得了！

戈林子爵　对。我想象得出，她要是非让罗伯特上她的圈套，她会碰一鼻子灰的。精明的女人竟然犯下这样的大错，真是少见。

奇尔顿夫人　我不认为这种女人精明。我认为她们很愚蠢！

戈林子爵　往往是同一样东西。晚安，奇尔顿夫人！

奇尔顿夫人　晚安！

　　〔罗伯特·奇尔顿上

罗伯特·奇尔顿爵士　你要走吗？请等一会儿好吧！

戈林子爵　恐怕不行，谢谢了。我答应去哈特洛克斯家看看的。我听说他们请了一个演奏紫红匈牙利音乐的紫红匈牙利管弦乐队。以后见。晚安！（下。）

罗伯特·奇尔顿爵士　你今天晚上多么好看啊，格特鲁德！

奇尔顿夫人　罗伯特，这不是真的，对吗？你不会支持那个阿根廷投机项目吧？你可不能支持啊！

罗伯特·奇尔顿爵士　（吃惊）谁告诉你我要支持的？

奇尔顿夫人　刚刚从这里出去的那个女人，谢弗利太太，她现在就是这样称呼她自己的。她好像还拿这件事嘲弄

65

taunt me with it. Robert, I know this woman. You don't. We were at school together. She was untruthful, dishonest, an evil influence on every one whose trust or friendship she could win. I hated, I despised her. She stole things, she was a thief. She was sent away for being a thief. Why do you let her influence you?

SIR ROBERT CHILTERN: Gertrude, what you tell me may be true, but it happened many years ago, It is best forgotten! Mrs. Cheveley may have changed since then. No one should be entirely judged by their past.

LADY CHILTERN (*sadly*): One's past is what one is. It is the only way by which people should be judged.

SIR ROBERT CHILTERN: That is hard saying, Gertrude!

LADY CHILTERN: It is a true saying, Robert. And what did she mean by boasting that she had got you to lend your support, your name, to a thing I have heard you describe as the most dishonest and fraudulent scheme there has ever been in political life?

SIR ROBERT CHILTERN (*biting his lip*): I was mistaken in the view I took. We all may make mistakes.

LADY CHILTERN: But you told me yesterday that you had received the report from the Commission, and that it entirely condemned the whole thing.

SIR ROBERT CHILTERN (*walking up and down*): I have reasons now to believe that the Commission was prejudiced, or, at any rate, misinformed. Besides, Gertrude, public and private life are different things. They have different laws, and move on different lines.

LADY CHILTERN: They should both represent man at his highest. I see no difference between them.

SIR ROBERT CHILTERN (*stopping*): In the present

第 一 幕

我呢。罗伯特,我了解这个女人。你不了解。我们过去一起上过学。她这个人满口瞎话,不诚实,她总是把她骗得信任和友谊的人往坏处勾引。我恨她,看不起她。她偷东西,她是个贼。她就是因为行窃才被送到别的地方去了。你为什么让她影响了你呢?

罗伯特·奇尔顿爵士　格特鲁德,你跟我说的也许是对的,不过那是许多年以前的事了。过去的最好让它过去吧!谢弗利太太后来也许完全变了。你不能老揪着人家的过去不放。

奇尔顿夫人　(痛心地)一个人的过去就是他的现在。看人就是要看人的过去。

罗伯特·奇尔顿爵士　这话很苛刻,格特鲁德!

奇尔顿夫人　这是大实话,罗伯特。她夸口说得到了你的支持,公开支持她,可你支持的事情却是你政治生涯中最虚假、最骗人的项目——你亲口跟我说的,她是什么意思呢?

罗伯特·奇尔顿爵士　(咬着嘴唇)我过去的判断有错。我们大家都会犯错误。

奇尔顿夫人　可是你昨天还和我说,你已经收到了调查委员会的报告,那份报告完全否定了那个大骗局。

罗伯特·奇尔顿爵士　(踱来踱去)我现在有理由相信调查委员会怀有偏见,或者至少得到的情况有误。还有,格特鲁德,公众生活和私人生活不是一回事。它们遵循不同的法律,奉行不同的路线。

奇尔顿夫人　它们应该是人的最高境界。我看不出它们中间有什么区别。

罗伯特·奇尔顿爵士　(站住)在目前的情况下,在一件实

case, on a matter of practical politics, I have changed my mind. That is all.

LADY CHILTERN: All!

SIR ROBERT CHILTERN(*sternly*): Yes!

LADY CHILTERN: Robert! oh! it is horrible that I should have to ask you such a question—Robert, are you telling me the whole truth?

SIR ROBERT CHILTERN: Why do you ask me such a question?

LADY CHILTERN(*after a pause*): Why do you not answer it?

SIR ROBERT CHILTERN (*sitting down*): Gertrude, truth is a very complex thing, and politics is a very complex business. There are wheels within wheels. One may be under certain obligations to people that one must pay. Sooner or later in political life one has to compromise. Every one does.

LADY CHILTERN: Compromise? Robert, why do you talk so differently to-night from the way I have always heard you talk? Why are you changed?

SIR ROBERT CHILTERN: I am not changed. But circumstances alter things.

LADY CHILTERN: Circumstances should never alter principles.

SIR ROBERT CHILTERN: But if I told you—

LADY CHILTERN: What?

SIR ROBERT CHILTERN: That it was necessary, vitally necessary?

LADY CHILTERN: It can never be necessary to do what is not honourable. Or if it be necessary, then what is it that I have loved! But it is not, Robert; tell me it is not. Why should it be? What gain would you get? Money?

际政治事情上,我改变了想法。就这么回事。

奇尔顿夫人　就这么回事!

罗伯特·奇尔顿爵士　(坚定地)是的!

奇尔顿夫人　罗伯特!噢!我问你这样一个问题实在是不得已,可是,罗伯特,你是在把全部真相都告诉我吗?

罗伯特·奇尔顿爵士　你为什么问这样一个问题?

奇尔顿夫人　(停顿稍许)你为什么不回答呢?

罗伯特·奇尔顿爵士　(坐下)格特鲁德,真理是非常复杂的事情,政治是非常复杂的生意。事情是错综复杂的。一个人受了人家的恩惠就得偿还。在政治生活中,一个人迟早得搞妥协。每个人都如此。

奇尔顿夫人　妥协?罗伯特,你今晚说话为什么跟过去我听到的完全不一样了?你为什么完全变了?

罗伯特·奇尔顿爵士　我没有变。可是种种情况把事情改变了。

奇尔顿夫人　什么情况都永远不能改变原则。

罗伯特·奇尔顿爵士　可是要是我告诉你——

奇尔顿夫人　什么?

罗伯特·奇尔顿爵士　那是必要的,绝对必要的呢?

奇尔顿夫人　不管干出什么不光彩的事情,都是绝对不行的。如果那样干是必要的,那我所爱过的究竟是什么呀!可那不是必要的,罗伯特,告诉我那不是必要的。那怎么会是必要的呢?你那样做会得到什么?钱吗?

We have no need of that! And money that comes from a tainted source is a degradation. Power? But power is nothing in itself. It is power to do good that is fine—that, and that only. What is it, then? Robert, tell me why you are going to do this dishonourable thing!

SIR ROBERT CHILTERN: Gertrude, you have no right to use that word. I told you it was a question of rational compromise. It is no more than that.

LADY CHILTERN: Robert, that is all very well for other men, for men who treat life simply as a sordid speculation; but not for you, Robert, not for you. You are different. All your life you have stood apart from others. You have never let the world soil you. To the world, as to myself, you have been an ideal always. Oh! be that ideal still. That great inheritance throw not away—that tower of ivory do not destroy. Robert, men can love what is beneath them—things unworthy, stained, dishonoured. We women worship when we love; and when we lose our worship, we lose everything. Oh! don't kill my love for you, don't kill that!

SIR ROBERT CHILTERN: Gertrude!

LADY CHILTERN: I know that there are men with horrible secrets in their lives—men who have done some shameful thing, and who in some critical moment have to pay for it, by doing some other act of shame—oh! don't tell me you are such as they are! Robert, is there in your life any secret dishonour or disgrace? Tell me, tell me at once, that—

SIR ROBERT CHILTERN: That what?

LADY CHILTERN (*speaking very slowly*): That our lives may drift apart.

SIR ROBERT CHILTERN: Drift apart?

第 一 幕

我们根本不需要钱!来自肮脏渠道的钱是一种堕落。权力吗?可是权力本身什么都不是啊。权力只有用来干好事才正当——这也是唯一的。它还能是别的什么吗?罗伯特,告诉我你为什么要去干这种不光彩的事情!

罗伯特·奇尔顿爵士　格特鲁德,你说不光彩是没有道理的。我跟你说了这是一个理性妥协的问题。仅仅是这样一个问题。

奇尔顿夫人　罗伯特,这话让别人说很合适,让那些只把生活当做不折不扣的投机生意来做的人说这种话吧;但是你不能说,罗伯特,你不能说这样的话。你和那样的人不一样。你一辈子都应该与众不同。你永远都不能让这个世界把你弄脏了。对这个世界,对你本人,你就总是一种理想。噢!当好这样的理想吧。伟大的遗产是丢不得的——象牙之塔不能摧毁。罗伯特,男人可以爱不如他的东西——不值钱的、肮脏的、不光彩的东西。我们女人崇拜我们爱的东西;我们没有了崇拜,我们就失去了一切。哦!别扼杀了我对你的爱,别扼杀啊!

罗伯特·奇尔顿爵士　格特鲁德!

奇尔顿夫人　我知道男人的生活里隐藏着可怕的秘密——那种男人干了某件可耻的事情,在某个关键时刻得靠做另一件可耻的事情来偿还——噢!别告诉我你也是那种人!罗伯特,你生活里有什么丢人或可耻的秘密吗?告诉我,立即告诉我,说——

罗伯特·奇尔顿爵士　说什么?

奇尔顿夫人　(说得一字一顿)我们的生活也许会成为泡影。

罗伯特·奇尔顿爵士　泡影?

LADY CHILTERN: That they may entirely separate. It would be better for us both.

SIR ROBERT CHILTERN: Gertrude, there is nothing in my past life that you might not know.

LADY CHILTERN: I was sure of it, Robert, I was sure of it. But why did you say those dreadful things, things so unlike your real self? Don't let us ever talk about the subject again. You will write, won't you, to Mrs. Cheveley, and tell her that you cannot support this scandalous scheme of hers? If you have given her any promise you must take it back, that is all!

SIR ROBERT CHILTERN: Must I write and tell her that?

LADY CHILTERN: Surely, Robert! What else is there to do?

SIR ROBERT CHILTERN: I might see her personally. It would be better.

LADY CHILTERN: You must never see her again, Robert. She is not a woman you should ever speak to. She is not worthy to talk to a man like you. No; you must write to her at once, now, this moment, and let your letter show her that your decision is quite irrevocable!

SIR ROBERT CHILTERN: Write this moment!

LADY CHILTERN: Yes.

SIR ROBERT CHILTERN: But it is so late. It is close on twelve.

LADY CHILTERN: That makes no matter. She must know at once that she has been mistaken in you—and that you are not a man to do anything base or underhand or dishonourable. Write here, Robert. Write that you decline to support this scheme of hers, as you hold it to be a dishonest scheme. Yes—write the word dishonest. She

第 一 幕

奇尔顿夫人　完全成为两个泡沫。那样对我们俩也许更好。

罗伯特·奇尔顿爵士　格特鲁德,我过去的生活没有什么你不可以知道的。

奇尔顿夫人　我很放心,罗伯特,我完全放心这点。可是你为什么说出那样可怕的话来,那些话和你真实的生活不相称呀？我们不再谈这件事情了。你写信告诉谢弗利太太,告诉她你不会支持她那个可耻的计划,不行吗？如果你已经答应了她什么,你务必马上撤回来,没有别的好说！

罗伯特·奇尔顿爵士　我必须写信告诉她吗？

奇尔顿夫人　必须写,罗伯特！还有别的选择吗？

罗伯特·奇尔顿爵士　我可以和她单独见面。那样也许更好办。

奇尔顿夫人　你一定不能和她再见面,罗伯特。她这个女人你根本就不应该和她说话。她不配和你这样的男人说话。不！你必须立即给她写信,就现在,就这会儿,写信让她明白你的决定是不可改变的！

罗伯特·奇尔顿爵士　这会儿就写！

奇尔顿夫人　是的。

罗伯特·奇尔顿爵士　可是已经晚了。十二点就关门了。

奇尔顿夫人　没关系。她必须马上明白她错看了你——明白你这个人不会干任何下流、龌龊、可耻的事情。就在这里写,罗伯特。写你拒绝支持她的那个计划,因为你认为那是一个弄虚作假的计划。是的——写上"弄虚

73

knows what that word means. (SIR ROBERT CHILTERN *sits down and writes a letter. His wife takes it up and reads it.*) Yes; that will do. (*Rings bell.*) And now the envelope. (*He writes the envelope slowly. Enter* MASON.) Have this letter sent at once to Claridge's Hotel. There is no answer. (*Exit* MASON. LADY CHILTERN *kneels down beside her husband and puts her arms around him.*) Robert, love gives one an instinct to things. I feel to-night that I have saved you from something that might have been a danger to you, from something that might have made men honour you less than they do. I don't think you realise sufficiently, Robert, that you have brought into the political life of our time a nobler atmosphere, a finer attitude towards life, a freer air of purer aims and higher ideals—I know it, and for that I love you, Robert.

SIR ROBERT CHILTERN: Oh, love me always, Gertrude, love me always!

LADY CHILTERN: I will love you always, because you will always be worthy of love. We must love the highest when we see it! (*Kisses him and rises and goes out.*)

> SIR ROBERT CHILTERN *walks up and down for a moment; then sits down and buries his face in his hands. The Servant enters and begins putting out the lights.* SIR ROBERT CHILTERN *looks up.*

SIR ROBERT CHILTERN: Put out the lights, Mason, put out the lights!

> *The Servant puts out the lights. The room becomes almost dark. The only light there is comes from the great chandelier that hangs over the staircase and illumines the tapestry of the Triumph of Love.*

ACT DROP

作假"这个词儿。她很明白这个词儿是什么意思。(罗伯特·奇尔顿爵士坐下写信。他妻子拿起信看过。)对了,这样就行了。(按响铃。)把信皮写好。(他慢慢地写好信皮。梅森上。)马上把这封信送到柯拉奇旅馆。不用等回话。(梅森下。奇尔顿夫人跪在她的丈夫身边,用胳膊搂住他。)罗伯特,爱能使人对事情产生本能。今天晚上我觉得我让你避免了某些危及你人生的东西,让你避免了某些人们会因此小看你的东西。我看你还没有完全认识到,罗伯特,你已经给我们时代的政治生活带来了一种更加高贵的气氛,一种对生活更加善待的态度,一种目的更纯、理想更高的自由空气——可我知道这点,我爱你就是为了这点,罗伯特。

罗伯特·奇尔顿爵士　喔,永远爱我,格特鲁德,永远爱我吧!

奇尔顿夫人　我会永远爱你,因为你永远值得我爱。我们认清了爱,我们就加倍需要爱!(吻过他,站起身,下。)

〔罗伯特·奇尔顿爵士来回踱了一会儿;然后坐下用手把脸捂上。仆人上,开始熄灭蜡烛。罗伯特·奇尔顿露开脸看。

罗伯特·奇尔顿爵士　把蜡烛熄灭,梅森,快把蜡烛熄灭!

〔仆人把蜡烛熄灭。屋子几乎完全暗下来。唯一的亮光来自楼梯上方那盏枝形吊灯,它把《维纳斯的胜利》挂毯照得一清二楚。

幕　落

ACT TWO

SCENE: Morning-room at Sir Robert Chiltern's house.

> LORD GORING, *dressed in the height of fashion, is lounging in an arm-chair.* SIR ROBERT CHILTERN *is standing in front of the fireplace. He is evidently in a state of great mental excitement and distress. As the scene progresses he paces nervously up and down the room.*

LORD GORING: My dear Robert, it's a very awkward business, very awkward indeed. You should have told your wife the whole thing. Secrets from other people's wives are a necessary luxury in modern life. So, at least, I am always told at the club by people who are bald enough to know better. But no man should have a secret from his own wife. She invariably finds it out. Women have a wonderful instinct about things. They can discover everything except the obvious.

SIR ROBERT CHILTERN: Arthur, I couldn't tell my wife. When could I have told her? Not last night. It would have made a lifelong separation between us, and I would have lost the love of the one woman in the world I worship, of the only woman who had ever stirred love within me. Last night it would have been quite impossible. She would have turned from me in horror... in horror and in contempt.

LORD GORING: Is Lady Chiltern as perfect as all that?

SIR ROBERT CHILTERN: Yes; my wife is as perfect as

第 二 幕

场景:罗伯特·奇尔顿爵士府上早晨用的起居室。

〔戈林子爵,穿戴得非常入时,吊儿郎当地坐在扶手椅子里。罗伯特·奇尔顿爵士站在壁炉前面。他显然处于极度的精神紧张和压抑之中。随着布景显现,他在屋子里不安地踱来踱去。

戈林子爵　我亲爱的罗伯特,这是一笔非常笨拙的生意,的确非常笨拙。你应该把全部事实告诉你的妻子。在现代生活里,他人妻子的秘密是必不可少的奢侈品。至少我在俱乐部里经常听见懂得更多的上年纪的人说这种话。可是男人谁都不应该跟自己的妻子保守秘密。她不知怎样就发现了。女人对事情有一种奇妙的本能。她们什么都能发现,就是明摆着的东西视而不见。

罗伯特·奇尔顿爵士　亚瑟,我不能和我妻子说啊。什么时候我能跟她说呢? 昨天夜里不能说吧。一旦说了,那会让我们两个从此分手,我会失去这世界上我所崇拜的女人的爱,她是唯一在我心里激起我的爱的女人啊。昨天晚上是根本说不得的。她一旦听说了她会极端地厌恶我……又厌恶我又蔑视我。

戈林子爵　奇尔顿夫人就完美无缺到这种地步吗?

罗伯特·奇尔顿爵士　是的;我妻子就完美到了这种地步。

all that.

LORD GORING (*taking off his left-hand glove*): What a pity! I beg your pardon, my dear fellow, I didn't quite mean that. But if what you tell me is true, I should like to have a serious talk about life with Lady Chiltern.

SIR ROBERT CHILTERN: It would be quite useless.

LORD GORING: May I try?

SIR ROBERT CHILTERN: Yes; but nothing could make her alter her views.

LORD GORING: Well, at the worst it would simply be a psychological experiment.

SIR ROBERT CHILTERN: All such experiments are terribly dangerous.

LORD GORING: Everything is dangerous, my dear fellow. If it wasn't so, life wouldn't be worth living... Well, I am bound to say that I think you should have told her years ago.

SIR ROBERT CHILTERN: When? When we were engaged? Do you think she would have married me if she had known that the origin of my fortune is such as it is, the basis of my career such as it is, and that I had done a thing that I suppose most men would call shameful and dishonourable?

LORD GORING (*slowly*): Yes; most men would call it ugly names. There is no doubt of that.

SIR ROBERT CHILTERN (*bitterly*): Men who every day do something of the same kind themselves. Men who, each one of them, have worse secrets in their own lives.

LORD GORING: That is the reason they are so pleased to find out other people's secrets. It distracts public attention from their own.

SIR ROBERT CHILTERN: And, after all, whom did I

第 二 幕

戈林子爵 （脱下他左手的手套）多么遗憾啊！对不起,我亲爱的老兄,我根本不是那个意思。不过,如果你跟我所说的都是真的,那我应该和奇尔顿夫人严肃地谈谈生活。

罗伯特·奇尔顿爵士 谈话根本不管用的。

戈林子爵 我试试行吗？

罗伯特·奇尔顿爵士 不妨一试。不过什么也改变不了她的看法。

戈林子爵 噢,最差也不过是一次心理实验嘛。

罗伯特·奇尔顿爵士 所有这种实验都是非常危险的。

戈林子爵 每件事情都是危险的,我亲爱的老兄。如果不是这样,那么生活就不值得生活了……噢,可我还是要说,我认为你多年前就应该告诉她。

罗伯特·奇尔顿爵士 什么时候？我们定下终身的时候吗？她如果知道我时来运转的根底原来如此,我平步青云的根基原来如此,我原来干了一件我想大多数人都会称为羞耻和丢人的事情,那么她还会嫁给我吗？

戈林子爵 （慢慢地）是啊。多数人都会叫出一连串难听的名字。这是毫无疑问的。

罗伯特·奇尔顿爵士 （恶狠狠地）其实那些人自己每天都在干同样肮脏的事情。他们每个人的生活里都藏着更肮脏的秘密。

戈林子爵 这也正是他们乐此不疲专找别人的秘密的原因。这样才能让公众的注意力避开他们自己。

罗伯特·奇尔顿爵士 而且,我所做的事情究竟伤害谁了

wrong by what I did? No one.

LORD GORING (*looking at him steadily*): Except yourself, Robert.

SIR ROBERT CHILTERN (*after a pause*): Of course I had private information about a certain transaction contemplated by the Government of the day, and I acted on it. Private information is practically the source of every large modern fortune.

LORD GORING (*tapping his boot with his cane*): And public scandal invariably the result.

SIR ROBERT CHILTERN (*pacing up and down the room*): Arthur, do you think that what I did nearly eighteen years ago should be brought up against me now? Do you think it fair that a man's whole career should be ruined for a fault done in one's boyhood almost? I was twenty-two at the time, and I had the double misfortune of being well-born and poor, two unforgivable things nowadays. Is it fair that the folly, the sin of one's youth, if men choose to call it a sin, should wreck a life like mine, should place me in the pillory, should shatter all that I have worked for, all that I have built up? Is it fair, Arthur?

LORD GORING: Life is never fair, Robert. And perhaps it is a good thing for most of us that it is not.

SIR ROBERT CHILTERN: Every man of ambition has to fight his century with its own weapons. What this century worships is wealth. The God of this century is wealth. To succeed one must have wealth. At all costs one must have wealth.

LORD GORING: You underrate yourself, Robert. Believe me, without your wealth you could have succeeded just as well.

呢？谁都没有伤害啊。

戈林子爵　（目不转睛地看着他）就伤害了你自己，罗伯特。

罗伯特·奇尔顿爵士　（稍停）当然，我当时的确私下了解到一桩政府正在关注的生意，而且做了手脚。现代社会每一笔成功的大买卖都得靠秘密的信息。

戈林子爵　（用手杖轻轻敲着靴子）那也是社会丑闻的必然结果。

罗伯特·奇尔顿爵士　（在屋子里踱来踱去）亚瑟，你认为我十八年前所干的事情，现在该得到报应了吗？你真的认为一个人几乎还是在他童年犯下的过错，会毁掉他整个生涯吗？我那时也就二十二岁，不幸的是我出身好，却很穷，这两点在今天是无法原谅的东西。年轻时做的蠢事，犯下的罪孽——如果人家愿意称之为罪孽的话——就硬要把像我这样人的生活毁了，硬把我套进颈手枷里，硬要打碎我奋斗来的一切，让我辛苦经营的一切化为泡影，难道这公道吗？这公道吗，亚瑟？

戈林子爵　生活从来就不公道，罗伯特。对我们大多数人来说，生活不公道也许是一件好事。

罗伯特·奇尔顿爵士　每一个雄心勃勃的人都应该用他所处世纪的武器为他的世纪而战。这个世纪崇拜的是财富。这个世纪的上帝就是财富。要成功就得有财富。不管付出什么代价，你必须有财富。

戈林子爵　你低估了你自己，罗伯特。相信我，没有你那些财富，你同样会取得成功。

SIR ROBERT CHILTERN: When I was old, perhaps. When I had lost my passion for power, or could not use it. When I was tired, worn out, disappointed. I wanted my success when I was young. Youth is the time for success. I couldn't wait.

LORD GORING: Well, you certainly have had your success while you are still young. No one in our day has had such a brilliant success. Under-Secretary for Foreign Affairs at the age of forty—that's good enough for any one. I should think.

SIR ROBERT CHILTERN: And if it is all taken away from me now? If I lose everything over a horrible scandal? If I am hounded from public life?

LORD GORING: Robert, how could you have sold yourself for money?

SIR ROBERT CHILTERN (*excitedly*): I did not sell myself for money. I bought success at a great price. That is all.

LORD GORING (*gravely*): Yes; you certainly paid a great price for it. But what first made you think of doing such a thing?

SIR ROBERT CHILTERN: Baron Arnheim.

LORD GORING: Damned scoundrel!

SIR ROBERT CHILTERN: No; he was a man of a most subtle and refined intellect. A man of culture, charm, and distinction. One of the most intellectual men I ever met.

LORD GORING: Ah! I prefer a gentlemanly fool any day. There is more to be said for stupidity than people imagine. Personally, I have a great admiration for stupidity. It is a sort of fellow-feeling, I suppose. But how did he do it? Tell me the whole thing.

SIR ROBERT CHILTERN (*throws himself into an arm-*

罗伯特·奇尔顿爵士　那也许要等到我老的时候吧。等到我失去了对权力的激情,或者不能使用它的时候。等到我疲倦了,磨秃了,失望了。可我年轻的时候就想成功。青春才是成功的好时机。我等不得啊。

戈林子爵　得了,你的确在你还年轻的时候就获得了成功。我们今天没有几个人获得这样骄人的成功。四十岁就当上了外交部的副部长——依我看这对谁来说都应该感到满足。

罗伯特·奇尔顿爵士　可是如果这一切现在都从我这里夺走呢?如果我因为一件可怕的丑闻失去一切呢?如果我被赶出公众生活呢?

戈林子爵　罗伯特,你怎么能把自己卖给金钱呢?

罗伯特·奇尔顿爵士　(激动地)我没有把自己卖给金钱。我用大价钱买到了成功。就这么回事。

戈林子爵　(正经地)是的,你为它的确花了大价钱。可是一开始什么因素让你想到干这样的事呢?

罗伯特·奇尔顿爵士　安海姆男爵。

戈林子爵　该死的流氓!

罗伯特·奇尔顿爵士　不;他是一个明察毫厘才智超凡的人。一个有教养、有魅力、有个性的人。是我见过的最有智慧的人。

戈林子爵　啊!我什么时候都更喜欢具有绅士风度的糊涂蛋。糊涂蛋可说可论的内容远比人们想象得多。就个人而言,我对糊涂行为羡慕不已。我琢磨这也许是一种同情吧。不过他是怎么达到目的的呢?把整个事情告诉我。

罗伯特·奇尔顿爵士　(一下坐在写字台旁边的扶手椅子里)一

chair by the writing-table): One night after dinner at Lord Radley's the Baron began talking about success in modern life as something that one could reduce to an absolutely definite science. With that wonderfully fascinating quiet voice of his he expounded to us the most terrible of all philosophies, the philosophy of power, preached to us the most marvellous of all gospels, the gospel of gold. I think he saw the effect he had produced on me, for some days afterwards he wrote and asked me to come and see him. He was living then in Park Lane, in the house Lord Woolcomb has now. I remember so well how, with a strange smile on his pale, curved lips, he led me through his wonderful picture gallery, showed me his tapestries, his enamels, his jewels, his carved ivories, made me wonder at the strange loveliness of the luxury in which he lived; and then told me that luxury was nothing but a background, a painted scene in a play, and that power, power over other men, power over the world, was the one thing worth having, the one supreme pleasure worth knowing, the one joy one never tired of, and that in our century only the rich possessed it.

LORD GORING (*with great deliberation*): A thoroughly shallow creed.

SIR ROBERT CHILTERN (*rising*): I didn't think so then. I don't think so now. Wealth has given me enormous power. It gave me at the very outset of my life freedom, and freedom is everything. You have never been poor, and never known what ambition is. You cannot understand what a wonderful chance the Baron gave me. Such a chance as few men get.

LORD GORING: Fortunately for them, if one is to judge by results. But tell me definitely, how did the Baron

第 二 幕

天晚上在拉德利勋爵府上,男爵开始谈起现代生活中的成功问题,认为这已是一个人完全依靠科学可以做到的事情。他用非常迷人的平静的声音向我们讲述所有哲学中最可怕的哲学,权力的哲学,对我们宣传所有福音中最奇怪的福音,金子的福音。我想他看见他的布道在我身上发生的效果,因为几天以后他写信要我去见他。他那时住在公园巷,伍尔科姆勋爵府上现在就在那里。我记得非常清楚他苍白的脸上那种古怪的微笑,翘上去的嘴角,他领着我穿过他的画室,让我看他的挂毯,他的搪瓷制品,他的珠宝,他的镂雕象牙,终使得我对他生活其中的豪华奢侈羡慕不已;随后他告诉我奢侈只不过是一种背景,是剧本中的布景,只有权力,万人之上的权力,左右世界的权力,才是值得享有的东西,值得知道的至高快乐,是人乐此不疲的欢乐,是我们这个世纪只有富人才拥有的东西。

戈林子爵　(非常郑重地)一种浅薄之极的信条。

罗伯特·奇尔顿爵士　(起立)我当时并不这样认为。我现在也不这样认为。财富给了我很大的权力。它让我一开始生活就享有了自由,而自由就是一切。你从来就没有受过穷,从来不知道胸怀抱负是什么意思。你不理解男爵给了我多么美妙的机会。这样的机会很少有人得到啊。

戈林子爵　如果根据结果来看,没有那些玩艺儿倒是万幸了。不过明明白白地告诉我,男爵到底是怎么说服你

finally persuade you to—well, to do what you did?

SIR ROBERT CHILTERN: When I was going away he said to me that if I ever could give him any private information of real value he would make me a very rich man. I was dazed at the prospect he held out to me, and my ambition and my desire for power were at that time boundless. Six weeks later certain private documents passed through my hands.

LORD GORING (*keeping his eyes steadily fixed on the carpet*): State documents?

SIR ROBERT CHILTERN: Yes.

LORD GORING *sighs, then passes his hand across his forehead and looks up.*

LORD GORING: I had no idea that you, of all men in the world, could have been so weak, Robert, as to yield to such a temptation as Baron Arhneim held out to you.

SIR ROBERT CHILTERN: Weak? Oh, I am sick of hearing that phrase. Sick of using it about others. Weak! Do you really think, Arthur, that it is weakness that yields to temptation? I tell you that there are terrible temptations that it requires strength, strength and courage, to yield to. To stake all one's life on a single moment, to risk everything on one throw, whether the stake be power or pleasure, I care not—there is no weakness in that. There is a horrible, a terrible courage. I had that courage. I sat down the same afternoon and wrote Baron Arnheim the letter this woman now holds. He made three-quarters of a million over the transaction.

LORD GORING: And you?

SIR ROBERT CHILTERN: I received from the Baron £110,000.

LORD GORING: You were worth more, Robert.

第 二 幕

去——哦,去干你所干的事情的?

罗伯特·奇尔顿爵士　我要离去时,他跟我说,如果我能给他什么货真价实的秘密信息,他能让我成为一个阔佬儿。他给我指出的前景令我向往,我当时对权力的欲望没有止境。六个星期后,一些秘密文件从我的手里传了出去。

戈林子爵　（两眼死死盯着地毯）国家文件吗?

罗伯特·奇尔顿爵士　是的。

〔戈林子爵叹了口气,然后用手在额前挥了一下,眼往上看。

戈林子爵　我真不明白,你这人上之人,是这般软弱,罗伯特,竟然在安海姆男爵给你下的钓饵前上了钩。

罗伯特·奇尔顿爵士　软弱?哦,我特别反感这个词儿。反感对别人使用这个词儿。软弱!亚瑟,你真的认为在钓饵前上钩是软弱行为吗?我跟你说,世上成千上万的可怕钓饵是需要力量——力量和勇气——才敢上钩的。把全部生命在瞬间押上去,孤注一掷,不管所押的赌注是力量还是快活,我都不在乎——这中间根本就没有软弱。这需要惊人的、可怕的勇气。我有这个勇气。在同一个下午,我坐下来给安海姆男爵写了那封现在落在这个女人手里的信。他在那笔生意里赚到了七十五万英镑钱。

戈林子爵　你呢?

罗伯特·奇尔顿爵士　我从男爵那里得到了十一万英镑。

戈林子爵　你还应该多得,罗伯特。

SIR ROBERT CHILTERN: No; that money gave me exactly what I wanted, power over others. I went into the House immediately. The Baron advised me in finance from time to time. Before five years I had almost trebled my fortune. Since then everything that I have touched has turned out a success. In all things connected with money I have had a luck so extraordinary that sometimes it has made me almost afraid. I remember having read somewhere, in some strange book, that when the gods wish to punish us they answer our prayers.

LORD GORING: But tell me, Robert, did you never suffer any regret for what you had done?

SIR ROBERT CHILTERN: No. I felt that I had fought the century with its own weapons, and won.

LORD GORING(*sadly*): You thought you had won.

SIR ROBERT CHILTERN: I thought so. (*After a long pause*): Arthur, do you despise me for what I have told you?

LORD GORING(*with deep feeling in his voice*): I am very sorry for you, Robert, very sorry indeed.

SIR ROBERT CHILTERN: I don't say that I suffered any remorse. I didn't. Not remorse in the ordinary, rather silly sense of the word. But I have paid conscience money many times. I had a wild hope that I might disarm destiny. The sum Baron Arnheim gave me I have distributed twice over in public charities since then.

LORD GORING (*looking up*): In public charities? Dear me! what a lot of harm you must have done, Robert!

SIR ROBERT CHILTERN: Oh, don't say that, Arthur; don't talk like that!

LORD GORING: Never mind what I say, Robert! I am

罗伯特·奇尔顿爵士　不;那笔钱正好是我想要的,在别人之上的权力。我马上进了议院。男爵在经济方面一次又一次给我出主意。不到五年,我的财产几乎翻了三倍。从那以后,我所染指的每件事都最后获得成功。在所有和金钱有关系的事情上我都吉星高照,有时我都会因此感到害怕。我记得在一本很怪的书里什么地方看到,诸神要是打算惩罚我们,他们就会回答我们的祈祷。

戈林子爵　可是告诉我,罗伯特,你从来没有为你所做的事感到后悔吗?

罗伯特·奇尔顿爵士　没有。我觉得我已经为这个世纪用它的武器去战斗,并且打赢了。

戈林子爵　(悲痛地)你以为你打赢了。

罗伯特·奇尔顿爵士　我是这样认为的。(停顿许久后)亚瑟,我跟你说了这些,你会看不起我吗?

戈林子爵　(声音里深带感情地说)我为你感到非常遗憾,罗伯特,真的非常遗憾。

罗伯特·奇尔顿爵士　我得说我没有任何悔恨的痛苦。我没有过。从悔恨这个词儿平常而愚蠢的意义上讲,我没有过任何悔恨。不过我已经多次付出过良心钱了。我一心希望我能够让命运感到无奈。安海姆男爵给我的那笔钱,我已经向公共慈善机构捐献了两次钱了。

戈林子爵　(抬头看)向公共慈善机构捐钱?天哪!你干了多少有害的事情了,罗伯特!

罗伯特·奇尔顿爵士　哦,别这样说话,亚瑟;别这样说话!

戈林子爵　别在乎我说了什么,罗伯特!我总是说些我不

always saying what I shouldn't say. In fact, I usually say what I really think. A great mistake nowadays. It makes one so liable to be understood. As regards this dreadful business, I will help you in whatever way I can. Of course you know that.

SIR ROBERT CHILTERN: Thank you, Arthur, thank you. But what is to be done? What can be done?

LORD GORING (*leaning back with his hands in his pockets*): Well, the English can't stand a man who is always saying he is in the right, but they are very fond of a man who admits that he has been in the wrong. It is one of the best things in them. However, in your case, Robert, a confession would not do. The money, if you will allow me to say so, is... awkward. Besides, if you did make a clean breast of the whole affair, you would never be able to talk morality again. And in England a man who can't talk morality twice a week to a large, popular, immoral audience is quite over as a serious politician. There would be nothing left for him as a profession except Botany or the Church. A confession would be of no use. It would ruin you.

SIR ROBERT CHILTERN: It would ruin me. Arthur, the only thing for me to do now is to fight the thing out.

LORD GORING (*rising from his chair*): I was waiting for you to say that, Robert. It is the only thing to do now. And you must begin by telling your wife the whole story.

SIR ROBERT CHILTERN: That I will not do.

LORD GORING: Robert, believe me, you are wrong.

SIR ROBERT CHILTERN: I couldn't do it. It would kill her love for me. And now about this woman, this Mrs. Cheveley. How can I defend myself against her? You

应该说的话。事实上,我通常说的是我的真实想法。当今之日,这可是个大毛病啊。这样很容易让人看透了。至于这件棘手的事情,我会尽我所能帮助你的。你当然知道这点。

罗伯特·奇尔顿爵士　谢谢你,亚瑟,谢谢你。可是干什么呢?还能干什么呢?

戈林子爵　(两手插在口袋里往后仰着身体)哦,英国人受不了一个总说自己是正确的人,但是他们非常喜欢承认自己是犯过错误的人。这是英国人的最好东西。但是,照你的情况看,罗伯特,忏悔是要不得的。那笔钱,如果你允许我这样说的话,是……很要命的。还有,你如果把这件事如数抖搂,那你可就永远不能再谈道德了。在英国,一个人要以一本正经的政治家身份,不能在众多的平庸而不道德的观众面前一星期谈两次道德,那就全完了。作为职业,他将一无所有,只好去讲讲植物学或者教堂问题。忏悔是毫无用处的。那只会把你毁了。

罗伯特·奇尔顿爵士　那会把我毁了。亚瑟,我现在唯一能做的事情就是斗争到底。

戈林子爵　(从椅子上站起来)我等的就是你这句话,罗伯特。这是现在惟一可干的事情。你必须准备把全部事情都告诉你的妻子。

罗伯特·奇尔顿爵士　我办不到啊。

戈林子爵　罗伯特,相信我,你不说是不对的。

罗伯特·奇尔顿爵士　我办不到啊。那会把她对我的爱扼杀了。现在主要是这个女人,这个谢弗利太太。我怎

knew her before, Arthur, apparently.

LORD GORING: Yes.

SIR ROBERT CHILTERN: Did you know her well?

LORD GORING (*arranging his necktie*): So little that I got engaged to be married to her once, when I was staying at the Tenbys'. The affair lasted for three days... nearly.

SIR ROBERT CHILTERN: Why was it broken off?

LORD GORING (*airily*): Oh, I forget. At least, it makes no matter. By the way, have you tried her with money? She used to be confoundedly fond of money.

SIR ROBERT CHILTERN: I offered her any sum she wanted. She refused.

LORD GORING: Then the marvellous gospel of gold breaks down sometimes. The rich can't do everything, after all.

SIR ROBERT CHILTERN: Not everything. I suppose you are right. Arthur, I feel that public disgrace is in store for me. I feel certain of it. I never knew what terror was before. I know it now. It is as if a hand of ice were laid upon one's heart. It is as if one's heart were beating itself to death in some empty hollow.

LORD GORING (*striking the table*): Robert, You must fight her. You must fight her.

SIR ROBERT CHILTERN: But how?

LORD GORING: I can't tell you how at present. I have not the smallest idea. But every one has some weak point. There is some flaw in each one of us. (*Strolls over to the fireplace and looks at himself in the glass.*) My father tells me that even I have faults. Perhaps I have. I don't know.

SIR ROBERT CHILTERN: In defending myself against

么保护自己跟她斗争呢？你过去显然认识她，亚瑟。

戈林子爵　是的。

罗伯特·奇尔顿爵士　你了解她深吗？

戈林子爵　（整了整领带）我曾经差一点和她订了婚，那时我呆在坦比斯家。那件风流韵事只持续了三天……差不多三天。

罗伯特·奇尔顿爵士　为什么分手了？

戈林子爵　（快活地）哦，我忘了。至少那事不足挂齿。喂，你给她使过钱吗？她过去见钱就眼红。

罗伯特·奇尔顿爵士　她要多少，我给多少。可她拒绝了。

戈林子爵　那么神通广大的金子福音有时也不灵嘛。有钱还不是万能的。

罗伯特·奇尔顿爵士　不是万能的。我看你是对的。亚瑟，我觉得在公众面前身败名裂是不可避免了。我真的感觉到了。我过去从来不知道什么是害怕。可我现在知道了。它像一只冰冷的手抓住了我的心。我仿佛觉得心在什么空荡荡的地方怦怦直跳。

戈林子爵　（拍了一下桌子）罗伯特，你必须和她做斗争。你一定要跟她斗争。

罗伯特·奇尔顿爵士　可是怎么个斗法？

戈林子爵　眼下我还没法告诉你怎么办。我一点儿主意也没有。不过每个人都有某个弱点。我们每个人都有缺点。（大步走向壁炉，在镜子里看自己。）我父亲跟我说就是我也有毛病。也许我有。我不清楚。

罗伯特·奇尔顿爵士　为了保卫我自己跟谢弗利太太斗

Mrs. Cheveley I have a right to use any weapon I can find, have I not?

LORD GORING (*still looking in the glass*): In your place I don't think I should have the smallest scruple in doing so. She is thoroughly well able to take care of herself.

SIR ROBERT CHILTERN (*sits down at the table and takes a pen in his hand*): Well, I shall send a cipher telegram to the Embassy at Vienna, to inquire if there is anything known against her. There may be some secret scandal she might be afraid of.

LORD GORING (*settling his buttonhole*): Oh, I should fancy Mrs. Cheveley is one of those very modern women of our time who find a new scandal as becoming as a new bonnet, and air them both in the Park every afternoon at five-thirty. I am sure she adores scandals, and that the sorrow of her life at present is that she can't manage to have enough of them.

SIR ROBERT CHILTERN (*writing*): Why do you say that?

LORD GORING (*turning round*): Well, she wore far too much rouge last night, and not quite enough clothes. That is always a sign of despair in a woman.

SIR ROBERT CHILTERN (*striking a bell*): But it is worth while my wiring to Vienna, is it not?

LORD GORING: It is always worth while asking a question, though it is not always worth while answering one.

Enter MASON.

SIR ROBERT CHILTERN: Is Mr. Trafford in his room?
MASON: Yes, Sir Robert.

SIR ROBERT CHILTERN (*puts what he has written into

争,不管什么武器,我都有权利使用,对吗?

戈林子爵 (仍然看着镜子)从你那方面看,我认为这样干用不着一点顾虑。她有足够的能力把自己保护好。

罗伯特·奇尔顿爵士 (坐在桌子前,手拿起一支笔)哦,我要给维也纳使馆发去一封密码电报,调查一下是不是知道有关她的情况。也许能弄到一些她很害怕的秘密丑闻。

戈林子爵 (整理他的扣眼)喔,我倒认为谢弗利太太本来就是一个非常现代的女性,把新丑闻看得像一顶新帽子一样难得,恨不得每天下午五点半到公园里把这两样东西炫耀一番。我相信她对丑闻情有独钟,现在正发愁她生活里碰破脑袋都找不到呢。

罗伯特·奇尔顿爵士 (写电文)你为什么说这种话?

戈林子爵 (转过身来)噢,她昨天夜里往嘴上抹口红太多了,衣服倒不算很讲究。这样子往往表明女人陷入绝望了。

罗伯特·奇尔顿爵士 (按响铃)那还用往维也纳发电文吗?

戈林子爵 打听情况什么时候都值得,虽然回复往往不合算。

〔梅森上

罗伯特·奇尔顿爵士 特拉福德先生在他房间里吗?

梅森 是的,罗伯特爵士。

罗伯特·奇尔顿爵士 (把他所写的东西塞进信封里,随后细心

an envelope, which he then carefully closes): Tell him to have this sent off in cipher at once. There must not be a moment's delay.

MASON: Yes, Sir Robert.

SIR ROBERT CHILTERN: Oh! just give that back to me again.

> *Writes something on the envelope.* MASON *then goes out with the letter.*

SIR ROBERT CHILTERN: She must have had some curious hold over Baron Arnheim. I wonder what it was.

LORD GORING (*smiling*): I wonder.

SIR ROBERT CHILTERN: I will fight her to the death, as long as my wife knows nothing.

LORD GORING (*strongly*): Oh, fight in any case—in any case.

SIR ROBERT CHILTERN (*with a gesture of despair*): If my wife found out, there would be little left to fight for. Well, as soon as I hear from Vienna, I shall let you know the result. It is a chance, just a chance, but I believe in it. And as I fought the age with its own weapons, I will fight her with her weapons. It is only fair, and she looks like a woman with a past, doesn't she?

LORD GORING: Most pretty women do. But there is a fashion in pasts just as there is a fashion in frocks. Perhaps Mrs. Cheveley's past is merely a slightly *décolleté* one, and they are excessively popular nowadays. Besides, my dear Robert, I should not build too high hopes on frightening Mrs. Cheveley. I should not fancy Mrs. Cheveley is a woman who would be easily frightened. She has survived all her creditors, and she shows wonderful presence of mind.

SIR ROBERT CHILTERN: Oh! I live on hopes now. I

地粘上)告诉他把这个用密码立即发出去。马上就发,千万别耽搁。

梅森　是的,罗伯特爵士。

罗伯特·奇尔顿爵士　哦!发完把原件还给我。

〔在信封上写了些什么。梅森然后拿上信下。

罗伯特·奇尔顿爵士　她一定非常巧妙地把安海姆男爵牢牢控制了。我纳闷是什么高招。

戈林子爵　(微笑)我也纳闷呢。

罗伯特·奇尔顿爵士　只要我的妻子不知情,我就要跟她斗争到底。

戈林子爵　(强烈地)噢,什么情况下都要斗争——无论什么情况下都要斗。

罗伯特·奇尔顿爵士　(作一绝望姿势)如果我的妻子知道了,斗争的余地就很少喽。哦,我听到维也纳的消息后立即把结果告诉你。这是碰运气,碰运气而已,不过我相信它。我既然能用时代的武器跟时代斗争,那我也能用她的武器和她斗争。这是非常公平的,她看样子像一个有点儿来历的女人,对吗?

戈林子爵　多数漂亮女人都有些来历。不过如同女人的衣服讲究时尚一样,来历也是有时尚的。也许谢弗利太太的来历是袒胸露肩的那种,如今袒胸露肩却满大街都是了。还有,我亲爱的罗伯特,我没有太指望能把谢弗利太太唬住。依我看,谢弗利太太不是一个能够被轻易吓唬住的主儿。她把所有的债主都甩掉了。她的脑子相当好使。

罗伯特·奇尔顿爵士　噢!我现在就靠希望活着了。我一

clutch at every chance. I feel like a man on a ship that is sinking. The water is round my feet, and the very air is bitter with storm. Hush! I hear my wife's voice.

  Enter LADY CHILTERN *in walking dress.*

LADY CHILTERN: Good-afternoon, Lord Goring.

LORD GORING: Good-afternoon, Lady Chiltern! Have you been in the Park?

LADY CHILTERN: No; I have just come from the Woman's Liberal Association, where, by the way, Robert, your name was received with loud applause, and now I have come in to have my tea. (*To* LORD GORING): You will wait and have some tea, won't you?

LORD GORING: I'll wait for a short time, thanks.

LADY CHILTERN: I will be back in a moment. I am only going to take my hat off.

LORD GORING (*in his most earnest manner*): Oh! please don't. It is so pretty. One of the prettiest hats I ever saw. I hope the Woman's Liberal Association received it with loud applause.

LADY CHILTERN (*with a smile*): We have much more important work to do than look at each other's bonnets, Lord Goring.

LORD GORING: Really? What sort of work?

LADY CHILTERN: Oh! dull, useful, delightful things, Factory Acts, Female Inspectors, the Eight Hours' Bill, the Parliamentary Franchise... Everything, in fact, that you would find thoroughly uninteresting.

LORD GORING: And never bonnets?

LADY CHILTERN (*with mock indignation*): Never bonnets, never!

  LADY CHILTERN *goes out through the door leading to her boudoir.*

见运气就要碰一碰。我觉得自己像一个人呆在下沉的船上。水都淹到我的脚面了,天空偏偏刮起了风暴。嘘!我听见我妻子的声音了。

〔奇尔顿夫人穿着便装上。

奇尔顿夫人 下午好,戈林子爵。

戈林子爵 下午好,奇尔顿夫人!你在公园里呆着吗?

奇尔顿夫人 没有。我刚从妇女自由协会来,喂,罗伯特,你的名字在那里赢得了热烈掌声,我这会儿是回来喝茶的。(对戈林子爵)你等会儿来些茶点吧,好吗?

戈林子爵 我等一小会儿,谢谢。

奇尔顿夫人 我一会儿就回来。我得赶紧去把我的帽子取下来。

戈林子爵 (作出一副非常诚实的样子)喔!别取下来。这帽子漂亮极了。这是我见过的最漂亮的帽子了。我想妇女自由协会是热烈欢迎它的。

奇尔顿夫人 (莞尔一笑)我们有很多重要的事情可做,哪顾得上彼此打量,戈林子爵。

戈林子爵 真的吗?什么样的工作呢?

奇尔顿夫人 哦!单调、有用、有趣的事情,比如工厂法案啦,妇女检查员啦,八小时工作法啦,议院公民特权啦,等等,什么事情都有,不过你一点不会对这些事情发生兴趣的。

戈林子爵 你从来不管女帽的事吗?

奇尔顿夫人 (假作生气状)从来不管女帽的事,从来不管!

〔奇尔顿夫人穿过门,走向自己的闺房。

SIR ROBERT CHILTERN(*takes* LORD GORING's hand): You have been a good friend to me, Arthur, a thoroughly good friend.

LORD GORING: I don't know that I have been able to do much for you, Robert, as yet. In fact, I have not been able to do anything for you, as far as I can see. I am thoroughly disappointed with myself.

SIR ROBERT CHILTERN: You have enabled me to tell you the truth. That is something. The truth has always stifled me.

LORD GORING: Ah! the truth is a thing I get rid of as soon as possible! Bad habit, by the way. Makes one very unpopular at the club... with the older members. They call it being conceited. Perhaps it is.

SIR ROBERT CHILTERN: I would to God that I had been able to tell the truth... to the truth. Ah! that is the great thing in life, to live the truth. (*Sighs, and goes towards the door.*) I'll see you soon again, Arthur, shan't I?

LORD GORING: Certainly. Whenever you like. I'm going to look in at the Bachelors' Ball to-night, unless I find something better to do. But I'll come round to-morrow morning. If you should want me to-night by any chance, send round a note to Curzon Street.

SIR ROBERT CHILTERN: Thank you.

  As he reaches the door, LADY CHILTERN *enters from her boudoir.*

LADY CHILTERN: You are not going, Robert?

SIR ROBERT CHILTERN: I have some letters to write, dear.

LADY CHILTERN(*going to him*): You work too hard, Robert. You seem never to think of yourself, and you are

罗伯特·奇尔顿爵士 （拉住戈林子爵的手）你一直是我的好朋友，亚瑟，真正的好朋友。

戈林子爵 我到现在还不明白我能给你们做点什么呢，罗伯特。事实上，就我现在能看到的，我是爱莫能助呀。我对自己感到彻底失望了。

罗伯特·奇尔顿爵士 你让我终于跟你说了实情。这就是收获啊。那真相总是让我喘不过气来。

戈林子爵 啊！真相这玩艺儿我是能躲多远就躲多远！嘿，坏习惯。这让你在俱乐部里很没有人缘……和老一点的会员就合不来。他们叫这种毛病是自负。也许还就是那么回事呢。

罗伯特·奇尔顿爵士 我要是能把真相讲出来，踏踏实实地生活，那么让我见上帝都行啊！踏踏实实地生活是生活的头等大事啊。（连连叹气，向门走去）我很快就会见到你，亚瑟，对吗？

戈林子爵 当然了。你多会儿想见都行。如果找不到更好的事情可做，我今晚就到单身汉舞会消磨时光。不过我明天早上就过来。要是你今天夜里突然想见我，叫人到柯曾街打声招呼就行。

罗伯特·奇尔顿爵士 谢谢你。

〔他走到门前时，奇尔顿夫人从她的闺房上。

奇尔顿夫人 你要离去吗，罗伯特？

罗伯特·奇尔顿爵士 我有一些信需要写，亲爱的。

奇尔顿夫人 （走向他）你工作得太累了，罗伯特。你好像从

looking so tired.

SIR ROBERT CHILTERN: It is nothing, dear, nothing. (*He kisses her and goes out.*)

LADY CHILTERN (*to* LORD GORING): Do sit down. I am so glad you have called. I want to talk to you about... well, not about bonnets, or the Woman's Liberal Association. You take far too much interest in the first subject, and not nearly enough in the second.

LORD GORING: You want to talk to me about Mrs. Cheveley?

LADY CHILTERN: Yes. You have guessed it. After you left last night I found out that what she had said was really true. Of course I made Robert write her a letter at once, withdrawing his promise.

LORD GORING: So he gave me to understand.

LADY CHILTERN: To have kept it would have been the first stain on a career that has been stainless always. Robert must be above reproach. He is not like other men. He cannot afford to do what other men do. (*She looks at* LORD GORING, *who remains silent.*) Don't you agree with me? You are Robert's greatest friend. You are our greatest friend, Lord Goring. No one, except myself, knows Robert better than you do. He has no secrets from me, and I don't think he has any from you.

LORD GORING: He certainly has no secrets from me. At least I don't think so.

LADY CHILTERN: Then am I not right in my estimate of him? I know I am right. But speak to me frankly.

LORD GORING (*looking straight at her*): Quite frankly?

LADY CHILTERN: Surely. You have nothing to conceal, have you?

来没有想到过你自己,你看上去十分疲劳。

罗伯特·奇尔顿爵士　没什么,亲爱的,没什么。(他吻了她,下。)

奇尔顿夫人　(走向戈林子爵)请坐吧。你来坐坐我很高兴。我想和你谈谈……哦,不是帽子的事,也不是妇女自由协会的事。你对第一件事很感兴趣,对第二件事却几乎兴趣索然。

戈林子爵　你想和我谈谈谢弗利太太吗?

奇尔顿夫人　是的。你猜对了。你昨天晚上走后,我发现她所说的全是真的。我当然逼着罗伯特马上给她写了一封信,把他的许诺撤回了。

戈林子爵　罗伯特都告诉我了。

奇尔顿夫人　如果答应了她,那就会让他一贯洁白的生涯有了第一个污点,永远去不掉了。罗伯特必须做到无可指责。他和别人不一样。别人能干的,他可干不得。(她看了看默不作声的戈林子爵。)你同意我的看法吗?你是罗伯特的知心朋友。你是我们俩的知心朋友,戈林子爵。除了我,谁都没有你了解罗伯特。他和我没有什么秘密可言,我想他和你也一样。

戈林子爵　他当然不会向我保守秘密。至少我是这样想的。

奇尔顿夫人　那么说我对他的估计有误差了。我还以为我不会错的。不过和我坦率地说吧。

戈林子爵　(直视着她)毫无保留地说吗?

奇尔顿夫人　毫无保留。你没有什么可隐藏的,对吗?

103

LORD GORING: Nothing. But, my dear Lady Chiltern, I think, if you will allow me to say so, that in practical life—

LADY CHILTERN (*smiling*): Of which you know so little, Lord Goring—

LORD GORING: Of which I know nothing by experience, though I know something by observation. I think that in practical life there is something about success, actual success, that is a little unscrupulous, something about ambition that is unscrupulous always. Once a man has set his heart and soul on getting to a certain point, if he has to climb the crag, he climbs the crag; if he has to walk in the mire—

LADY CHILTERN: Well?

LORD GORING: He walks in the mire. Of course I am only talking generally about life.

LADY CHILTERN (*gravely*): I hope so. Why do you look at me so strangely, Lord Goring?

LORD GORING: Lady Chiltern, I have sometimes thought that... perhaps you are a little hard in some of your views on life. I think that... often you don't make sufficient allowances. In every nature there are elements of weakness, or worse than weakness. Supposing, for instance, that—that any public man, my father, or Lord Merton, or Robert, say, had, years ago, written some foolish letter to some one...

LADY CHILTERN: What do you mean by a foolish letter?

LORD GORING: A letter gravely compromising one's position. I am only putting an imaginary case.

LADY CHILTERN: Robert is as incapable of doing a foolish thing as he is of doing a wrong thing.

戈林子爵　没有什么。可是,我亲爱的奇尔顿夫人,我想,如果你允许我这样说的话,在实际生活中——

奇尔顿夫人　(莞尔一笑)实际生活你知道得可怜,戈林子爵——

戈林子爵　按经历讲,我对此是一无所知,不过从旁观的角度讲,我还是知道一些的。我认为,在实际生活里,关于成功,真正的成功,是有些说头的,其中有点违反道德的东西,有些总是和不大道德的野心有关系的东西在里面。一个人一旦下决心要达到某个地点,比如他不得不爬上石崖,那他就得爬上去;如果他不得不往泥坑里走——

奇尔顿夫人　说吧?

戈林子爵　他就得走进泥坑。当然我只是在泛泛地谈生活问题。

奇尔顿夫人　(严肃地)希望如此。你为什么这么奇怪地看着我,戈林子爵?

戈林子爵　奇尔顿夫人,我有时想呢……也许你对生活的某些观点有点苛求。我认为……往往你宽容得不够。任何本性都有软弱的成分,或者比软弱还糟糕的东西。比方说,有人——任何公众人物,我父亲,或默顿勋爵,或罗伯特,多年前,写了一封糊涂的信给某个人……

奇尔顿夫人　你所说的糊涂信是指什么?

戈林子爵　一封严重有损于他的身份的信。我只是举一个虚构的例子。

奇尔顿夫人　罗伯特绝不会干这种傻事,如同他不会干什么错事一样。

LORD GORING (*after a long pause*): Nobody is incapable of doing a foolish thing. Nobody is incapable of doing a wrong thing.

LADY CHILTERN: Are you a Pessimist? What will the other dandies say? They will all have to go into mourning.

LORD GORING (*rising*): No, Lady Chiltern, I am not a Pessimist. Indeed I am not sure that I quite know what pessimism really means. All I do know is that life cannot be understood without much charity, cannot be lived without much charity. It is love, and not German philosophy, that is the true explanation of this world, whatever may be the explanation of the next. And if you are ever in trouble, Lady Chiltern, trust me absolutely, and I will help you in every way I can. If you ever want me, come to me for my assistance, and you shall have it. Come at once to me.

LADY CHILTERN (*looking at him in surprise*): Lord Goring, you are talking quite seriously. I don't think I ever heard you talk seriously before.

LORD GORING (*laughing*): You must excuse me, Lady Chiltern. It won't occur again, if I can help it.

LADY CHILTERN: But I like you to be serious.

Enter MABEL CHILTERN, in the most ravishing frock.

MABEL CHILTERN: Dear Gertrude, don't say such a dreadful thing to Lord Goring. Seriousness would be very unbecoming to him. Good-afternoon, Lord Goring! Pray be as trivial as you can.

LORD GORING: I should like to, Miss Mabel, but I am afraid I am... a little out of practice this morning; and besides, I have to be going now.

戈林子爵　（停顿许久）任何人都会干出傻事。任何人都会干错事。

奇尔顿夫人　你是个悲观主义者吗？别的花花公子会怎么说呢？他们就只好去等死了。

戈林子爵　（站起）不，奇尔顿夫人，我不是一个悲观主义者。当然我也不十分清楚悲观主义到底是什么意思。就我所知道的，人不懂得爱就不懂得生活，不懂得爱就不会生活。不管对另一个世界的解释是什么，对这个世界的真实解释只能是爱，不会是德国的哲学。如果你有了什么麻烦，请你绝对相信我好了，我会从各方面帮助你的。如果你需要我，叫我来帮助你，你肯定会得到的。尽快来找我。

奇尔顿夫人　（惊讶地看着他）戈林子爵，你说得也太一本正经了。想想看，我过去可从来没有听见你这么严肃地谈过话。

戈林子爵　（大笑）你只好原谅我了，奇尔顿夫人。只要我能把握住，我以后再不会这样说话了。

奇尔顿夫人　不过我倒是喜欢你严肃一点。

〔梅布尔·奇尔顿上，穿着十分抢眼的上衣。

梅布尔·奇尔顿　亲爱的格特鲁德，别对戈林子爵说这种话。他这个人不适合一本正经。下午好，戈林子爵！你爱怎么随便就怎么随便好了。

戈林子爵　我应该随便才好，梅布尔小姐，不过今天早上……我有点荒疏了。还有呢，我现在也该走了。

107

MABEL CHILTERN: Just when I have come in! What dreadful manners you have! I am sure you were very badly brought up.

LORD GORING: I was.

MABEL CHILTERN: I wish I had brought you up!

LORD GORING: I am so sorry you didn't.

MABEL CHILTERN: It is too late now, I suppose?

LORD GORING (*smiling*): I am not so sure.

MABEL CHILTERN: Will you ride to-morrow morning?

LORD GORING: Yes, at ten.

MABEL CHILTERN: Don't forget.

LORD GORING: Of course I shan't. By the way, Lady Chiltern, there is no list of your guests in *The Morning Post* of to-day. It has apparently been crowded out by the County Council, or the Lambeth Conference, or something equally boring. Could you let me have a list? I have a particular reason for asking you.

LADY CHILTERN: I am sure Mr. Trafford will be able to give you one.

LORD GORING: Thanks, so much.

MABEL CHILTERN: Tommy is the most useful person in London.

LORD GORING (*turning to her*): And who is the most ornamental?

MABEL CHILTERN (*triumphantly*): I am.

LORD GORING: How clever of you to guess it! (*Takes up his hat and cane.*) Good-bye, Lady Chiltern! You will remember what I said to you, won't you?

LADY CHILTERN: Yes; but I don't know why you said it to me.

LORD GORING: I hardly know myself. Good-bye, Miss Mabel!

第　二　幕

梅布尔·奇尔顿　我一来你就要走！你的行为也太那个了吧！我看你小时候的教养一定很差。

戈林子爵　没错。

梅布尔·奇尔顿　但愿是我从小带你就好了！

戈林子爵　很遗憾你没有带我！

梅布尔·奇尔顿　我说现在带就太晚了不成？

戈林子爵　（微笑）我心里没有底儿。

梅布尔·奇尔顿　你明天早上骑马去吗？

戈林子爵　是的，十点钟。

梅布尔·奇尔顿　可别忘了啊。

戈林子爵　我当然忘不了。喂，奇尔顿夫人，今天的《早邮报》上没有你的客人名单。这显然是被郡委员会或者兰贝斯会议①或者同样讨厌的东西给挤掉了。你给我一份名单好吗？我有点特殊原因，你得给我一份。

奇尔顿夫人　我一定让特拉福德先生给你一份。

戈林子爵　非常感谢。

梅布尔·奇尔顿　汤米是全伦敦最有用的人了。

戈林子爵　（转向她）那谁是穿戴最入时的呢？

梅布尔·奇尔顿　（得意洋洋地）我呀。

戈林子爵　你真聪明，猜对了！（拿起他的帽子和手杖。）再见，奇尔顿夫人！你记住我说过的话了吧，是吗？

奇尔顿夫人　是的；不过我不知道你为什么跟我说这个。

戈林子爵　我自己也说不清楚。再见，梅布尔小姐！

----

① 指英国国教各主教每十年一次在伦敦举行的讨论会，属教会决策性会议，因在兰贝斯宫开，故叫做"兰贝斯会议"。

109

MABEL CHILTERN (*with a little moue of disappointment*): I wish you were not going. I have had four wonderful adventures this morning; four and a half, in fact. You might stop and listen to some of them.

LORD GORING: How very selfish of you to have four and a half! There won't be any left for me.

MABEL CHILTERN: I don't want you to have any. They would not be good for you.

LORD GORING: That is the first unkind thing you have ever said to me. How charmingly you said it! Ten tomorrow.

MABEL CHILTERN: Sharp.

LORD GORING: Quite sharp. But don't bring Mr. Trafford.

MABEL CHILTERN (*with a little toss of her head*): Of course I shan't bring Tommy Trafford. Tommy Trafford is in great disgrace.

LORD GORING: I am delighted to hear it. (*Bows and goes out.*)

MABEL CHILTERN: Gertrude, I wish you would speak to Tommy Trafford.

LADY CHILTERN: What has poor Mr. Trafford done this time? Robert says he is the best secretary he has ever had.

MABEL CHILTERN: Well, Tommy has proposed to me again. Tommy really does nothing but propose to me. He proposed to me last night in the music-room, when I was quite unprotected, as there was an elaborate trio going on. I didn't dare to make the smallest repartee, I need hardly tell you. If I had, it would have stopped the music at once. Musical people are so absurdly unreasonable. They always want one to be perfectly dumb at the very

第 二 幕

梅布尔·奇尔顿　（带点失望的怪相）我不愿意你离去。我今天上午经历了四次美妙的冒险——事实上是四次半——你不妨留步听一听啊。

戈林子爵　你多么自私啊,独占了四次半！这下我就摊不上了。

梅布尔·奇尔顿　我就不愿意你摊上。你摊上没有什么好处。

戈林子爵　这种不友好的话,我还是第一次听你跟我说。你说得可真动听啊！明天十点钟见。

梅布尔·奇尔顿　准时啊。

戈林子爵　一定准时。不过别把特拉福德先生带去啊。

梅布尔·奇尔顿　（把头稍稍扬了扬）我当然要把汤米·特拉福德带上。汤米·特拉福德太受冷落了。

戈林子爵　我就高兴听这话。（鞠躬,下。）

梅布尔·奇尔顿　格特鲁德,我希望你跟汤米·特拉福德讲一讲。

奇尔顿夫人　可怜的特拉福德这次又干什么了？罗伯特说汤米是他使过的最好的秘书。

梅布尔·奇尔顿　哦,汤米又向我求婚了。汤米就只会向我求婚。他昨天夜晚在音乐室向我求婚,我当时一点儿防范也没有,因为一组三重唱正在进行。我不用说你也知道,我简直没有办法搪塞一下。如果我回答他,那音乐就全停下来了。忙着音乐的人就是不能像常人一样讲道理。他们总是要求在人家渴望什么也听不见

moment when one is longing to be absolutely deaf. Then he proposed to me in broad daylight this morning, in front of that dreadful statue of Achilles. Really, the things that go on in front of that work of art are quite appalling. The police should interfere. At luncheon I saw by the glare in his eye that he was going to propose again, and I just managed to check him in time by assuring him that I was a bimetallist. Fortunately I don't know what bimetallism means. And I don't believe anybody else does either. But the observation crushed Tommy for ten minutes. He looked quite shocked. And then Tommy is so annoying in the way he proposes. If he proposed at the top of his voice, I should not mind so much, That might produce some effect on the public. But he does it in a horrid confidential way. When Tommy wants to be romantic he talks to one just like a doctor. I am very fond of Tommy, but his methods of proposing are quite out of date. I wish, Gertrude, you would speak to him, and tell him that once a week is quite often enough to propose to any one, and that it should always be done in a manner that attracts some attention.

LADY CHILTERN: Dear Mabel, don't talk like that. Besides, Robert thinks very highly of Mr. Trafford. He believes he has a brilliant future before him.

MABEL CHILTERN: Oh! I wouldn't marry a man with a future before him for anything under the sun.

LADY CHILTERN: Mabel!

MABEL CHILTERN: I know, dear. You married a man with a future, didn't you! But then Robert was a genius, and you have a noble, self-sacrificing character. You can stand geniuses. I have no character at all, and Robert is the only genius I could ever bear. As a rule, I think they

时哑口无言。后来他在今天早上大白天的又向我求婚,还当着那尊可怕的阿基里斯塑像。真的,当着一件艺术品继续干那种事情太别扭了。连警察都会来干涉的。用午餐时,我从他的眼光里看出来他又准备求婚了,我赶紧声明我是复本位制论者才把他暂时制止住了。好在我也不知道什么是复本位制,而且我也不相信别人知道这个。不过那番见解让汤米整整十分钟不知所措。他看上去相当傻。后来汤米求婚的方式烦死人了。如果他大声求婚,那我倒不会很在乎。那样能让众人有些印象。可是他就是用那种很亲切可近的样子求婚。汤米想表现得浪漫时,他说话就像一个医生。我很喜欢汤米,可是他求婚的方式太过时了。格特鲁德,我希望你跟他说一说,告诉他一星期求一次婚就足够了,而且求婚的样子要能把大家的注意力吸引住才好。

奇尔顿夫人　亲爱的梅布尔,别用这种口气讲话。再说了,罗伯特对特拉福德先生的评价很高。他相信特拉福德先生很有前途。

梅布尔·奇尔顿　哦!我才不嫁给天下有什么前途的男人呢。

奇尔顿夫人　梅布尔!

梅布尔·奇尔顿　我懂,亲爱的。我知道你嫁了一个前程似锦的男人,对不对?可是罗伯特是个天才,你又生性高贵,富有牺牲精神。你能受得了天才人物。我这人一点个性都没有,罗伯特是我唯一能受得了的天才。

are quite impossible. Geniuses talk so much, don't they? Such a bad habit! And they are always thinking about themselves, when I want them to be thinking about me. I must go round now and rehearse at Lady Basildon's. You remember, we are having tableaux, don't you? The Triumph of something, I don't know what! I hope it will be triumph of me. Only triumph I am really interested in at present. (*Kisses* LADY CHILTERN *and goes out*; *then comes running back*). Oh, Gertrude, do you know who is coming to see you? That dreadful Mrs. Cheveley, in a most lovely gown. Did you ask her?

LADY CHILTERN(*rising*): Mrs. Cheveley! Coming to see me? Impossible!

MABEL CHILTERN: I assure you she is coming upstairs, as large as life and not nearly so natural.

LADY CHILTERN: You need not wait, Mabel. Remember, Lady Basildon is expecting you.

MABEL CHILTERN: Oh! I must shake hands with Lady Markby. She is delightful. I love being scolded by her.

Enter MASON.

MASON: Lady Markby. Mrs. Cheveley.

Enter LADY MARKBY *and* MRS. CHEVELEY.

LADY CHILTERN(*advancing to meet them*): Dear Lady Markby, how nice of you to come and see me! (*Shakes hands with her, and bows somewhat distantly to* MRS. CHEVELEY.) Won't you sit down, Mrs. Cheveley?

MRS. CHEVELEY: Thanks. Isn't that Miss Chiltern? I should like so much to know her.

LADY CHILTERN: Mabel, Mrs. Cheveley wishes to know you. (MABEL CHILTERN *gives a little nod*.)

MRS. CHEVELEY(*sitting down*): I thought your frock so charming, last night, Miss Chiltern. So simple and...

一般说来，他们是让人受不了的。天才们总是喋喋不休，对不对？再坏不过的毛病！我想要他们想一想我时，他们却只想着他们自己。我现在得去巴西尔顿夫人家排练了。你可记得，我们的一些场面很生动，是吧？有些东西胜利了，我不知道是什么！我希望我会取得胜利。我现在真正感兴趣的是胜利。（亲吻过奇尔顿夫人，下；随后又反回来。）哦，格特鲁德，你知道谁来看望你了吗？那个可怕的谢弗利太太，穿着非常可爱的晚礼服。是你请她来的吗？

奇尔顿夫人　（起立）谢弗利太太！来看望我？不可能！

梅布尔·奇尔顿　我向你保证她正在上楼，大活人一个，就是有点不够自然。

奇尔顿夫人　你不必等着了，梅布尔。别忘了，巴西尔顿夫人还在等你呢。

梅布尔·奇尔顿　噢！我一定要和马克比夫人握握手。她讨人喜欢。我爱听她挖苦几句。

〔梅森上。

梅森　马克比夫人到。谢弗利太太到。

〔马克比夫人和谢弗利太太上。

奇尔顿夫人　（上前迎接她们）亲爱的马克比夫人，劳你大驾来看我，太好了！（和马克比夫人握手，并朝谢弗利太太冷冷地点点头。）干什么不坐下，谢弗利太太？

谢弗利太太　谢谢。这不就是奇尔顿小姐吗？我早想认识她了。

奇尔顿夫人　梅布尔，谢弗利太太想认识你。（梅布尔·奇尔顿点了一下头。）

谢弗利太太　（坐下）我看你昨天晚上穿的衣服非常好看，

suitable.

MABEL CHILTERN: Really? I must tell my dressmaker. It will be such a surprise to her. Good-bye, Lady Markby!

LADY MARKBY: Going already?

MABEL CHILTERN: I am so sorry but I am obliged to. I am just off to rehearsal. I have got to stand on my head in some tableaux.

LADY MARKBY: On your head, child? Oh! I hope not. I believe it is most unhealthy. (*Takes a seat on the sofa next* LADY CHILTERN.)

MABEL CHILTERN: But it is for an excellent charity; in aid of the Undeserving, the only people I am really interested in. I am the secretary, and Tommy Trafford is treasurer.

MRS. CHEVELEY: And what is Lord Goring?

MABEL CHILTERN: Oh! Lord Goring is president.

MRS. CHEVELEY: The post should suit him admirably, unless he has deteriorated since I knew him first.

LADY MARKBY (*reflecting*): You are remarkably modern, Mabel. A little too modern, perhaps. Nothing is so dangerous as being too modern. One is apt to grow old-fashioned quite suddenly. I have known many instances of it.

MABEL CHILTERN: What a dreadful prospect!

LADY MARKBY: Ah! my dear, you need not be nervous. You will always be as pretty as possible. That is the best fashion there is, and the only fashion that England succeeds in setting.

MABEL CHILTERN (*with a curtsey*): Thank you so much, Lady Markby, for England... and myself. (*Goes out.*)

第 二 幕

奇尔顿小姐。款式非常简朴却又……那么得体。

梅布尔·奇尔顿　真的吗?我一定把这话说给我的裁缝听。她听了准会大吃一惊的。再见,马克比夫人!

马克比夫人　这就走吗?

梅布尔·奇尔顿　很失礼,可是我非走不可。我得去按一定舞台造型做头朝下练习。

马克比夫人　头朝下练习,孩子?哦!可别那样。我相信那对身体没有好处。(在奇尔顿夫人身边坐下。)

梅布尔·奇尔顿　可这是为了一次盛大的善举啊;为了帮助那些被忽略的人,我就对这些人真有兴趣。我是秘书,汤米·特拉福德是司库。

谢弗利太太　戈林子爵是什么?

梅布尔·奇尔顿　哦!戈林子爵是主席。

谢弗利太太　如果我第一次见他以后没有退步的话,他干这个主席是很合适的。

马克比夫人　(思考状)你真够摩登的,梅布尔。也许有点过分摩登了。摩登过了头可是再危险不过了。你很快会一下子变得古板起来的。这样的人我见得多了去了。

梅布尔·奇尔顿　多可怕的一幅前景!

马克比夫人　啊!亲爱的,你用不着担心。你多会儿都是个美人儿。美人儿才是最时髦的,也是英国长盛不衰的唯一美景。

梅布尔·奇尔顿　(行屈膝礼)为英国,也为了我自己,我应该多多感谢你。(下。)

117

LADY MARKBY (*turning to* LADY CHILTERN): Dear Gertrude, we just called to know if Mrs. Cheveley's diamond brooch has been found.

LADY CHILTERN: Here?

MRS. CHEVELEY: Yes. I missed it when I got back to Claridge's, and I thought I might possibly have dropped it here.

LADY CHILTERN: I have heard nothing about it. But I will send for the butler and ask. (*Touches the bell.*)

MRS. CHEVELEY: Oh, pray don't trouble, Lady Chiltern. I dare say I lost it at the Opera, before we came on here.

LADY MARKBY: Ah yes, I suppose it must have been at the Opera. The fact is, we all scramble and jostle so much nowadays that I wonder we have anything at all left on us at the end of an evening. I know myself that, when I am coming back from the Drawing room, I always feel as if I hadn't a shred on me, except a small shred of decent reputation, just enough to prevent the lower classes making painful observations through the windows of the carriage. The fact is that our Society is terribly over-populated. Really, some one should arrange a proper scheme of assisted emigration. It would do a great deal of good.

MRS. CHEVELEY: I quite agree with you, Lady Markby. It is nearly six years since I have been in London for the Season, and I must say Society has become dreadfully mixed. One sees the oddest people everywhere.

LADY MARKBY: That is quite true, dear. But one needn't know them. I'm sure I don't know half the people who come to my house. Indeed, from all I hear, I shouldn't like to.

第 二 幕

马克比夫人　（转向奇尔顿夫人）亲爱的格特鲁德，我们来访，主要是看看谢弗利太太的胸针掉在这里了没有？

奇尔顿夫人　掉在这里？

谢弗利太太　是的。我回到柯拉里奇旅馆发现我把它丢了，我想了想可能是掉在这里了。

奇尔顿夫人　我没有听说谁拾到了。不过我这就叫管家来问问。（按响铃。）

谢弗利太太　噢，别麻烦了，奇尔顿夫人。也许我在来这里之前掉在歌剧院了呢。

马克比夫人　可也是，我看准是掉在歌剧院了。实际上我们现在到哪里都挤挤抗抗的，到了一天的夜晚我看我们身上就所剩无几了。我知道我自己从宫廷会客室出来后，只觉得身子好像什么都给挤掉了，就还剩了一点点体面的名声，刚刚够挡住下层阶级从马车窗户往里面争着抢着观看。显然我们的上流社会人满为患了。真的，应该有人站出来弄一个援助移民计划。那才叫干了一件大好事情呢。

谢弗利太太　我很同意你的看法，马克比夫人。我有差不多六年时间是在伦敦过社交季节了，我不得不说，上流社会变得鱼目混杂了。到处都能看见古里古怪的人。

马克比夫人　一点没错，亲爱的。不过你用不着答理他们。我相信到我家来聚会的人我连一半也不认识。就我所听说的，我真的就不喜欢答理他们。

Enter MASON.

LADY CHILTERN: What sort of brooch was it that you lost, Mrs. Cheveley?

MRS. CHEVELEY: A diamond snake-brooch with a ruby, a rather large ruby.

LADY MARKBY: I thought you said there was a sapphire on the head, dear?

MRS. CHEVELEY (*smiling*): No, Lady Markby—a ruby.

LADY MARKBY (*nodding her head*): And very becoming, I am quite sure.

LADY CHILTERN: Has a ruby and diamond brooch been found in any of the rooms this morning, Mason?

MASON: No, my lady.

MRS. CHEVELEY: It really is of no consequence, Lady Chiltern. I am so sorry to have put you to any inconvenience.

LADY CHILTERN (*coldly*): Oh, it has been no inconvenience. That will do, Mason. You can bring tea. (*Exit* MASON.)

LADY MARKBY: Well, I must say it is most annoying to lose anything. I remember once at Bath, years ago, losing in the Pump Room an exceedingly handsome cameo bracelet that Sir John had given me. I don't think he has ever given me anything since, I am sorry to say. He has sadly degenerated. Really, this horrid House of Commons quite ruins our husbands for us. I think the Lower House by far the greatest blow to a happy married life that there has been since that terrible thing called the Higher Education of Women was invented.

LADY CHILTERN: Ah! it is heresy to say that in this house, Lady Markby. Robert is a great champion of the

〔梅森上。

奇尔顿夫人　你丢掉的是怎样一只胸针,谢弗利太太?

谢弗利太太　钻石蛇形胸针,镶着一枚红宝石,一块很大的红宝石。

马克比夫人　我听你说过上面镶着一块蓝宝石,亲爱的?

谢弗利太太　(莞尔一笑)不是,马克比夫人——是一块红宝石。

马克比夫人　(点点头)我只知道看上去非常顺眼。

奇尔顿夫人　今天早上在什么房间里发现了一枚胸针吗,梅森?

梅森　没有,夫人。

谢弗利太太　这事真的没有什么,奇尔顿夫人。给你添了这么多麻烦,我感到十分过意不去。

奇尔顿夫人　(冷冷地)喔,没有多少麻烦。那就这样吧,梅森。你上些茶点吧。(梅森下。)

马克比夫人　哦,说真的,丢东西是最让人恼火的事情了。我记得有一次在巴思,多年前,我把约翰爵士送给我的一个绝好的浮雕宝石手镯丢在了那个水泵屋里。说来遗憾,他后来就再也没有送给我任何东西。他可悲地退化了。真的,这可怕的下议院把我们的丈夫完全给毁了。自从所谓的"妇女高等教育"那可怕的玩艺儿发明出来,下议院对幸福的婚姻生活是最最大的打击。

奇尔顿夫人　啊! 这话在这家可是异端邪说啊,马克比夫人。罗伯特就是主张"妇女高等教育"的大斗士,所以

121

Higher Education of Woman, and so, I am afraid, am I.

MRS. CHEVELEY: The higher education of men is what I should like to see. Men need it so sadly.

LADY MARKBY: They do, dear. But I am afraid such a scheme would be quite unpractical. I don't think man has much capacity for development. He has got as far as he can, and that is not far, is it? With regard to women, well, dear Gertrude, you belong to the younger generation, and I am sure it is all right if you approve of it. In my time, of course, we were taught not to understand anything. That was the old system, and wonderfully interesting it was. I assure you that the amount of things I and my poor dear sister were taught not to understand was quite extraordinary. But modern women understand everything, I am told.

MRS. CHEVELEY: Except their husbands. That is the one thing the modern woman never understands.

LADY MARKBY: And a very good thing too, dear, I dare say. It might break up many a happy home if they did. Not yours, I need hardly say, Gertrude. You have married a pattern husband. I wish I could say as much for myself. But since Sir John has taken to attending the debates regularly, which he never used to do in the good old days, his language has become quite impossible. He always seems to think that he is addressing the House, and consequently whenever he discusses the state of the agricultural labourer, or the Welsh Church, or something quite improper of that kind, I am obliged to send all the servants out of the room. It is not pleasant to see one's own butler, who has been with one for twenty-three years, actually blushing at the sideboard, and the footmen making contortions in corners like persons in circuses. I

呢,我恐怕也算一个了。

谢弗利太太　男人的高等教育我是很赞成的。男人非常需要高等教育。

马克比夫人　他们的确需要,亲爱的。不过我看这样的计划未必行得通。我认为男人没有什么发展的潜力。他已经走到了头了,还不算太远,是吗?至于女人呢,哦,亲爱的格特鲁德,你属于年轻的一代,我认为你如果赞成是很正常的。我们那时候,家里根本就告诉我们什么也别懂才好。旧的那套就是这样的,想来也真是不可思议。我跟你说啊,家里不让我和我妹妹知道的东西是非常不寻常的东西。但是现代妇女什么都懂,我知道这个。

谢弗利太太　就是不懂他们的丈夫。这是现代妇女唯一不懂的东西。

马克比夫人　要我说,她们不懂丈夫才好呢。她们要是懂了,那会让许多幸福家庭破裂的。我得声明,你的家庭是个例外,格特鲁德。你嫁了一个模范丈夫。我自己如果有这样的福气就好了。可是自从约翰爵士经常参加辩论以来——他过去从来不这样的——他的语言就变得让人受不了了。他总以为在向议院发表演说,因此他一说到农业劳力状况,或者威尔士教会,或者这类不合时宜的话题,我就得把仆人们打发到屋外去。看见跟了自己二三十年的管家在餐具柜旁边脸红脖子粗,男仆在角落里像马戏团的演员一样忸怩作态,终归不是愉快的事情。听我说没错,他们要是不赶快把约

assure you my life will be quite ruined unless they send John at once to the Upper House. He won't take any interest in politics then, will he? The House of Lords is so sensible. An assembly of gentlemen. But in his present state, Sir John is really a great trial. Why, this morning before breakfast was half over, he stood up on the hearth-rug, put his hands in his pockets, and appealed to the country at the top of his voice. I left the table as soon as I had my second cup of tea, I need hardly say. But his violent language could be heard all over the house! I trust, Gertrude, that Sir Robert is not like that?

LADY CHILTERN: But I am very much interested in politics, Lady Markby. I love to hear Robert talk about them.

LADY MARKBY: Well, I hope he is not as devoted to Blue Books as Sir John is. I don't think they can be quite improving reading for any one.

MRS. CHEVELEY (*languidly*): I have never read a Blue Book. I prefer books...in yellow covers.

LADY MARKBY (*genially unconscious*): Yellow is a gayer colour, is it not? I used to wear yellow a good deal in my early days, and would do so now if Sir John was not so painfully personal in his observations, and a man on the question of dress is always ridiculous, is he not?

MRS. CHEVELEY: Oh, no! I think men are the only authorities on dress.

LADY MARKBY: Really? One wouldn't say so from the sort of hats they wear? Would one?

The butler enters, followed by the footman. Tea is set on a small table close to LADY CHILTERN.

LADY CHILTERN: May I give you some tea, Mrs. Cheveley?

翰弄到上议院去,我的生活非得毁掉不可。那时他对政治就不会有什么兴趣了。是吗?上议院是理智的。全是一伙绅士。可是约翰目前的状态真是活受罪。唉,今天早上早餐吃到一半时,他就去站到壁炉前的地毯上,两只手插进口袋里,扯足嗓门向全国发表讲演。不用说,我喝完了第二杯茶就赶快离开了餐桌。但是,他大叫大吼的话语在整座房子里都能听到!格特鲁德,我相信罗伯特不会是这个样子吧?

奇尔顿夫人　可是我对政治就非常有兴趣啊,马克比夫人。我很喜欢听罗伯特谈论政治。

马克比夫人　哦,那我也希望他别像约翰爵士那样对蓝皮书①爱不释手。我认为读它们不会让人有什么长进。

谢弗利太太　(懒洋洋地)我从来不看蓝皮书。我宁愿看看……黄皮书。

马克比夫人　(略带迷糊地)黄色的确更喜兴,不是吗?我年轻时经常穿黄色衣服,而且要是约翰爵士不那么带着个人色彩进行挑剔,我还会穿黄色衣服的。男人对穿戴的问题总是荒唐可笑的,对不对?

谢弗利太太　哦,不!我认为男人才对穿戴有评价的资格。

马克比夫人　真的吗?你看看他们戴的帽子就不会说这种话了!对吗?

〔管家上,男仆跟上。茶点放在奇尔顿夫人身旁的小桌子上。

奇尔顿夫人　我给你些茶点好吗,谢弗利太太?

---

① 英美等国政府就某一专题发表的封皮为蓝色的正式报告书或外交书。

MRS. CHEVELEY: Thanks. (*The butler hands* MRS. CHEVELEY *a cup of tea on a salver.*)

LADY CHILTERN: Some tea, Lady Markby?

LADY MARKBY: No thanks, dear. (*The servants go out.*) The fact is, I have promised to go round for ten minutes to see poor Lady Brancaster, who is in very great trouble. Her daughter, quite a well-brought-up girl, too, has actually become engaged to be married to a curate in Shropshire. It is very sad, very sad indeed. I can't understand this modern mania for curates. In my time we girls saw them, of course, running about the place like rabbits. But we never took any notice of them, I need hardly say. But I am told that nowadays country society is quite honeycombed with them. I think it most irreligious. And then the eldest son has quarrelled with his father, and it is said that when they meet at the club Lord Brancaster always hides himself behind the money article in *The Times*. However, I believe that is quite a common occurrence nowadays and that they have to take in extra copies of *The Times* at all the clubs in St. James's Street; there are so many sons who won't have anything to do with their fathers, and so many fathers who won't speak to their sons. I think myself, it is very much to be regretted.

MRS. CHEVELEY: So do I. Fathers have so much to learn from their sons nowadays.

LADY MARKBY: Really, dear? What?

MRS. CHEVELEY: The art of living. The only really Fine Art we have produced in modern times.

LADY MARKBY (*shaking her head*): Ah! I am afraid Lord Brancaster knew a good deal about that. More than this poor wife ever did. (*Turning to* LADY CHILTERN):

谢弗利太太　谢谢。(管家用碟子把茶杯递给谢弗利太太。)

奇尔顿夫人　喝些茶吗,马克比夫人?

马克比夫人　不用,谢谢,亲爱的。(两个仆人下。)事实上我已经答应花上十分八分钟去看看可怜的布兰卡斯特夫人,她的麻烦太大了。她的女儿也算出身名门了,却偏偏和希罗普郡的助理牧师订了婚,就要出嫁了。这的确是非常非常伤心的事情。我真不明白现代人怎么就疯狂地爱上了助理牧师。我们那时候,我们姑娘家看见他们当然像兔子一样满地跑。可是用不着说,我们根本就看不上他们。不过我听说今天的乡村社会到处都是他们的影子。我认为这是最最不合宗教的。后来长子又和他父亲闹不和。据说他们父子在俱乐部相遇,布兰卡斯特勋爵总是埋头看《泰晤士报》上的财产文章。不管怎样,我相信这种事情在今天不足为奇,圣詹姆士街的各家俱乐部都不得不多订几份《泰晤士报》;说不清有多少儿子和老子闹翻了脸,也说不清多少老子不和儿子说话。我心里想啊,这也实在让人遗憾了。

谢弗利太太　我也有同感。做父亲的当今之日向儿子学习的东西太多了。

马克比夫人　真的吗,亲爱的?学什么呢?

谢弗利太太　生活的艺术呀。这是在现代生活里我们制造出来的唯一真正的艺术。

马克比夫人　(摇摇头)啊!恐怕布兰卡斯特勋爵对此早深有体会了。比他可怜的妻子知道的还要多啊。(转向奇

You know Lady Brancaster, don't you, dear?

LADY CHILTERN: Just slightly. She was staying at Langton last autumn, when we were there.

LADY MARKBY: Well, like all stout women, she looks the very picture of happiness, as no doubt you noticed. But there are many tragedies in her family, besides this affair of the curate. Her own sister, Mrs. Jekyll, had a most unhappy life; through no fault of her own, I am sorry to say. She ultimately was so broken-hearted that she went into a convent, or on to the operatic stage, I forget which. No; I think it was decorative art-needlework she took up. I know she had lost all sense of pleasure in life. (*Rising*): And now, Gertrude, if you will allow me, I shall leave Mrs. Cheveley in your charge and call back for her in a quarter of an hour. Or perhaps, dear Mrs. Cheveley, you wouldn't mind waiting in the carriage while I am with Lady Brancaster. As I intend it to be a visit of condolence, I shan't stay long.

MRS. CHEVELEY (*rising*): I don't mind waiting in the carriage at all, provided there is somebody to look at one.

LADY MARKBY: Well, I hear the curate is always prowling about the house.

MRS. CHEVELEY: I am afraid I am not fond of girl friends.

LADY CHILTERN (*rising*): Oh, I hope Mrs. Cheveley will stay here a little. I should like to have a few minutes' conversation with her.

MRS. CHEVELEY: How very kind of you, Lady Chiltern! Believe me, nothing would give me greater pleasure.

LADY MARKBY: Ah! no doubt you both have many

第 二 幕

尔顿夫人)亲爱的,你认识布兰卡斯特夫人,对不?

谢弗利太太　还算熟悉吧。她去年秋天在朗顿小住时,我们在那里。

马克比夫人　哦,像所有结实的女人一样,她看上去是满身幸福的样子,你肯定注意到了这点,可是她家里悲剧发生了一起又一起。除了助理牧师这件韵事,她自己的妹妹杰尔基太太生活得也很不幸。问题倒不是出在她身上,遗憾就在这里。她心死如灰,进了修道院,要不到歌剧舞台上了,我记不得是哪个了。不对,我认为她去干装饰刺绣艺术活儿了。我知道她对生活的乐趣失去了感觉。(站起)格特鲁德,如果你允许,现在我要把谢弗利太太留给你照顾一下,一刻钟后我来接她回去。或许,亲爱的谢弗利太太,在我探望布兰卡斯特夫人时,你可以在马车里等着我。我只是去礼节性地安慰一下,呆不长的。

谢弗利太太　(站起)我不在乎在马车里等着,只要有人陪着我就行。

马克比夫人　哦,我听说那位助理牧师在家里四处走动。

谢弗利太太　恐怕我不喜欢姑娘朋友作陪。

奇尔顿夫人　(站起)噢,我看谢弗利太太就呆在这里吧。我正好和她说几分钟话。

谢弗利太太　你太好了,奇尔顿夫人!真的,干什么都没有和你说会儿话更让我高兴的了。

马克比夫人　啊!你们俩正好说说你们同窗学友的美好时

pleasant reminiscences of your schooldays to talk over together. Good-bye, dear Gertrude! Shall I see you at Lady Bonar's to-night? She has discovered a wonderful new genius. He does... nothing at all, I believe. That is a great comfort, is it not?

LADY CHILTERN: Robert and I are dining at home by ourselves to-night, and I don't think I shall go anywhere afterwards. Robert, of course, will have to be in the House. But there is nothing interesting on.

LADY MARKBY: Dining at home by yourselves? Is that quite prudent? Ah, I forgot, your husband is an exception. Mine is the general rule, and nothing ages a woman so rapidly as having married the general rule.

Exit LADY MARKBY.

MRS. CHEVELEY: Wonderful woman, Lady Markby, isn't she? Talks more and says less than anybody I ever met. She is made to be a public speaker. Much more so than her husband, though he is a typical Englishman, always dull and usually violent.

LADY CHILTERN (*makes no answer, but remains standing. There is a Pause. Then the eyes of the two women meet.* LADY CHILTERN *looks stern and pale.* MRS. CHEVELEY *seems rather amused*): Mrs. Cheveley, I think it is right to tell you quite frankly that, had I known who you really were, I should not have invited you to my house last night.

MRS. CHEVELEY (*with an impertinent smile*): Really?

LADY CHILTERN: I could not have done so.

MRS. CHEVELEY: I see that after all these years you have not changed a bit, Gertrude.

LADY CHILTERN: I never change.

MRS. CHEVELEY (*elevating her eyebrows*): Then life

光。再见,亲爱的格特鲁德!今晚我在博纳夫人那里还能见到你吗?她发现了一个了不起的新天才。罗伯特也不会……有什么事吧,我想,这是多么大的安慰,不是吗?

奇尔顿夫人　罗伯特和我今晚自己在家里用餐,我看用过餐不会到哪里去了。罗伯特当然要到议院去的。不过让人感兴趣的东西也不多。

马克比夫人　你们俩自己在家里用餐?太节俭了吧?呵,我忘了,你丈夫是一个例外。我那位是庸人,再没有跟庸人结婚能让女人迅速衰老了。

〔马克比夫人下。

谢弗利太太　多古怪的女人,我是说马克比夫人,不是吗?我从来没有见过像她这样聊天多说话少的人呢。她天生就是一个在公众场合聊天的人。比她丈夫活跃得多,尽管他是一个典型的英国人,却总是索然无味,还特别暴躁。

奇尔顿夫人　(停顿一会儿。没有作答,但是仍然站着。随后两个女人的眼光相遇。奇尔顿夫人看上去坚定而苍白。谢弗利太太似乎颇感有趣。)谢弗利太太,我认为还是有话跟你直说好,要是我早知道你到底是谁,那我是不会邀请你昨天晚上来做客的。

谢弗利太太　(带着得意的笑容)是吗?

奇尔顿夫人　我要是不请就好了。

谢弗利太太　我发现这么多年过去了,你一点都没有变,格特鲁德。

奇尔顿夫人　我永远不会变的。

谢弗利太太　(挑起眉毛)那么说,生活就没有教会你任何东

has taught you nothing?

LADY CHILTERN: It has taught me that a person who has once been guilty of a dishonest and dishonourable action may be guilty of it a second time, and should be shunned.

MRS. CHEVELEY: Would you apply that rule to every one?

LADY CHILTERN: Yes, to every one, without exception.

MRS. CHEVELEY: Then I am sorry for you, Gertrude, very sorry for you.

LADY CHILTERN: You see now, I am sure, that for many reasons any further acquaintance between us during your stay in London is quite impossible?

MRS. CHEVELEY (*leaning back in her chair*): Do you know, Gertrude, I don't mind your talking morality a bit. Morality is simply the attitude we adopt towards people whom we personally dislike. You dislike me. I am quite aware of that. And I have always detested you. And yet I have come here to do you a service.

LADY CHILTERN (*contemptuously*): Like the service you wished to render my husband last night, I suppose. Thank heaven, I saved him from that.

MRS. CHEVELEY (*starting to her feet*): It was you who made him write that insolent letter to me? It was you who made him break his promise?

LADY CHILTERN: Yes.

MRS. CHEVELEY: Then you must make him keep it. I give you till to-morrow morning—no more. If by that time your husband does not solemnly bind himself to help me in this great scheme in which I am interested—

LADY CHILTERN: This fraudulent speculation—

西吗？

奇尔顿夫人　生活告诉我，一个人一旦犯过不诚实的和丢脸行为的罪，那他还会犯第二次，别人还是躲开他为好。

谢弗利太太　你认为这个法则对谁都一样吗？

奇尔顿夫人　是的，对谁都一样，一无例外。

谢弗利太太　那我只有为你难过了，格特鲁德，非常为你难过。

奇尔顿夫人　你现在明白，我可以肯定说，你在伦敦期间，不管有多少理由，我们都不会再见面了吧？

谢弗利太太　(仰靠在沙发上)格特鲁德，你可知道，我压根就不在乎你谈论道德问题。道德只是我们对自己不喜欢的人所采取的态度。你不喜欢我，我非常明白这点。我也总是厌恶你呀。可是我还是要来为你做点好事。

奇尔顿夫人　(蔑视地)我想你的好事，就像你昨天晚上为我丈夫所做的一样吧。谢天谢地，我总算把他从你的好事里解救出来了。

谢弗利太太　(吃惊地站了起来)是你让他给我写那封侮辱信的？是你让他收回他的许诺的吗？

奇尔顿夫人　是的。

谢弗利太太　那么你必须让他信守他的许诺。我给你时间到明天早上——绝不再多。如果到那时候你丈夫还不认真地支持那个与我利益密切相关的伟大计划——

奇尔顿夫人　那个骗人的投机项目——

MRS. CHEVELEY: Call it what you choose. I hold your husband in the hollow of my hand, and if you are wise you will make him do what I tell him.

LADY CHILTERN (*rising and going towards her*): You are impertinent. What has my husband to do with you? With a woman like you?

MRS. CHEVELEY (*with a bitter laugh*): In this world like meets with like. It is because your husband is himself fraudulent and dishonest that we pair so well together. Between you and him there are chasms. He and I are closer than friends. We are enemies linked together. The same sin binds us.

LADY CHILTERN: How dare you class my husband with yourself? How dare you threaten him or me? Leave my house. Yon are unfit to enter it.

SIR ROBERT CHILTERN *enters from behind. He hears his wife's last words, and sees to whom they are addressed. He grows deadly pale.*

MRS. CHEVELEY: Your house! A house bought with the price of dishonour. A house, everything in which has been paid for by fraud. (*Turns round and sees* SIR ROBERT CHILTERN.) Ask him what the origin of his fortune is! Get him to tell you how he sold to a stockbroker a Cabinet secret. Learn from him to what you owe your position.

LADY CHILTERN: It is not true! Robert! It is not true!

MRS. CHEVELEY (*pointing at him with outstretched finger*): Look at him! Can he deny it! Does he dare to?

SIR ROBERT CHILTERN: Go! Go at once. You have done your worst now.

MRS. CHEVELEY: My worst? I have not yet finished

谢弗利太太　你爱怎么叫都行。我早把你丈夫捏在手心里了,如果你还算明智的话,你应该告诉他照我说的办。

奇尔顿夫人　(站起来向她走去)你别太放肆。我丈夫和你有什么相干？和你这样的女人有什么相干？

谢弗利太太　(露出一丝冷笑)这个世界是讲物以类聚的。因为你的丈夫他本人就行骗,不诚实,我们正好是一对儿。你和他之间是有断层的。他和我亲密得胜过朋友。我们是拴在一起的敌人。同样的罪恶把我们捆在一块儿了。

奇尔顿夫人　你怎么敢把我丈夫和你扯在一起？你竟然敢对他和我如此威胁吗？离开我的家,你不配走进这个家门。

〔罗伯特·奇尔顿爵士从后面上。他听见了他妻子最后几句话,看见了她在对谁说话,脸色立时变得煞白。

谢弗利太太　你的家！一个用来路不明的钱买来的家。家里的每一件东西都是用骗来的钱买的。(转过身看见了罗伯特·奇尔顿爵士。)问一问他的财产是从哪里来的！让他告诉你他如何把内阁秘密卖给了一个证券经纪人。听他说说他现在的地位多亏了什么。

奇尔顿夫人　这不是真的！罗伯特！这不是真的！

谢弗利太太　(伸直手指指向罗伯特)看着他！看他能否认得了！看他敢否认吗？

罗伯特·奇尔顿爵士　滚！马上滚。你的最坏表演现在到头了。

谢弗利太太　我的最坏表演？我和你还没有算清账,和你

with you, with either of you. I give you both till to-morrow at noon. If by then you don't do what I bid you to do, the whole world shall know the origin of Robert Chiltern.

SIR ROBERT CHILTERN *strikes the bell. Enter* MASON.

SIR ROBERT CHILTERN: Show Mrs. Cheveley out.

MRS. CHEVELEY *starts; then bows with somewhat exaggerated politeness to* LADY CHILTERN. *who makes no sign of response. As she passes by* SIR ROBERT CHILTERN, *who is standing close to the door, she pauses for a moment and looks him straight in the face. She then goes out, followed by the servant, who closes the door after him. The husband and wife are left alone.* LADY CHILTERN *stands like some one in a dreadful dream. Then she turns round and looks at her husband. She looks at him with strange eyes, as though she was seeing him for the first time.*

LADY CHILTERN: Yon sold a Cabinet secret for money! You began your life with fraud! You built up your career on dishonour! Oh, tell me it is not true! Lie to me! Lie to me! Tell me it is not true.

SIR ROBERT CHILTERN: What this woman said is quite true. But, Gertrude, listen to me. You don't realise how I was tempted. Let me tell you the whole thing. (*Goes towards her.*)

LADY CHILTERN: Don't come near me. Don't touch me. I feel as if you had soiled me for ever. Oh! what a mask you have been wearing all these years! A horrible painted mask! You sold yourself for money. Oh! a common thief were better. You put yourself up to sale to the highest bidder! You were bought in the market. You

们两个都没有算清账呢。我给你们俩时间到明天中午。如果那时你们还没有按我说的去做,那么整个世界将会知道罗伯特·奇尔顿的底细。

〔罗伯特·奇尔顿爵士打响铃。梅森上。

罗伯特·奇尔顿爵士 把谢弗利太太领出去。

〔谢弗利太太颇感惊讶,随后向奇尔顿夫人行了一个有点夸张的礼,奇尔顿夫人没有答理。她走过站在门边的罗伯特·奇尔顿爵士时,直视着他的脸。然后她走了出去,仆人在后边,把门关上。丈夫和妻子这时呆在房间,奇尔顿夫人站着像在做噩梦,转过身,看着她的丈夫。她用陌生的眼光看着他,仿佛她是第一次看见他。

奇尔顿夫人 你用内阁秘密卖过钱啊!你靠行骗开始你的生活啊!你用卑鄙的手段经营你的生涯啊!噢,跟我说那不是真的!是向我撒谎!快告诉我那不是真的!

罗伯特·奇尔顿爵士 这个女人所说的全部都是真的。不过,格特鲁德,听我说,你不明白我是如何受了诱惑的。让我告诉你全部真相吧。(向她走去。)

奇尔顿夫人 别走近我。别动我。我觉得好像你早把我弄脏了。噢!这么多年来,你一直戴着什么样的脸谱啊!一张可怕的化装的脸谱啊!你把自己卖成了钱。噢!连一个惯偷都不如啊。你把自己标上最高价出卖了!你把自己卖进了市场了。你向全世界撒谎。可是你用

lied to the whole world. And yet you will not lie to me.

SIR ROBERT CHILTERN (*rushing towards her*): Gertrude! Gertrude!

LADY CHILTERN (*thrusting him back with outstretched hands*): No, don't speak! Say nothing! Your voice wakes terrible memories—memories of things that made me love you—memories of words that made me love you—memories that now are horrible to me. And how I worshipped you! You were to me something apart from common life, a thing pure, noble, honest, without stain. The world seemed to me finer because you were in it, and goodness more real because you lived. And now—oh, when I think that I made of a man like you my ideal! the ideal of my life!

SIR ROBERT CHILTERN: There was your mistake. There was your error. The error all women commit. Why can't you women love us, faults and all? Why do you place us on monstrous pedestals? We have all feet of clay, women as well as men; but when we men love women, we love them knowing their weaknesses, their follies, their imperfections, love them all the more, it may be; for that reason. It is not the perfect, but the imperfect, who have need of love. It is when we are wounded by our own hands, or by the hands of others, that love should come to cure us—else what use is love at all? All sins, except a sin against itself, Love should forgive. All lives, save loveless lives, true Love should pardon. A man's love is like that. It is wider, larger, more human than a woman's. Women think that they are making ideals of men. What they are making of us are false idols merely. You made your false idol of me, and I had not the courage to come down, show you my wounds, tell you

不着向我撒谎了。

罗伯特·奇尔顿爵士　(冲向她)格特鲁德！格特鲁德！

奇尔顿夫人　(伸直手臂往后推他)不，不用说了！什么也别说！你的声音只会唤起各种可怕的往事——让我爱上你的往事，让我爱上你的旧话——现在让我不寒而栗的往事。我过去是多么崇拜你啊！你是我平常生活中不同寻常的东西，一样纯洁、高贵、诚实、洁白无瑕的东西。在我看来，这世界有了你好像格外美好，因为你活着德性更真切。可现在——喔，我想都不敢想，我把你当成了我的理想！我生活的理想啊！

罗伯特·奇尔顿爵士　这中间有你的误会，也有你的错误。那是所有女人都会犯的错误。为什么你们女人爱我们不把过错都算上？为什么你们把我们摆在了可怕的受人尊敬的地位？我们都有一双泥捏的脚，男人女人都一样；可是我们男人爱上女人时，明明知道她们的弱点、她们的愚蠢、她们的缺陷，我们也照爱不误，而且正因如此才更爱她们。需要爱的不是完美无缺的人，而是有这样那样毛病的人。当我们被我们自己的手或者别人的手所伤害时，爱应该来治我们的伤口——否则爱还有什么用途？所有罪恶，除了罪上加罪，爱都应该原谅。所有生命，除了没有爱的生命，真正的爱都应该饶恕。男人的爱就是这样的爱。这种爱比女人的爱更宽广，更巨大，更有人情。女人总以为她们在把男人理想化。实际上她们把我们搞得完全成了虚假的偶像。你把我弄成了你的虚假偶像，而我又没有勇气从神坛上走下来，让你看看我的伤口，告诉你我的弱点。我害

my weaknesses. I was afraid that I might lose your love, as I have lost it now. And so, last night you ruined my life for me—yes, ruined it! What this woman asked of me was nothing compared to what she offered to me. She offered security, peace, stability. The sin of my youth, that I had thought was buried, rose up in front of me, hideous, horrible, with its hands at my throat. I could have killed it for ever, sent it back into its tomb, destroyed its record, burned the one witness against me. You prevented me. No one but you, you know it. And now what is there before me but public disgrace, ruin, terrible shame, the mockery of the world, a lonely dishonoured life, a lonely dishonoured death, it may be, some day? Let women make no more ideals of men! let them not put them on altars and bow before them or they may ruin other lives as completely as you—you whom I have so wildly loved—have ruined mine!

He passes from the room. LADY CHILTERN *rushes towards him, but the door is closed when she reaches it. Pale with anguish, bewildered, helpless, she sways like a plant in the water. Her hands, outstretched, seem to tremble in the air like blossoms in the wind. Then she flings herself down beside a sofa and buries her face. Her sobs are like the sobs of a child.*

ACT DROP

怕我也许会失去了你的爱,就像我现在已经失去了你的爱。所以,你昨天晚上毁了我的生活——是的,毁了我的生活!和这个女人所给予我的相比,她所要求的根本算不了什么。她给了我安全,和平,稳定。我年轻时作的孽,我原以为已经深埋了,却突然暴露在了我的面前,可恶,可怕,它的脏手紧紧扼住了我的脖子。我本可以把它杀死,送进坟墓里;毁掉蛛丝马迹,把那份证据烧成灰烬。可是你阻止了我。就是你阻止了我,你明白这个。现在等待我的只有当众露丑,毁灭,可怕的羞耻,世人的嘲笑,一种孤独的不光彩生活,也许还有哪天等待我的一种孤独的不光彩的死?女人还是别再把男人理想化的好!女人还是别把男人摆到神坛上顶礼膜拜的好,要不她们会像你一样彻底地把别的男人的生活给毁了——我爱你爱得那么刻骨铭心——你却彻底把我毁了!

〔他走过房间。奇尔顿夫人冲向他,但是等她到了门前,门已经关上了。她的脸色因痛苦而苍白、迷惑、无助,像水里的一株禾苗摇摇晃晃,她的两只手伸出去,好像风中的花儿在颤抖。然后她无力地倒在了沙发旁,把脸埋了起来。她抽泣得像孩子那样委屈。

幕　落

ACT THREE

SCENE: The Library in Lord Goring's house in Curzon Street, London. An Adam room. On the right is the door leading into the hall. On the left, the door of the smoking-room. A pair of folding doors at the back open into the drawing-room. The fire is lit. Phipps, the butler, is arranging some newspapers on the writing-table. The distinction of Phipps is his impassivity. He has been termed by enthusiasts the Ideal Butler. The Sphinx is not so incommunicable. He is a mask with a manner. Of his intellectual or emotional life, history knows nothing. He represents the dominance of form.

> *Enter* LORD GORING *in evening dress with a buttonhole. He is wearing a silk hat and Inverness cape. White-gloved, he carries a Louis Seize cane. His are all the delicate fopperies of Fashion. One sees that he stands in immediate relation to modern life, makes it indeed, and so masters it. He is the first well-dressed philosopher in the history of thought.*

LORD GORING: Got my second buttonhole for me, Phipps?

PHIPPS: Yes, my lord. (*Takes his hat, cane, and cape, and presents new buttonhole on salver.*)

LORD GORING: Rather distinguished thing, Phipps. I am the only person of the smallest importance in London at present who wears a buttonhole.

第 三 幕

场景：伦敦柯曾街戈林子爵的住宅。一间亚当式的屋子①，右边是通着大厅的门，左边是通向吸烟室的门。后面两个折叠门通向会客室。炉火正旺。管家菲普斯在写字台上整理着一些报纸。菲普斯的明显特征就是惟命是从。热心人称他为"理想管家"。这个斯芬克斯②并不难沟通。他是个有一种式样的脸谱。无人知道他的智力水平和感情生活。他是形式的代表。

〔戈林子爵穿着扣眼插花的夜礼服上。他戴着一顶绸丝帽，一件长披风，手戴白手套，携带一根路易十六世风格的手杖。他的装束全然一派十分讲究的纨绔习气。一眼便可看出他和现代生活十分贴近，既赶时髦，又让时髦为己所用。他是思想史上第一位讲究穿戴的哲学家。

戈林子爵　给我准备第二朵扣眼插花了吗，菲普斯？

菲普斯　准备了，老爷。（从戈林子爵那里接过帽子、手杖和长披风，随后用托盘递上新的扣眼插花。）

戈林子爵　非常标新立异的东西，菲普斯。我是伦敦城眼下区区小人物中唯一戴扣眼插花的人。

---

① 亚当式的屋子(Adam room)，当指十八世纪英国建筑师罗伯特·亚当和约翰·亚当兄弟设计的建筑风格。

② 斯芬克斯(Sphinx)，带翼的狮身女怪。传说她常叫过路人猜谜，猜不出的人即遭杀害。另指埃及吉萨地方金字塔附近的狮身人面巨像。王尔德有一首长诗专写斯芬克斯，可见他对斯芬克斯的兴趣，这里指管家菲普斯给人的印象，兼有以上两层意思。

PHIPPS: Yes, my lord. I have observed that.

LORD GORING (*taking out old buttonhole*): You see, Phipps, Fashion is what one wears oneself. What is unfashionable is what other people wear.

PHIPPS: Yes, my lord.

LORD GORING: Just as vulgarity is simply the conduct of other people.

PHIPPS: Yes, my lord.

LORD GORING (*putting in new buttonhole*): And falsehoods the truths of other people.

PHIPPS: Yes, my lord.

LORD GORING: Other people are quite dreadful. The only possible society is oneself.

PHIPPS: Yes, my lord.

LORD GORING: To love oneself is the beginning of a lifelong romance, Phipps.

PHIPPS: Yes, my lord.

LORD GORING (*looking at himself in the glass*): Don't think I quite like this buttonhole, Phipps. Makes me look a little too old. Makes me almost in the prime of life, eh, Phipps?

PHIPPS: I don't observe any alteration in your lordship's appearance.

LORD GORING: You don't, Phipps?

PHIPPS: No, my lord.

LORD GORING: I am not quite sure. For the future a more trivial buttonhole, Phipps, on Thursday evenings.

PHIPPS: I will speak to the florist, my lord. She has had a loss in her family lately, which perhaps accounts for the lack of triviality your lordship complains of in the buttonhole.

LORD GORING: Extraordinary thing about the lower

第 三 幕

菲普斯　是的,老爷。我注意到这点了。

戈林子爵　(取下旧的扣眼插花)你看,菲普斯,所谓时髦就是一个人自己所爱穿戴的。所谓不赶时髦就是别人所喜欢穿戴的。

菲普斯　没错儿,老爷。

戈林子爵　正像庸俗只是别人的行为一样。

菲普斯　没错儿,老爷。

戈林子爵　(把新扣眼插花戴上)也正像虚伪是别人的真实一样。

菲普斯　没错儿,老爷。

戈林子爵　别人是非常可怕的,唯一可行的社会就是一个人自己。

菲普斯　没错儿,老爷。

戈林子爵　爱自己才是一辈子浪漫的开始,菲普斯。

菲普斯　没错儿,老爷。

戈林子爵　(在镜子里照自己)别以为我很喜欢这朵扣子插花,菲普斯,它让我看起来有点见老。让我几乎进入了壮年时期了,对吗,菲普斯?

菲普斯　从老爷的样子上,我看不出有什么变化。

戈林子爵　你看不出吗,菲普斯?

菲普斯　看不出来,老爷。

戈林子爵　我也搞不清楚了。以后每逢星期四晚上,准备一朵更活泼的扣眼插花,菲普斯。

菲普斯　我会跟花商讲好的,老爷。她最近家里死了亲人,

classes in England—they are always losing their relations.

PHIPPS: Yes, my lord! They are extremely fortunate in that respect.

LORD GORING (*turns round and looks at him. PHIPPS remains impassive*): Hum! Any letters, Phipps?

PHIPPS: Three, my lord. (*Hands letters on a salver.*)

LORD GORING (*takes letters*): Want my cab round in twenty minutes.

PHIPPS: Yes, my lord. (*Goes towards door.*)

LORD GORING (*holds up letter in pink envelope*): Ahem, Phipps, when did this letter arrive?

PHIPPS: It was brought by hand just after your lordship went to the club.

LORD GORING: That will do. (*Exit* PHIPPS.) Lady Chiltern's handwriting on Lady Chiltern's pink notepaper. That is rather curious. I thought Robert was to write. Wonder what Lady Chiltern has got to say to me? (*Sits at bureau and opens letter, and reads it.*) 'I want you. I trust you. I am coming to you. Gertrude.' (*Puts down the letter with a puzzled look. Then takes it up, and reads it again slowly.*) 'I want you. I trust you. I am coming to you.' She has found out everything! Poor woman! Poor woman! (*Pulls out watch and looks at it.*) But what an hour to call! Ten o'clock! I shall have to give up going to the Berkshires. However, it is always nice to be expected, and not to arrive. I am not expected at the Bachelors', so I shall certainly go there. Well, I will make her stand by her husband. That is the only thing for any woman to do. It is the growth of the moral sense of women that makes marriage such a hopeless, one-sided institution. Ten o'clock. She should be here

也许因为这个原因她提供的花儿少了些老爷您抱怨的活泼劲儿。

戈林子爵　这是英国下层阶级特有的事情——他们总是死掉自己的亲人。

菲普斯　没错儿,老爷!他们在这方面是再幸运不过了。

戈林子爵　(转身看着菲普斯。菲普斯保持一副惟命是从的样子。)喂!有信吗,菲普斯?

菲普斯　有三封信,老爷。(用托盘送上信。)

戈林子爵　(取信)二十分钟后给我备好马车。

菲普斯　好的,老爷。(走向门口。)

戈林子爵　(拿起粉色信皮的信)喂,菲普斯,这封信什么时候来的?

菲普斯　你刚刚离开到俱乐部时有人亲自送来的。

戈林子爵　知道了。(菲普斯下。)奇尔顿夫人亲自写在奇尔顿夫人用的粉色信纸上。这倒是满怪的。我原以为罗伯特会给我写信来呢。奇尔顿夫人会有什么话写给我呢?(坐在写字台前,拆封,念信。)"我需要你,我信任你。我就去找你。格特鲁德。"(一脸迷惑地把信放在了写字台上。然后拿起来又逐字逐句地念信。)"我需要你。我信任你。我就去找你。"她全都知道了!可怜的女人哪!可怜的女人哪!(掏出表,看时间。)这个时间还要来访啊!都十点钟了!我只好放弃到伯克希尔家去的打算了。不过让人干等着而又不去,总是很好玩的。单身俱乐部没人等我,所以我不如到那里去。哦,我要让她支持她的丈夫才行。这是任何女人都应该做的事情。只有女人的道德感加强了,才能使婚姻成为这样一种没有希望、一厢情愿的制度。十点了。她很快就到这里来

soon. I must tell Phipps I am not in to any one else. (*Goes towards bell.*)

    Enter PHIPPS.

PHIPPS: Lord Caversham.

LORD GORING: Oh, why will parents always appear at the wrong time? Some extraordinary mistake in nature, I suppose. (*Enter* LORD CAVERSHAM.) Delighted to see you, my dear father. (*Goes to meet him.*)

LORD CAVERSHAM: Take my cloak off.

LORD GORING: Is it worth while, father?

LORD CAVERSHAM: Of course it is worth while, sir. Which is the most comfortable chair?

LORD GORING: This one, father. It is the chair I use myself, when I have visitors.

LORD CAVERSHAM: Thank ye. No draught, I hope, in this room?

LORD GORING: No, father.

LORD CAVERSHAM (*sitting down*): Glad to hear it. Can't stand draughts. No draughts at home.

LORD GORING: Good many breezes, father.

LORD CAVERSHAM: Eh? Eh? Don't understand what you mean. Want to have a serious conversation with you, sir.

LORD GORING: My dear father! At this hour?

LORD CAVERSHAM: Well, sir, it is only ten o'clock. What is your objection to the hour? I think the hour is an admirable hour!

LORD GORING: Well, the fact is, father, this is not my day for talking seriously. I am very sorry, but it is not my day.

LORD CAVERSHAM: What do you mean, sir?

LORD GORING: During the Season, father, I only talk

了。我得告诉菲普斯,不管谁来访,都要说我不在家。(要去按门铃。)

〔菲普斯上。

菲普斯　卡弗沙姆伯爵来了。

戈林子爵　哦,当父母的为什么总是在不该来的时候来呢?我看这是天生的特有误会。(卡弗沙姆上。)很高兴看见你,我亲爱的老爸。(上前迎接。)

卡弗沙姆伯爵　给我把外衣脱下来。

戈林子爵　值得花这趟时间吗,老爸?

卡弗沙姆伯爵　当然值得,先生。哪把椅子坐着最舒服?

戈林子爵　这把,老爸。客人来访时,我总坐这把椅子。

卡弗沙姆伯爵　谢谢。这房间里不会有过堂风吧?

戈林子爵　没有,老爸。

卡弗沙姆伯爵　(坐下)那就好。我受不了过堂风。

戈林子爵　就是有不少温和的微风,老爸。

卡弗沙姆伯爵　是吗?是吗?不明白你在说些什么。就是想和你好好谈谈,先生。

戈林子爵　我亲爱的老爸啊!在这个钟点吗?

卡弗沙姆伯爵　嘿,先生,现在才刚刚十点钟。十点钟你会有什么事情可做?我看这个钟点就最合适!

戈林子爵　哦,老爸呀,事实上今天不是我正儿八经说话的日子。我感到非常遗憾,可是我的日子不对。

卡弗沙姆伯爵　你这是什么意思,先生?

戈林子爵　社交活动期间,老爸,我只有每个月的第一个星

seriously on the first Tuesday in every month, from four to seven.

LORD CAVERSHAM: Well, make it Tuesday, sir, make it Tuesday.

LORD GORING: But it is after seven, father, and my doctor says I must not have any serious conversation after seven. It makes me talk in my sleep.

LORD CAVERSHAM: Talk in your sleep, sir? What does that matter? You are not married.

LORD GORING: No, father, I am not married.

LORD CAVERSHAM: Hum! That is what I have come to talk to you about, sir. You have got to get married, and at once. Why, when I was your age, sir, I had been an inconsolable widower for three months, and was already paying my addresses to your admirable mother. Damme, sir, it is your duty to get married. You can't be always living for pleasure. Every man of position is married nowadays. Bachelors are not fashionable any more. They are a damaged lot. Too much is known about them. You must get a wife, sir. Look where your friend Robert Chiltern has got to by probity, hard work, and a sensible marriage with a good woman. Why don't you imitate him, sir? Why don't you take him for your model?

LORD GORING: I think I shall, father.

LORD CAVERSHAM: I wish you would, sir. Then I should be happy. At present I make your mother's life miserable on your account. You are heartless, sir, quite heartless.

LORD GORING: I hope not, father.

LORD CAVERSHAM: And it is high time for you to get married. You are thirty-four years of age, sir.

LORD GORING: Yes, father, but I only admit to thir-

期二是正儿八经谈话的日子,还只在四点至七点之间。

卡弗沙姆伯爵　嘿,全当星期二好了,先生,全当星期二好了。

戈林子爵　可是现在已经是七点以后了,老爸,我的医生说,七点以后我一定不能正儿八经地谈话。要不然,我会在睡觉时说胡话的。

卡弗沙姆伯爵　会在睡觉时说话吗,先生?那有什么关系?你还没有结婚。

戈林子爵　没有,老爸,我是没有结婚。

卡弗沙姆伯爵　哼!这正是我要跟你谈话的内容,先生。你应该结婚了,马上就结婚。咳,我像你这岁数,先生,我早做了三个月悲伤不已的鳏夫,而且已经和你尊敬的母亲来往许多次了。该死,先生,结婚是你的责任。你不能总是嘻嘻哈哈地活着。现如今,每个有身份的男人都要结婚。单身汉不再是时髦了。他们是一伙受伤害的人。他们的那些事谁都知道。你一定要娶个媳妇,先生。看看你的朋友罗伯特·奇尔顿爵士走得端行得正,工作努力,娶了一个好媳妇,结了一门明智的婚姻,走了一条正道。你为什么不能学学他的样子呢,先生?你为什么不把他当做你的好榜样呢?

戈林子爵　我想我会的,老爸。

卡弗沙姆伯爵　我希望你这样,先生。你真那样我就高兴了。眼下就因为你的事情我让你母亲的日子过不安全。无情无义啊,先生,顶无情无义了。

戈林子爵　但愿不是那样,老爸。

卡弗沙姆伯爵　时间不等人,也是你结婚的时候了。你都三十四岁了。先生。

戈林子爵　是的,老爸,可是我得说我是三十二岁——我要

ty-two—thirty-one and a half when I have a really good buttonhole. This buttonhole is not... trivial enough.

Lord Caversham: I tell you you are thirty-four, sir. And there is a draught in your room, besides, which makes your conduct worse. Why did you tell me there was no draught, sir? I feel a draught, sir, I feel it distinctly.

Lord Goring: So do I, father. It is a dreadful draught. I will come and see you to-morrow, father. We can talk over anything you like. Let me help you on with your cloak, father.

Lord Caversham: No, sir; I have called this evening for a definite purpose, and I am going to see it through at all costs to my health or yours. Put down my cloak, sir.

Lord Goring: Certainly, father. But let us go into another room. (*Rings bell.*) There is a dreadful draught here. (*Enter* Phipps.) Phipps, is there a good fire in the smoking-room?

Phipps: Yes, my lord.

Lord Goring: Come in there, father. Your sneezes are quite heartrending.

Lord Caversham: Well, sir, I suppose I have a right to sneeze when I choose?

Lord Goring (*apologetically*): Quite so, father. I was merely expressing sympathy.

Lord Caversham: Oh, damn sympathy. There is a great deal too much of that sort of thing going on nowadays.

Lord Goring: I quite agree with you, father. If there was less sympathy in the world there would be less trouble in the world.

Lord Caversham (*going towards the smoking-room*):

第 三 幕

是戴上一朵真正合适的扣眼插花,也就三十一岁半。这朵插花不够……活泼。

卡弗沙姆伯爵　我跟你说三十四岁了,先生。还有,你这房间里有一股过堂风,显得你的行为越发不像样子了。你为什么跟我说这里没有过堂风呢,先生?我感觉到有股过堂风,先生,我明显感觉到了。

戈林子爵　我也感觉到了,老爸。还是一股可怕的过堂风呢。我明天会去看你的,老爸。那时你爱说什么我们谈什么。让我给你穿上外衣吧,老爸。

卡弗沙姆伯爵　不,先生。我今天晚上来看你是有特别目的的,不管你和我的身体受什么伤害,我非看到目的达到不可。把我的外衣放下,先生。

戈林子爵　当然没问题,老爸。不过让我们到另一个房间去吧。(按响铃。)这里的过堂风太大了。(菲普斯上)菲普斯,吸烟室的火旺吗?

菲普斯　火旺,老爷。

戈林子爵　到那里去吧,老爸。你一打喷嚏我就心里难受。

卡弗沙姆伯爵　嘿,先生,我想我打喷嚏的自由还是有的吧?

戈林子爵　(辩护)那当然,老爸。我只是表示一下同情。

卡弗沙姆伯爵　哦,关心个屁。现如今这种同情都臭满街了。

戈林子爵　我完全同意你的看法,老爸。这世上要是少一些同情,这世上的麻烦会少得多。

卡弗沙姆伯爵　(向吸烟室走去)你这话似是而非,先生。我

That is a paradox, sir. I hate paradoxes.

LORD GORING: So do I, father. Everybody one meets is a paradox nowadays. It is a great bore. It makes society so obvious.

LORD CAVERSHAM (*turning round, and looking at his son beneath his bushy eyebrows*): Do you always really understand what you say, sir?

LORD GORING (*after some hesitation*): Yes, father, if I listen attentively.

LORD CAVERSHAM (*indignantly*): If you listen attentively!... Conceited young puppy!

Goes off grumbling into the smoking-room.
PHIPPS *enters.*

LORD GORING: Phipps, there is a lady coming to see me this evening on particular business. Show her into the drawing-room when she arrives. You understand?

PHIPPS: Yes, my lord.

LORD GORING: It is a matter of the gravest importance, Phipps.

PHIPPS: I understand, my lord.

LORD GORING: No one else is to be admitted, under any circumstances.

PHIPPS: I understand, my lord. (*Bell rings.*)

LORD GORING: Ah! that is probably the lady. I shall see her myself.

Just as he is going towards the door LORD CAVERSHAM *enters from the smoking-room.*

LORD CAVERSHAM: Well, sir? am I to wait attendance on you?

LORD GORING (*considerably perplexed*): In a moment, father. Do excuse me. (LORD CAVERSHAM *goes back.*) Well, remember my instructions, Phipps—into

讨厌似是而非的话。

戈林子爵　我也讨厌，老爸。时下是人都会说几句似是而非的话。真让人受不了。这都成了社会风气了。

卡弗沙姆伯爵　（转身，刷子般的眉毛下一双眼睛瞪着他的儿子）你明白你嘴里经常在说些什么吗？

戈林子爵　（犹豫少许）知道，父亲，如果我用心听着的话。

卡弗沙姆伯爵　（气愤地）如果你用心听的话！……不知天高地厚的臭小子！

〔嘟嘟囔囔走进了吸烟室。菲普斯上。

戈林子爵　菲普斯，今天晚上有位夫人要来跟我谈件重要的事。她来了你把她带到会客厅去。你听明白了吗？

菲普斯　明白了，老爷。

戈林子爵　一件非常重要的事情，菲普斯。

菲普斯　我明白了，老爷。

戈林子爵　不管因为什么事情，不要让任何人进来。

菲普斯　我明白了，老爷。（铃响。）

戈林子爵　啊！来人也许就是那个夫人。我会亲自去见她的。（他正要去门边迎接，卡弗沙姆伯爵从吸烟室上。）

卡弗沙姆伯爵　嘿，先生？我在等你过来呢。

戈林子爵　（一时不知所措）等一会儿，老爸。就等我一会儿。（卡弗沙姆伯爵下。）喂，记住我的话，菲普斯——带

155

that room.

PHIPPS: Yes, my lord.

LORD GORING *goes into the smoking-room. HAROLD, the footman, shows* MRS. CHEVELEY *in. Lamia-like, she is in green and silver. She has a cloak of black satin, lined with dead rose-leaf silk.*

HAROLD: What name, madam?

MRS. CHEVELEY (*to* PHIPPS, *who advances towards her*): Is Lord Goring not here? I was told he was at home?

PHIPPS: His lordship is engaged at present with Lord Caversham, madam.

Turns a cold, glassy eye on HAROLD, *who at once retires.*

MRS. CHEVELEY (*to herself*): How very filial!

PHIPPS: His lordship told me to ask you, madam, to be kind enough to wait in the drawing-room for him. His lordship will come to you there.

MRS. CHEVELEY (*with a look of surprise*): Lord Goring expects me?

PHIPPS: Yes, madam.

MRS. CHEVELEY: Are you quite sure?

PHIPPS: His lordship told me that if a lady called I was to ask her to wait in the drawing-room. (*Goes to the door of the drawing-room and opens it.*) His lordship's directions on the subject were very precise.

MRS. CHEVELEY (*to herself*): How thoughtful of him! To expect the unexpected shows a thoroughly modern intellect. (*Goes towards the drawing-room and looks in.*) Ugh! How dreary a bachelor's drawing-room always looks. I shall have to alter this. (PHIPPS *brings the lamp from the writing-table.*) No, I don't care for that lamp. It

第 三 幕

进会客厅呀。

菲普斯　记住了,老爷。

〔戈林子爵走进吸烟室。男仆哈罗德带谢弗利太太上,谢弗利太太妖里妖气,身着绿色和银色搭配的服装。她的外衣是黑缎做的,里子是死玫瑰叶色绸。

哈罗德　请问芳名,夫人?

谢弗利太太　(直向迎过来的菲普斯走去)戈林子爵不在这里吗?我听说他在家的。

菲普斯　我家老爷眼下正在跟卡弗沙姆伯爵说话呢,夫人。

〔她朝哈罗德瞪起冷冷的无情的眼看了看,哈罗德慌忙退下了。

谢弗利太太　(自言自语)多么孝顺啊!

菲普斯　我家老爷告诉我请你到会客厅去等他。我家老爷一会儿就来这里见你。

谢弗利太太　(脸上露出惊讶的神色)戈林子爵知道我要来吗?

菲普斯　是的,夫人。

谢弗利太太　你敢肯定吗?

菲普斯　我家老爷告诉我说,一位夫人来访时,我要把她带到会客厅等着。(走向会客厅门前,把门打开。)我家老爷关于这事吩咐得十分明确。

谢弗利太太　(自言自语)他想得多么周到啊!能预料到不速之客要来,这完全是现代人的智商。(走向会客厅往里看。)嚄!单身汉的会客厅看上去总是死气沉沉。我要把这里改变一下。(菲普斯从写字台上把灯拿过来。)不,我

157

is far too glaring. Light some candles.

PHIPPS(*replaces lamp*): Certainly, madam.

MRS. CHEVELEY: I hope the candles have very becoming shades.

PHIPPS: We have had no complaints about them, madam, as yet.

Passes into the drawing-room and begins to light the candles.

MRS. CHEVELEY(*to herself*): I wonder what woman he is waiting for to-night. It will be delightful to catch him. Men always look so silly when they are caught. And they are always being caught. (*Looks about room and approaches the writing-table.*) What a very interesting room! What a very interesting picture! Wonder what his correspondence is like. (*Takes up letters.*) Oh, what a very uninteresting correspondence! Bills and cards, debts and dowagers! Who on earth writes to him on pink paper? How silly to write on pink paper! It looks like the beginning of a middle-class romance. Romance should never begin with sentiment. It should begin with science and end with a settlement. (*Puts letter down, then takes it up again.*) I know that handwriting. That is Gertrude Chiltern's. I remember it perfectly. The ten commandments in every stroke of the pen, and the moral law all over the page. Wonder what Gertrude is writing to him about? Something horrid about me, I suppose. How I detest that woman! (*Reads it.*) 'I trust you. I want you. I am coming to you. Gertrude.' 'I trust you. I want you. I am coming to you.'

A look of triumph comes over her face. She is just about to steal the letter, when PHIPPS *comes in.*

PHIPPS: The candles in the drawing-room are lit,

不喜欢那种灯。它的光太刺眼。点上一些蜡烛吧。

菲普斯　（拿走灯）当然可以，夫人。

谢弗利太太　我希望蜡烛的光柔和得多。

菲普斯　我们对蜡烛挺满意的，夫人。

〔穿过会客厅，开始把蜡烛点上。

谢弗利太太　（自言自语）我纳闷儿他今晚在等什么女人。把他逮住真是好玩。他们男人被逮住时很傻。他们还总是让人逮住。（打量屋子，走向写字台。）多有意思的房间啊！多么有意思的画！这是一封什么来信！（拿起信。）哦，一封多么没有意思的来信！账单和名片，借款和未亡人！谁用粉色纸给他写信呢？真傻，怎么能用粉色纸写信啊！这看起来倒像开始一个中产阶级的浪漫故事。浪漫故事永远不应该以感情开始。它应该以科学开始，以财产授予结束。（把信放下，随后又拿起来。）我认识这笔迹。这是格特鲁德·奇尔顿的笔迹。我记得十分清楚。十条戒律用钢笔写得一笔一画，整页上都是道德准则。格特鲁德为什么会给他写信呢？我猜一定是说我的什么坏话的。这个女人多么可恶！（念信。）"我信任你。我需要你。我就去找你。格特鲁德。""我信任你。我需要你。我就去找你。"①

〔她脸上露出得意之色。她刚想偷走那封信，这时菲普斯上。

菲普斯　会客厅的蜡烛点上了，夫人，按你吩咐点的。

---

① 这几句话的顺序和之前和之后的都不一样，不知是排字错还是作者故意所为。

159

madam, as you directed.

MRS. CHEVELEY: Thank you. (*Rises hastily and slips the letter under a large silver-cased blotting-book that is lying on the table.*)

PHIPPS: I trust the shades will be to your liking, madam. They are the most becoming we have. They are the same as his lordship uses himself when he is dressing for dinner.

MRS. CHEVELEY (*with a smile*): Then I am sure they will be perfectly right.

PHIPPS (*gravely*): Thank you, madam.

MRS. CHEVELEY *goes into the drawing-room.* PHIPPS *closes the door and retires. The door is then slowly opened, and* MRS. CHEVELEY *comes out and creeps stealthily towards the writing-table. Suddenly voices are heard from the smoking-room.* MRS. CHEVELEY *grows pale, and stops. The voices grow louder, and she goes back into the drawing-room, biting her lip.*

Enter LORD GORING *and* LORD CAVERSHAM.

LORD GORING (*expostulating*): My dear father, if I am to get married, surely you will allow me to choose the time, place, and person? Particularly the person.

LORD CAVERSHAM (*testily*): That is a matter for me, sir. You would probably make a very poor choice. It is I who should be consulted, not you. There is property at stake. It is not a matter for affection. Affection comes later on in married life.

LORD GORING: Yes: In married life affection comes when people thoroughly dislike each other, father, doesn't it? (*Puts on* LORD CAVERSHAM's *cloak for him.*)

第 三 幕

谢弗利太太　谢谢你。(赶紧站起来,把信压在写字台上一本翻旧的银套书下。)

菲普斯　我相信蜡烛光线很合你的意,夫人。蜡烛的光线是我们最合适的。我家老爷参加晚餐穿戴时就是使用这种烛光的。

谢弗利太太　(面带微笑)那么我敢说它们是无可挑剔的了。

菲普斯　谢谢你,夫人。

〔谢弗利太太走进会客厅。菲普斯关上门,下。那门紧接着又慢慢打开,谢弗利太太出来蹑手蹑脚地向那张写字台走去。突然,吸烟室传出来说话的声音。谢弗利太太脸色变白,停住脚步。声音越来越大,她咬着嘴唇慌忙退回会客厅。

〔戈林子爵和卡弗沙姆伯爵上。

戈林子爵　(规劝的口气)我亲爱的老爸,如果我准备结婚,那你也得让我选好时间、地点和人吧?尤其是人的问题。

卡弗沙姆伯爵　(暴躁地)这事归我办好了,先生。你很可能挑瞎了眼。这事该由我来操持,而不是你。这关系着财产的风险。这和感情不搭界。感情婚后自然就来了。

戈林子爵　是的。婚后彼此根本不喜欢时感情就来了,老爸,对不?(帮着卡弗沙姆伯爵穿上外衣。)

LORD CAVERSHAM: Certainly, sir. I mean certainly not, sir. You are talking very foolishly to-night. What I say is that marriage is a matter for common sense.

LORD GORING: But women who have common sense are so curiously plain, father, aren't they? Of course I only speak from hearsay.

LORD CAVERSHAM: No woman, plain or pretty, has any common sense at all, sir. Common sense is the privilege of our sex.

LORD GORING: Quite so. And we men are so self-sacrificing that we never use it, do we, father?

LORD CAVERSHAM: I use it, sir. I use nothing else.

LORD GORING: So my mother tells me.

LORD CAVERSHAM: It is the secret of your mother's happiness. You are very heartless, sir, very heartless.

LORD GORING: I hope not, father.

Goes out for a moment. Then returns, looking rather put out, with SIR ROBERT CHILTERN.

SIR ROBERT CHILTERN: My dear Arthur, what a piece of good luck meeting you on the doorstep! Your servant had just told me you were not at home. How extraordinary!

LORD GORING: The fact is, I am horribly busy to-night, Robert, and I gave orders I was not at home to any one. Even my father had a comparatively cold reception. He complained of a draught the whole time.

SIR ROBERT CHILTERN: Ah! you must be at home to me, Arthur. You are my best friend. Perhaps by to-morrow you will be my only friend. My wife has discovered everything.

LORD GORING: Ah! I guessed as much!

SIR ROBERT CHILTERN(*looking at him*): Really! How!

卡弗沙姆伯爵　当然，先生。我的意思是说当然不是，先生。你今天晚上净说昏话。我要说的是，婚姻是一个常识问题。

戈林子爵　可是有常识的女人往往长得奇丑无比，老爸，对不？当然我也只是听别人说的。

卡弗沙姆伯爵　丑也好，俊也罢，女人压根就没有常识，先生。常识是我们男性的特权。

戈林子爵　太对了。而且我们男人往往勇于自我牺牲，从来就不屑使用常识，是吧，老爸？

卡弗沙姆伯爵　我使用常识，先生。我就使用它。不使用别的。

戈林子爵　这话是我妈跟我说的。

卡弗沙姆伯爵　这是你妈幸福的秘密。你无情无义啊，先生，你一点情义都没有呀。

戈林子爵　但愿不像你说的那样，老爸。

〔下去一会儿。然后和罗伯特·奇尔顿爵士上，一脸的烦恼。

罗伯特·奇尔顿爵士　我亲爱的亚瑟，在门口台阶上碰见你真是万幸。你的仆人刚刚告诉我说你不在家。真是不可思议！

戈林子爵　实际情况是我今天晚上忙死了，罗伯特。我吩咐仆人说我不在家。我的老爸都受到了冷落。他在这里时一直抱怨有过堂风。

罗伯特·奇尔顿爵士　啊！那你在家就是专门等我了，亚瑟。你是我的知心朋友。也许明天你就成了我唯一的朋友了。我的妻子什么都知道了。

戈林子爵　啊！我早猜到了！

罗伯特·奇尔顿爵士　(看着他)真的！怎么会呢！

LORD GORING (*after some hesitation*): Oh, merely by something in the expression of your face as you came in. Who told her?

SIR ROBERT CHILTERN: Mrs. Cheveley herself. And the woman I love knows that I began my career with an act of low dishonesty, that I built up my life upon sands of shame—that I sold, like a common huckster, the secret that had been intrusted to me as a man of honour. I thank heaven poor Lord Radley died without knowing that I betrayed him. I would to God I had died before I had been so horribly tempted, or had fallen so low. (*Burying his face in his hands.*)

LORD GORING (*after a pause*): You have heard nothing from Vienna yet, in answer to your wire?

SIR ROBERT CHILTERN (*looking up*): Yes; I got a telegram from the first secretary at eight o'clock to-night.

LORD GORING: Well?

SIR ROBERT CHILTERN: Nothing is absolutely known against her. On the contrary, she occupies a rather high position in society. It is a sort of open secret that Baron Arnheim left her the greater portion of his immense fortune. Beyond that I can learn nothing.

LORD GORING: She doesn't turn out to be a spy, then?

SIR ROBERT CHILTERN: Oh! spies are of no use nowadays. Their profession is over. The newspapers do their work instead.

LORD GORING: And thunderingly well they do it.

SIR ROBERT CHILTERN: Arthur, I am parched with thirst. May I ring for something? Some hock and seltzer?

LORD GORING: Certainly. Let me. (*Rings the bell.*)

SIR ROBERT CHILTERN: Thanks! I don't know what

第 三 幕

戈林子爵　（犹豫稍许）噢，一看你进来时的脸色就猜个八九不离十。谁告诉她的？

罗伯特·奇尔顿爵士　谢弗利太太亲自告诉她的。我深爱的女人这下知道我是以一种不光彩的行为开始我的生涯的，知道我的生活建立在羞耻的沙土上——知道我像小商贩一样，我出卖了我作为一个名誉的人所信赖保存的秘密。谢天谢地，可怜的拉德利勋爵至死不知道我出卖了他。早知道我会被诱惑得这么深，陷得这么深，还不如早早死了去见上帝呢。（把脸埋在两手里。）

戈林子爵　（停顿一会儿）你给维也纳发了电报，还没有听到回音吗？

罗伯特·奇尔顿爵士　（抬头看）听到了；今天晚上八点钟我收到了使馆一秘发来的回答。

戈林子爵　怎么样？

罗伯特·奇尔顿爵士　有关她不光彩的事没有半点了解。恰恰相反，她在那里的上流社会声誉很高。安海姆男爵把自己的绝大部分财产都留给了她，这已是公开的秘密了。此外我没有得到别的任何消息。

戈林子爵　没有办法说明她是一个间谍吗？

罗伯特·奇尔顿爵士　噢！间谍在今天也派不上什么用场了。他们的专业过时了。报纸代替他们干了。

戈林子爵　报纸还干得更绝呢。

罗伯特·奇尔顿爵士　亚瑟，我渴得要命。我可以按铃要点什么吗？来点白葡萄酒和矿泉水好吗？

戈林子爵　当然可以。我来要吧。（按响铃。）

罗伯特·奇尔顿爵士　谢谢！我不知道该怎么办了，亚瑟，

to do, Arthur, I don't know what to do, and you are my only friend. But what a friend you are—the one friend I can trust. I can trust you absolutely, can't I?

  Enter PHIPPS.

  LORD GORING: My dear Robert, of course. (*To* PHIPPS): Bring some hock and seltzer.

  PHIPPS: Yes, my lord.

  LORD GORING: And Phipps!

  PHIPPS: Yes, my lord.

  LORD GORING: Will you excuse me for a moment, Robert? I want to give some directions to my servant.

  SIR ROBERT CHILTERN: Gertainly.

  LORD GORING: When that lady calls, tell her that I am not expected home this evening. Tell her that I have been suddenly called out of town. You understand?

  PHIPPS: The lady is in that room, my lord. You told me to show her into that room, my lord.

  LORD GORING: You did perfectly right. (*Exit* PHIPPS.) What a mess I am in. No; I think I shall get through it. I'll give her a lecture through the door. Awkward thing to manage, though.

  SIR ROBERT CHILTERN: Arthur, tell me what I should do. My life seems to have crumbled about me. I am a ship without a rudder in a night without a star.

  LORD GORING: Robert, you love your wife, don't you?

  SIR ROBERT CHILTERN: I love her more than anything in the world. I used to think ambition the great thing. It is not. Love is the great thing in the world. There is nothing but love, and I love her. But I am defamed in her eyes. I am ignoble in her eyes. There is a

我不知道干什么好了,你是我唯一的朋友了。何止是朋友——唯一我可以信赖的朋友啊。我可以绝对地信任你,是吧?

〔菲普斯上。

戈林子爵　这还用说嘛,我亲爱的罗伯特。(向菲普斯)拿些白葡萄酒和矿泉水。

菲普斯　是的。

戈林子爵　菲普斯!

菲普斯　在,老爷。

戈林子爵　你稍等一会儿好吗,罗伯特?我想跟我的仆人说几句话。

罗伯特·奇尔顿爵士　当然可以。

戈林子爵　那位夫人来访时,告诉她我今天晚上没有在家等客人。告诉她我突然被人叫到城外去了。你听明白了吗?

菲普斯　那个夫人就在那间屋子里,老爷。你告诉我把她带到那里的,老爷。

戈林子爵　你做得很好。(菲普斯下。)我这下全乱套了。不,我想我要把这事理顺了。我要隔着门给她上一课。不过这事干起来还挺麻烦。

罗伯特·奇尔顿爵士　亚瑟,告诉我该怎么办。我的生活好像把我碾碎了。我这下成了一只茫茫黑夜里飘流的无舵的船了。

戈林子爵　罗伯特,你爱你的妻子,是吗?

罗伯特·奇尔顿爵士　在这个世界上,我爱她胜于爱任何东西。我过去曾经认为胸有大志才是了不起的东西。那算不上什么了不起的东西。爱才是这世界上了不起的东西。爱是唯一重要的东西,我爱她。可是我在她眼里不算人了。我在她眼里很卑鄙。我们俩之间现在出

wide gulf between us now. She had found me out, Arthur, she has found me out.

LORD GORING: Has she never in her life done some folly—some indiscretion—that she should not forgive your sin?

SIR ROBERT CHILTERN: My wife! Never! She does not know what weakness or temptation is. I am of clay like other men. She stands apart as good women do—pitiless in her perfection—cold and stern and without mercy. But I love her, Arthur. We are childless, and I have no one else to love, no one else to love me. Perhaps if God had sent us children she might have been kinder to me. But God has given us a lonely house. And she has cut my heart in two. Don't let us talk of it. I was brutal to her this evening. But I suppose when sinners talk to saints they are brutal always. I said to her things that were hideously true, on my side, from my standpoint, from the standpoint of men. But don't let us talk of that.

LORD GORING: Your wife will forgive you. Perhaps at this moment she is forgiving you. She loves you, Robert. Why should she not forgive?

SIR ROBERT CHILTERN: God grant it! God grant it! (*Buries his face in his hands.*) But there is something more I have to tell you, Arthur.

Enter PHIPPS *with drinks.*

PHIPPS(*hands hock and seltzer to* SIR ROBERT CHILTERN): Hock and seltzer, sir.

SIR ROBERT CHILTERN: Thank you.

LORD GORING: Is your carriage here, Robert?

SIR ROBERT CHILTERN: No, I walked from the club.

现了一条鸿沟。她知道我的底细,亚瑟,她知道我的底细了。

戈林子爵 她在生活中从来就没有干过什么蠢事吗——什么不检点的事——什么让她原谅你的过错的傻事?

罗伯特·奇尔顿爵士 我的妻子!从来没有!她根本就不知道什么是弱点和诱惑。我是泥土做的,和别的男人没有什么两样。她却像贤惠的女人一样冰清玉洁——完美无缺得不懂怜悯——冰冷而生硬,不懂怜爱人。可是我爱她,亚瑟。我们俩没有孩子,我没有儿女可爱,没有儿女爱我。要是上帝能让我们生养孩子,那么她也许会对我更温柔一些。可是上帝只给了我一座孤零零的住房。她把我的心切成了两半。我们不谈这事吧。我今天晚上对她很粗鲁。不过我想罪人对待圣人总是很粗鲁的。我从我的方面,从我的立场,从男人的立场,将可怕的事实告诉了她。不过我们不谈这个了。

戈林子爵 你的妻子会原谅你的。也许此时此刻她已经原谅你了。她爱你,罗伯特。她有什么理由不原谅你呢?

罗伯特·奇尔顿爵士 但愿上帝帮忙!但愿上帝帮忙啊!(把他的脸埋进两手里。)可是有些事情我不得不和你说说,亚瑟。

〔菲普斯上。

菲普斯 (给罗伯特·奇尔顿爵士送上白葡萄酒和矿泉水)白葡萄酒和矿泉水,老爷。

罗伯特·奇尔顿爵士 谢谢你。

戈林子爵 你的马车在这里吗,罗伯特?

罗伯特·奇尔顿爵士 不在。我是从俱乐部走来的。

Lord Goring: Sir Robert will take my cab, Phipps.
Phipps: Yes, my lord.
   Exit.

Lord Goring: Robert, you don't mind my sending you away?

Sir Robert Chiltern: Arthur, you must let me stay for five minutes. I have made up my mind what I am going to do to-night in the House. The debate on the Argentine Canal is to begin at eleven. (*A chair falls in the drawing-room.*) What is that!

Lord Goring: Nothing.

Sir Robert Chiltern: I heard a chair fall in the next room. Some one has been listening.

Lord Goring: No, no; there is no one there.

Sir Robert Chiltern: There is some one. There are lights in the room, and the door is ajar. Some one has been listening to every secret of my life. Arthur, what does this mean?

Lord Goring: Robert, you are excited, unnerved. I tell you there is no one in that room. Sit down, Robert.

Sir Robert Chiltern: Do you give me your word that there is no one there?

Lord Goring: Yes.

Sir Robert Chiltern: Your word of honour? (*Sits down.*)

Lord Goring: Yes.

Sir Robert Chiltern (*rises*): Arthur, let me see for myself.

Lord Goring: No, no.

Sir Robert Chiltern: If there is no one there why should I not look in that room? Arthur, you must let me go into that room and satisfy myself. Let me know that

第 三 幕

戈林子爵 罗伯特爵士要用马车,菲普斯。

菲普斯 知道了,老爷。

〔下。

戈林子爵 罗伯特,你不介意我送你走吧?

罗伯特·奇尔顿爵士 亚瑟,你一定要让我再呆五分钟。我已经拿定主意今天晚上在议院里怎么办了。关于阿根廷运河的辩论将在十一点开始。(会客厅传来椅子倒地的声音。)这是什么?

戈林子爵 没什么。

罗伯特·奇尔顿爵士 我听见隔壁的椅子倒地了。有人一直在偷听。

戈林子爵 没有,没有的事。隔壁没有人。

罗伯特·奇尔顿爵士 有人。那个屋子的灯光亮着,门虚掩着。有人一直在偷听我生活中的每个秘密。亚瑟,这是什么意思?

戈林子爵 罗伯特,是你在激动,在紧张。我跟你说那个房间没有人。坐下,罗伯特。

罗伯特·奇尔顿爵士 你真的告诉我,隔壁没有人吗?

戈林子爵 是的。

罗伯特·奇尔顿爵士 用你的荣誉担保吗?(坐下。)

戈林子爵 是的。

罗伯特·奇尔顿爵士 (站起)亚瑟,让我亲自看看。

戈林子爵 不,不。

罗伯特·奇尔顿爵士 如果隔壁没有人,那你为什么不让我看看?亚瑟,你一定要让我进去看看,那样我才放

no eavesdropper has heard my life's secret. Arthur, you don't realise what I am going through.

LORD GORING: Robert, this must stop. I have told you that there is no one in that room—that is enough.

SIR ROBERT CHILTERN (*rushes to the door of the room*): It is not enough. I insist on going into this room. You have told me there is no one there, so what reason can you have for refusing me?

LORD GORING: For God's sake, don't! There is some one there. Some one whom you must not see.

SIR ROBERT CHILTERN: Ah, I thought so!

LORD GORING: I forbid you to enter that room.

SIR ROBERT CHILTERN: Stand back. My life is at stake. And I don't care who is there. I will know who it is to whom I have told my secret and my shame. (*Enters room.*)

LORD GORING: Great heavens! his own wife!

> SIR ROBERT CHILTERN *comes back, with a look of scorn and anger on his face.*

SIR ROBERT CHILTERN: What explanation have you to give for the presence of that woman here?

LORD GORING: Robert, I swear to you on my honour that that lady is stainless and guiltless of all offence towards you.

SIR ROBERT CHILTERN: She is vile, an infamous thing!

LORD GORING: Don't say that, Robert! It was for your sake she came here. It was to try and save you she came here. She loves you and no one else.

SIR ROBERT CHILTERN: You are mad. What have I to do with her intrigues with you? Let her remain your mistress! You are well suited to each other. She, corrupt

第 三 幕

心。让我知道没有什么偷听者听见了我生活的秘密。亚瑟,你不明白我在怎么苦苦挣扎。

戈林子爵　罗伯特,别再胡来了。我告诉你没有人在隔壁——这就足够了。

罗伯特·奇尔顿爵士　(冲向门边)这根本不够。我坚持去隔壁看看。你告诉我那里没有人,可是你又为什么不让我过去看看呢?

戈林子爵　看在上帝的份上,别去好吧!隔壁是有人在那里。可那个人你千万不能见。

罗伯特·奇尔顿爵士　唉,我早想到是这么回事!

戈林子爵　我禁止你进那个房间。

罗伯特·奇尔顿爵士　闪开,我的生命危在旦夕。我不管谁在那里。我要知道是谁偷听到了我的秘密和羞耻。(进屋。)

戈林子爵　天哪!是他自己的老婆!

〔罗伯特·奇尔顿爵士上,脸上满是责备和气愤之色。

罗伯特·奇尔顿爵士　你如何向我解释那个女人竟然呆在那里?

戈林子爵　罗伯特,我以我的名誉发誓,那位夫人对你造成的所有冒犯都是清白和无辜的。

罗伯特·奇尔顿爵士　她是一个下流的不知廉耻的东西。

戈林子爵　别这样说话,罗伯特!她到这里来全是为了你。她到这里来是为了想办法拯救你。她爱你,比谁都爱你。

罗伯特·奇尔顿爵士　你疯了。她和你勾搭在一起,和我不得不做的事有什么关系?让她给你做主妇吧!你们才是互相般配的一对儿。她,堕落,不知羞耻——你

and shameful—you, false as a friend, treacherous as an enemy even—

LORD GORING: It is not true, Robert. Before heaven, it is not true. In her presence and in yours I will explain all.

SIR ROBERT CHILTERN: Let me pass, sir. You have lied enough upon your word of honour.

> SIR ROBERT CHILTERN *goes out.* LORD GORING *rushes to the door of the drawing-room, when* MRS. CHEVELEY *comes out, looking radiant and much amused.*

MRS. CHEVELEY (*with a mock curtsey*): Good-evening, Lord Goring!

LORD GORING: Mrs. Cheveley! Great heavens... May I ask what were you doing in my drawing-room?

MRS. CHEVELEY: Merely listening. I have a perfect passion for listening through keyholes. One always hears such wonderful things through them.

LORD GORING: Doesn't that sound rather like tempting Providence?

MRS. CHEVELEY: Oh! surely Providence can resist temptation by this time. (*Makes a sign to him to take her cloak off, which he does.*)

LORD GORING: I am glad you have called. I am going to give you some good advice.

MRS. CHEVELEY: Oh! pray don't. One should never give a woman anything that she can't wear in the evening.

LORD GORING: I see you are quite as wilful as you used to be.

MRS. CHEVELEY: Far more! I have greatly improved. I have had more experience.

第 三 幕

呢,作为朋友会玩虚假,作为敌人会耍诡计——
戈林子爵　这不是真的,罗伯特。对天发誓,这不是真的。当着她的面,也当着你的面,我来把一切解释清楚。
罗伯特·奇尔顿爵士　让我走,先生。你以你的名义说谎说得够多了。

　　〔罗伯特·奇尔顿爵士下。戈林子爵冲向客厅的门边,谢弗利太太正好出来,一脸的风光和得意。

谢弗利太太　(行了一个逢场作戏的屈膝礼)晚安,戈林子爵!
戈林子爵　谢弗利太太!老天爷……请问你到我的会客厅干什么来了?
谢弗利太太　听人说话而已。我就是喜欢在钥匙孔边听人讲话。在钥匙孔总能听到这样美妙的东西。
戈林子爵　你说这话难道就不怕冒犯老天爷吗?
谢弗利太太　哦!这次就是老天爷也没法阻止诱惑。(朝他示意给她脱下外衣,他照办了。)
戈林子爵　我对你的来访表示高兴。我正好给你提一些好建议。
谢弗利太太　哦!可别提什么建议。你千万别在晚上给女人提任何不能接受的建议。
戈林子爵　我看你还和过去一样任性。
谢弗利太太　哪里的话!我改进了许多。我经历得多了。

LORD GORING: Too much experience is a dangerous thing. Pray have a cigarette. Half the pretty women in London smoke cigarettes. Personally I prefer the other half.

MRS. CHEVELEY: Thanks. I never smoke. My dressmaker wouldn't like it, and a woman's first duty in life is to her dressmaker, isn't it? What the second duty is, no one has as yet discovered.

LORD GORING: You have come here to sell me Robert Chiltern's letter, haven't you?

MRS. CHEVELEY: To offer it to you on conditions! How did you guess that?

LORD GORING: Because you haven't mentioned the subject. Have you got it with you?

MRS. CHEVELEY (*sitting down*): Oh, no! A well-made dress has no pockets.

LORD GORING: What is your price for it?

MRS. CHEVELEY: How absurdly English you are! The English think that a cheque-book can solve every problem in life. Why, my dear Arthur, I have very much more money than you have, and quite as much as Robert Chiltern has got hold of. Money is not what I want.

LORD GORING: What do you want then, Mrs. Cheveley?

MRS. CHEVELEY: Why don't you call me Laura?

LORD GORING: I don't like the name.

MRS. CHEVELEY: You used to adore it.

LORD GORING: Yes; that's why. (MRS. CHEVELEY *motions to him to sit down beside her. He smiles, and does so.*)

MRS. CHEVELEY: Arthur, you loved me once.

LORD GORING: Yes.

第 三 幕

戈林子爵　经历太多危险就多。请抽支烟吧。伦敦城一半漂亮女人都吸烟。就个人而言,我更喜欢那另一半女人。

谢弗利太太　谢谢。我从来不吸烟。我的裁缝不喜欢吸烟,而女人生活的首要责任就是为了裁缝,不是吗?至于第二责任是什么,还没有人发现呢。

戈林子爵　你到这里来是要卖掉罗伯特·奇尔顿的信,对不对?

谢弗利太太　满足要求就交给你!你怎么猜到的?

戈林子爵　因为你一直没有提到这件事。你带来了吗?

谢弗利太太　(坐下)哦,没有!做工讲究的衣服是没有兜的。

戈林子爵　你为它开个价吧?

谢弗利太太　你们英国人真是不可理喻!英国人认为支票簿能解决每一个麻烦。唉,我亲爱的亚瑟,我的钱可比你多得多啊,跟罗伯特·奇尔顿所拥有的不相上下。钱已不是我所想要的了。

戈林子爵　那想要什么呢,谢弗利太太?

谢弗利太太　你为什么不叫我劳拉?

戈林子爵　我不喜欢那个名字。

谢弗利太太　你曾经深爱过它。

戈林子爵　是的。原因就在这里。(谢弗利太太示意他坐到她身边,他笑了笑,照办了。)

谢弗利太太　亚瑟,你曾经爱过我。

戈林子爵　是的。

MRS. CHEVELEY: And you asked me to be your wife.

LORD GORING: That was the natural result of my loving you.

MRS. CHEVELEY: And you threw me over because you saw, or said you saw, poor old Lord Mortlake trying to have a violent flirtation with me in the conservatory at Tenby.

LORD GORING: I am under the impression that my lawyer settled that matter with you on certain terms... dictated by yourself.

MRS. CHEVELEY: At that time I was poor; you were rich.

LORD GORING: Quite so. That is why you pretended to love me.

MRS. CHEVELEY (*shrugging her shoulders*): Poor old Lord Mortlake, who had only two topics of conversation, his gout and his wife! I never could quite make out which of the two he was talking about. He used the most horrible language about them both. Well, you were silly, Arthur. Why, Lord Mortlake was never anything more to me than an amusement. One of those utterly tedious amusements one only finds at an English country house on an English country Sunday. I don't think any one at all morally responsible for what he or she does at an English country house.

LORD GORING: Yes. I know lots of people think that.

MRS. CHEVELEY: I loved you, Arthur.

LORD GORING: My dear Mrs. Cheveley, you have always been far too clever to know anything about love.

MRS. CHEVELEY: I did love you. And you loved me. You know you loved me; and love is a very wonderful thing. I suppose that when a man has once loved a

谢弗利太太　你曾经要求我做你的妻子。

戈林子爵　那是我爱你的自然结果。

谢弗利太太　你抛弃了我是因为你看见,或者说你看见,可怜的莫特莱克勋爵在坦比的暖房里试图和我热烈地调情。

戈林子爵　我的印象中,我的律师按某些条件和你解决了这件事了……是你口述的。

谢弗利太太　那时我还很穷;你很富有。

戈林子爵　一点没有错。你就是因为这个才假装爱我的。

谢弗利太太　(耸了耸肩)可怜的莫特莱克勋爵,他只有两个话题:他的痛风和他的妻子!我始终就没有听明白他是在谈论其中的哪个。他一谈起这两个话题就使用那些最可怕的语言。哦,你当时很傻,亚瑟。唉,莫特莱克勋爵对我来说只是逗逗乐而已。那只不过是一个人在星期天的英国乡下住宅里躲都躲不掉的最无聊的乐趣。我根本不认为一个人应该为他或她在英国乡下住宅的所作所为负有任何道德责任。

戈林子爵　是的。我知道不少人都这样看。

谢弗利太太　我当时是爱你的,亚瑟。

戈林子爵　我亲爱的谢弗利太太,你总是精明过人,精明得连爱是什么都不懂了。

谢弗利太太　我当时真的爱你。你也爱过我。你知道我爱过你;爱是一种非常奇妙的东西。我琢磨一个男人一

woman, he will do anything for her, except continue to love her? (*Puts her hand on his.*)

LORD GORING (*taking his hand away quietly*): Yes; except that.

MRS. CHEVELEY (*after a pause*): I am tired of living abroad. I want to come back to London. I want to have a charming house here. I want to have a salon. If one could only teach the English how to talk, and the Irish how to listen, society here would be quite civilised. Besides, I have arrived at the romantic stage. When I saw you last night at the Chilterns', I knew you were the only person I had ever cared for, if I ever have cared for anybody, Arthur. And so, on the morning of the day you marry me, I will give you Robert Chiltern's letter. That is my offer. I will give it to you now, if you promise to marry me.

LORD GORING: Now?

MRS. CHEVELEY (*smiling*): To-morrow.

LORD GORING: Are you really serious?

MRS. CHEVELEY: Yes, quite serious.

LORD GORING: I should make you a very bad husband.

MRS. CHEVELEY: I don't mind bad husbands. I have had two. They amused me immensely.

LORD GORING: You mean that you amused yourself immensely, don't you?

MRS. CHEVELEY: What do you know about my married life?

LORD GORING: Nothing; but I can read it like a book.

MRS. CHEVELEY: What book?

LORD GORING (*rising*): *The Book of Numbers.*

旦爱过一个女人,那他就会为她干任何事情,除了继续爱她吗?(把她的手放在他的手上。)

戈林子爵　(抽掉他的手)是的,除了继续爱她。

谢弗利太太　(停了一会儿)我在国外呆腻了。我想回伦敦。我想在这里拥有一所迷人的住宅。我想拥有一个沙龙。如果有人能教会英国人如何谈话,教会爱尔兰人如何听人说话,这里的上流社会还是挺开化的。还有,我又到了谈情说爱的阶段。我昨天晚上在奇尔顿家看见你后,我知道你是唯一让我动过心的人,如果我过去对任何人动过心的话,亚瑟。所以,在你娶我的那天上午,我会把罗伯特·奇尔顿的信给你。这是我的求婚礼。如果你答应娶我,我现在就把它给你。

戈林子爵　现在吗?

谢弗利太太　(浅笑)明天。

戈林子爵　你是认真的吗?

谢弗利太太　是的,非常认真。

戈林子爵　我只能给你做一个坏丈夫。

谢弗利太太　我不在意坏丈夫。我已经嫁过两个坏丈夫。他们让我过得非常愉快。

戈林子爵　你是说你给自己找到了不同寻常的乐趣吧,对不?

谢弗利太太　你对我的婚姻生活知道多少?

戈林子爵　一无所知,可是我能把它当一本书读懂。

谢弗利太太　什么书?

戈林子爵　(站起)《民数记》。

MRS. CHEVELEY: Do you think it is quite charming of you to be so rude to a woman in your own house?

LORD GORING: In the case of very fascinating women, sex is a challenge, not a defence.

MRS. CHEVELEY: I suppose that is meant for a compliment. My dear Arthur, women are never disarmed by compliments. Men always are. That is the difference between the two sexes.

LORD GORING: Women are never disarmed by anything, as far as I know them.

MRS. CHEVELEY (*after a pause*): Then you are going to allow your greatest friend, Robert Chiltern, to be ruined, rather than marry some one who really has considerable attractions left. I thought you would have risen to some great height of self-sacrifice, Arthur. I think you should. And the rest of your life you could spend in contemplating your own perfections.

LORD GORING: Oh! I do that as it is. And self-sacrifice is a thing that should be put down by law. It is so demoralising to the people for whom one sacrifices oneself. They always go to the bad.

MRS. CHEVELEY: As if anything could demoralise Robert Chiltern! You seem to forget that I know his real character.

LORD GORING: What you know about him is not his real character. It was an act of folly done in his youth, dishonourable, I admit, shameful, I admit, unworthy of him, I admit, and therefore... not his true character.

MRS. CHEVELEY: How you men stand up for each other!

LORD GORING: How you women war against each other!

谢弗利太太　你认为在你自己的家里对一个女人如此粗鲁挺好玩吗？

戈林子爵　面对着十分令人陶醉的女人，性别是一种挑衅，而不是一种保护。

谢弗利太太　我看这就是一种恭维。我亲爱的亚瑟，女人在恭维面前从来不会束手就擒。男人却总是一听恭维就投降。男女之间的区别就在这里。

戈林子爵　就我所知，女人从来就不会束手就擒。

谢弗利太太　（稍停）那么说，你要眼看着你的好朋友罗伯特·奇尔顿毁掉，而不愿意和一个楚楚动人的女人结婚喽。我原以为你会作出很高的牺牲姿态的，亚瑟。我认为你应该这样。你以后的生活完全可以用来认真思考完善自己。

戈林子爵　噢！事实上我在完善自己。自我牺牲是一样应该通过法律加以取缔的东西。对接受自我牺牲的人来说，自我牺牲是非常不道德的。他们总是变坏。

谢弗利太太　好像还有什么东西能使罗伯特·奇尔顿道德堕落似的！你好像忘了我了解他的真正性格。

戈林子爵　你所了解的不是他的真正性格。那是他年轻时干的一件愚蠢的事情，我承认不光彩，我也承认很可耻，还承认不值得他干，所以……就不是他的真正性格。

谢弗利太太　你们男人彼此多么支持啊！

戈林子爵　你们女人却是互相拆台！

MRS. CHEVELEY (*bitterly*): I only war against one woman, against Gertrude Chiltern. I hate her. I hate her now more than ever.

LORD GORING: Because you have brought a real tragedy into her life, I suppose.

MRS. CHEVELEY (*with a sneer*): Oh, there is only one real tragedy in a woman's life. The fact that her past is always her lover, and her future invariably her husband.

LORD GORING: Lady Chiltern knows nothing of the kind of life to which you are alluding.

MRS. CHEVELEY: A woman whose size in gloves is seven and three quarters never knows much about anything. You know Gertrude has always worn seven and three-quarters? That is one of the reasons why there was never any moral sympathy between us... Well, Arthur, I suppose this romantic interview may be regarded as at an end. You admit it was romantic, don't you? For the privilege of being your wife I was ready to surrender a great prize, the climax of my diplomatic career. You decline. Very well. If Sir Robert doesn't uphold my Argentine scheme, I expose him. *Voila tout*.

LORD GORING: You mustn't do that. It would be vile, horrible, infamous.

MRS. CHEVELEY (*shrugging her shoulders*): Oh, don't use big words. They mean so little. It is a commercial transaction. That is all. There is no good mixing up sentimentality in it. I offered to sell Robert Chiltern a certain thing. If he won't pay me my price, he will have to pay the world a greater price. There is no more to be said. I must go. Good-bye. Won't you shake hands?

LORD GORING: With you? No. Your transaction with Robert Chiltern may pass as a loathsome commercial

谢弗利太太　（恶狠狠地）我只是跟一个女人作对,只和格特鲁德·奇尔顿作对。我恨她。我现在比过去更恨她。

戈林子爵　我想就是因为你给她的生活带来了真正的悲剧吧。

谢弗利太太　（嘲笑）哦,一个女人一辈子只有一出真正的悲剧。那就是她的过去老是她的情人,她的将来又老是她的丈夫。

戈林子爵　奇尔顿夫人对你所指的这种生活一点不懂。

谢弗利太太　一个手戴七又四分之三手套的女人永远不会懂多少东西。你可知道格特鲁德一直戴七又四分之三的手套吗?我们之间始终没有任何道德同情,这就是原因之一……哦,亚瑟,我想这次浪漫的会见可以结束了。你承认这次会见很浪漫,对吗?只要能成为你的妻子,我随时准备付出巨大代价,算我外交生涯的顶峰。可是你拒绝了。好吧好吧。如果罗伯特爵士不支持我的阿根廷计划,我就给他曝光。就这样。

戈林子爵　你千万别那样做。那样做未免太卑鄙、可怕、可耻了。

谢弗利太太　（耸了耸肩膀）哦,别使用这些大字眼儿。它们起不了什么作用。这是一笔商业生意。就这样。这中间不需要掺杂任何感情色彩。如果他不向我付出我所要的代价,那他就得向世界付出更大的代价。没有什么可说的了。我得走了。再见。难道你不和我握握手吗?

戈林子爵　和你吗?不。你和罗伯特·奇尔顿的生意也许

transaction of a loathsome commercial age; but you seem to have forgotten that you came here to-night to talk of love, you whose lips desecrated the word love, you to whom the thing is a book closely sealed, went this afternoon to the house of one of the most noble and gentle women in the world to degrade her husband in her eyes, to try and kill her love for him, to put poison in her heart, and bitterness in her life, to break her idol, and, it may be, spoil her soul. That I cannot forgive you. That was horrible. For that there can be no forgiveness.

MRS. CHEVELEY: Arthur, you are unjust to me. Believe me, you are quite unjust to me. I didn't go to taunt Gertrude at all. I had no idea of doing anything of the kind when I entered. I called with Lady Markby simply to ask whether an ornament, a jewel, that I lost somewhere last night, had been found at the Chilterns'. If you don't believe me, you can ask Lady Markby. She will tell you it is true. The scene that occurred happened after Lady Markby had left, and was really forced on me by Gertrude's rudeness and sneers. I called, oh! — a little out of malice if you like—but really to ask if a diamond brooch of mine had been found. That was the origin of the whole thing.

LORD GORING: A diamond snake-brooch with a ruby?

MRS. CHEVELEY: Yes. How do you know?

LORD GORING: Because it is found. In point of fact, I found it myself, and stupidly forgot to tell the butler anything about it as I was leaving. (*Goes over to the writing-table and pulls out the drawers.*) It is in this drawer. No, that one. This is the brooch, isn't it? (*Holds up the brooch.*)

会成为可恶的商业时代里一桩可恶的商业买卖。可是你好像忘了,你今天晚上是来这里谈论爱情的,你却满嘴糟蹋爱情这个字眼,爱情这事对你来说是本密封的天书,今天下午竟然跑到这世界上最高贵最贤惠的女人的家里去当着她的面贬低她的丈夫,竭力扼杀她对他的爱,往她的心里投放毒药,往她的生活里倾倒苦水,打碎她的偶像,也许还毁掉了她的心灵。这是我绝不原谅你的。这种做法令人恶心。这是无论如何都不能原谅的。

谢弗利太太　亚瑟,你委屈我了。相信我,你完全委屈我了。我根本没有去恶意攻击格特鲁德。我到她家去时根本没有任何要这样做的打算。我和马克比夫人去造访,只是问问我昨天夜里是不是掉在那儿一样装饰品,一样珠宝,问问奇尔顿家的人是不是见到了。如果你不相信我,你可以去问马克比夫人。她会告诉你真相的。那幕戏发生在马克比夫人离开以后,是格特鲁德态度粗鲁出言不逊把我逼到那步的。我去造访也许心怀一点你所谓的恶意,可是真的是去打听我的那枚胸针的下落的。这才是整件事情的根源。

戈林子爵　一枚镶嵌红宝石的钻石蛇形胸针吗?

谢弗利太太　是的。你怎么知道的?

戈林子爵　因为有人捡到了。事实上,是我自己捡到的,一时糊涂,离开时没有告诉管家这件事。(走向写字台前,把抽屉拉开。)它在这个抽屉里。不对,是那个抽屉里。这就是那枚胸针,对吗?(拿起胸针。)

MRS. CHEVELEY: Yes. I am so glad to get it back. It was...a present.

LORD GORING: Won't you wear it?

MRS. CHEVELEY: Certainly, if you pin it in. (LORD GORING *suddenly clasps it on her arm*.) Why do you put it on as a bracelet? I never knew it could be worn as a bracelet.

LORD GORING: Really?

MRS. CHEVELEY (*holding out her handsome arm*): No; but it looks very well on me as a bracelet, doesn't it?

LORD GORING: Yes; much better than when I saw it last.

MRS. CHEVELEY: When did you see it last?

LORD GORING (*calmly*): Oh, ten years ago, on Lady Berkshire, from whom you stole it.

MRS. CHEVELEY (*starting*): What do you mean?

LORD GORING: I mean that you stole that ornament from my cousin, Mary Berkshire, to whom I gave it when she was married. Suspicion fell on a wretched servant, who was sent away in disgrace. I recognised it last night. I determined to say nothing about it till I had found the thief. I have found the thief now, and I have heard her own confession.

MRS. CHEVELEY (*tossing her head*): It is not true.

LORD GORING: You know it is true. Why, thief is written across your face at this moment.

MRS. CHEVELEY: I will deny the whole affair from beginning to end. I will say that I have never seen this wretched thing, that it was never in my possession.

> MRS. CHEVELEY *tries to get the bracelet off her arm, but fails.* LORD GORING *looks on amused. Her thin fingers tear at the jewel to no purpose. A curse*

谢弗利太太　是的。我看见它失而复得真是太高兴了。这是……一件礼物。

戈林子爵　你不戴上它吗？

谢弗利太太　当然，如果你给我别上的话。(戈林子爵突然给她套在了胳膊上。)为什么你给我当手镯戴上？我从来不知道它还能当手镯戴呢。

戈林子爵　真的吗？

谢弗利太太　(伸出她漂亮的胳膊)真的不知道。不过这东西我戴在胳膊上还挺好看，不是吗？

戈林子爵　是的。比我最后那次看见它更好看。

谢弗利太太　你最后那次看见它是什么时候？

戈林子爵　(平静地)噢，十年前，伯克希尔夫人胳膊上，你就是从她那儿偷去的。

谢弗利太太　(惊慌地)你这话是什么意思？

戈林子爵　我的意思是说你从我的表姐伯克希尔夫人那里偷了这件装饰品，那是她结婚时我送给她的礼物。一个倒霉的仆人成了怀疑对象，被不光彩地打发回了家。昨天夜里我就认出来了。我拿定主意不找到偷东西的人绝不声张。我现在人赃俱获，还听到了她的亲口供认。

谢弗利太太　(往后甩了甩头)这不是真的。

戈林子爵　你知道这是真的。嚯，贼这个词儿这会儿就写在你的脸上呢。

谢弗利太太　我会彻底否定这件事情。我会说我根本就没有见过这件东西，我从来没有拿过它。

〔谢弗利太太竭力要把手镯从胳膊上脱下来，但是脱不掉。戈林子爵津津有味地看着。她纤细的手指徒劳地

breaks frore her.

LORD GORING: The drawback of stealing a thing, Mrs. Cheveley, is that one never knows how wonderful the thing that one steals is. You can't get that bracelet off, unless you know where the spring is. And I see you don't know where the spring is. It is rather difficult to find.

MRS. CHEVELEY: You brute! You coward! (*She tries again to unclasp the bracelet, but fails.*)

LORD GORING: Oh! don't use big words. They mean so little.

MRS. CHEVELEY (*again tears at the bracelet in a paroxysm of rage, with inarticulate sounds. Then stops, and looks at* LORD GORING): What are you going to do?

LORD GORING: I am going to ring for my servant. He is an admirable servant. Always comes in the moment one rings for him. When he comes I will tell him to fetch the police.

MRS. CHEVELEY (*trembling*): The police? What for?

LORD GORING: To-morrow the Berkshires will prosecute you. That is what the police are for.

MRS. CHEVELEY (*is now in an agony of physical terror. Her face is distorted. Her mouth awry. A mask has fallen from her. She is, for the moment, dreadful to look at*): Don't do that. I will do anything you want. Anything in the world you want.

LORD GORING: Give me Robert Chiltern's letter.

MRS. CHEVELEY: Stop! Stop! Let me have time to think.

LORD GORING: Give me Robert Chiltern's letter.

MRS. CHEVELEY: I have not got it with me. I will give it to you to-morrow.

揪扯着那件珠宝。她嘴里骂了一句。

戈林子爵　谢弗利太太,偷东西的不利条件是,行窃的人根本不知道他偷到了一件多么奇妙的东西。你不知道机关在哪里,你就无法把手镯取下来。我看你就不知道机关在哪里。想找到机关难啊。

谢弗利太太　你这畜生!你这懦夫!(她又使劲往下脱手镯,但白费力气。)

戈林子爵　喔!别使用这种大字眼儿。大字眼儿一点用也没有。

谢弗利太太　(又歇斯底里地往下脱手镯,嘴里嘟嘟囔囔个不停。然后停下,看着戈林子爵)你想要干什么?

戈林子爵　我要按铃叫我的仆人。他是非常本分的仆人。一按铃他就立刻进来。他进来后我告诉他去叫警察来。

谢弗利太太　(发抖)警察?叫警察干什么?

戈林子爵　明天伯克希尔家将对你进行控告。叫警察来就为这个。

谢弗利太太　(这时惊恐得全身发抖。她的脸变了形。她的嘴半张着。她换上了另一副面具。她这时看上去十分吓人。)别那样做。你要我干什么我就干什么。只要这世界允许的我都干。

戈林子爵　把罗伯特·奇尔顿的信给我。

谢弗利太太　住手!住手!让我多少想想好吧。

戈林子爵　给我罗伯特·奇尔顿的信。

谢弗利太太　我没有带在身上。我明天给你好吧。

LORD GORING: You know you are lying. Give it to me at once. (MRS. CHEVELEY *pulls the letter out, and hands it to him. She is horribly pale.*) This is it?

MRS. CHEVELEY (*in a hoarse voice*): Yes.

LORD GORING (*takes the letter, examines it, sighs, and burns it over the lamp*): For so-well dressed a woman, Mrs. Cheveley, you have moments of admirable common sense. I congratulate you.

MRS. CHEVELEY (*catches sight of* LADY CHILTERN'S *letter, the cover of which is just showing from under the blotting-book*): Please get me a glass of water.

LORD GORING: Certainly. (*Goes to the corner of the room and pours out a glass of water. While his back is turned* MRS. CHEVELEY *steals* LADY CHILTERN'S *letter. When* LORD GORING *returns with the glass she refuses it with a gesture.*)

MRS. CHEVELEY: Thank you. Will you help me on with my cloak?

LORD GORING: With pleasure. (*Puts her cloak on.*)

MRS. CHEVELEY: Thanks. I am never going to try to harm Robert Chiltern again.

LORD GORING: Fortunately you have not the chance, Mrs. Cheveley.

MRS. CHEVELEY: Well, if even I had the chance, I wouldn't. On the contrary, I am going to render him a great service.

LORD GORING: I am charmed to hear it. It is a reformation.

MRS. CHEVELEY: Yes. I can't bear so upright a gentleman, so honourable an English gentleman, being so shamefully deceived and so—

LORD GORING: Well?

第 三 幕

戈林子爵 你心里清楚你在撒谎。马上把它给我。(谢弗利太太把信掏出来,递给他。她脸色白得可怕。)是这个吗?

谢弗利太太 (声音沙哑地)是的。

戈林子爵 (拿过信,翻看一下,舒口气,在灯头上把信烧了。)谢弗利太太,就一个十分讲究穿戴的女人来说,你临场应付的常识是很机敏的。我祝贺你。

谢弗利太太 (看见奇尔顿夫人的信在那本翻旧的书下露出一角,计上心来)请给我一杯水喝。

戈林子爵 当然可以。(走向房间一角,倒了一杯水。他刚转过身去,谢弗利太太就把奇尔顿夫人的信偷在了手里。戈林子爵端着杯子回来时,她用手势拒绝了。)

谢弗利太太 谢谢你。帮我穿上我的外衣好吗?

戈林子爵 很高兴。(给她穿上外衣。)

谢弗利太太 谢谢。我永远不会再伤害罗伯特·奇尔顿了。

戈林子爵 可惜你没有机会了,谢弗利太太。

谢弗利太太 喔,就是有机会我也不干了。恰恰相反,我要为他好好效劳呢。

戈林子爵 听这话很舒心嘛。这叫悔过自新。

谢弗利太太 是的。我受不了如此正直的一位绅士,如此受人尊敬的一个英国绅士,正被人可耻地欺骗,而且——

戈林子爵 怎么啦?

MRS. CHEVELEY: I find that somehow Gertrude Chiltern's dying speech and confession has strayed into my pocket.

LORD GORING: What do you mean?

MRS. CHEVELEY (*with a bitter note of triumph in her voice*): I mean that I am going to send Robert Chiltern the love-letter his wife wrote to you to-night.

LORD GORING: Love-letter?

MRS. CHEVELEY (*laughing*): 'I want you. I trust you. I am coming to you. Gertrude.'

> LORD GORING *rushes to the bureau and takes up the envelope, finds it empty, and turns round.*

LORD GORING: You wretched woman, must you always be thieving? Give me back that letter. I'll take it from you by force. You shall not leave my room till I have got it.

> *He rushes towards her, but* MRS. CHEVELEY *at once puts her hand on the electric bell that is on the table. The bell sounds with shrill reverberations, and* PHIPPS *enters.*

MRS. CHEVELEY (*after a pause*): Lord Goring merely rang that you should show me out. Good-night, Lord Goring!

> *Goes out followed by* PHIPPS. *Her face is illumined with evil triumph. There is joy in her eyes. Youth seems to have come back to her. Her last glance is like a swift arrow.* LORD GORING *bites his lip, and lights a cigarette.*

ACT DROP

第 三 幕

谢弗利太太　我发现不知怎么格特鲁德·奇尔顿要命的情话和表白误进了我的口袋里。

戈林子爵　你这话是什么意思？

谢弗利太太　（声音里露出恶狠狠的得意）我的意思是说，我要给罗伯特·奇尔顿寄上他爱妻今晚写给你的那封情信。

戈林子爵　情信？

谢弗利太太　（大笑）"我需要你。我信任你。我就去找你。格特鲁德。"

〔戈林子爵冲向写字台，拿起信皮，发现里面没有信，转过身来。

戈林子爵　你这可怜的女人，非得每时每刻都偷东西不可吗？快把信给我。我要使用武力从你手里夺回来。我不得到它，你别想从这房间走掉。

〔他冲向谢弗利太太，但谢弗利太太马上按响了桌子上的电铃。铃声大作，菲普斯上。

谢弗利太太　（稍停）戈林子爵按铃要你送我走。晚安，戈林子爵！

〔谢弗利太太下，后面跟着菲普斯。她脸上露出恶毒的得意之色。她眼里满是喜悦。她好像青春再现。她的最后一瞥如同一支利箭。戈林子爵咬紧下嘴唇，点着了一根烟。

　　　　　　　　　　　　　　　　　　　幕　落

ACT FOUR

SCENE: Same as Act Two.

>LORD GORING *is standing by the fireplace with his hands in his pockets. He is looking rather bored.*
>LORD GORING (*pulls out his watch, inspects it, and rings the bell*): It is a great nuisance. I can't find any one in this house to talk to. And I am full of interesting information. I feel like the latest edition of something or other.
>*Enter servant.*

JAMES: Sir Robert is still at the Foreign Office, my lord.

LORD GORING: Lady Chiltern not down yet?

JAMES: Her ladyship has not yet left her room. Miss Chiltern has just come in from riding.

LORD GORING (*to himself*): Ah! that is something.

JAMES: Lord Caversham has been waiting some time in the library for Sir Robert. I told him your lordship was here.

LORD GORING: Thank you. Would you kindly tell him I've gone?

JAMES (*bowing*): I shall do so, my lord.

>*Exit servant.*

LORD GORING: Really, I don't want to meet my father three days running. It is a great deal too much excitement for any son. I hope to goodness he won't come up. Fathers should be neither seen nor heard. That is the only proper basis for family life. Mothers are different.

第 四 幕

场景：同第二幕

〔戈林子爵站在壁炉前,两手插在衣兜里。他看上去相当烦恼。

戈林子爵 （掏出表,看看时间,按响铃）真是讨厌透了。在这个家里竟然找不到一个人说话。可我有一肚子话要说呢。我觉得像什么不名之物的最新版本似的。

〔仆人上。

詹姆斯 罗伯特爵士仍然在外交部没有回来,老爷。

戈林子爵 奇尔顿夫人还没有下楼吗?

詹姆斯 我家夫人还没有离开她的房间。奇尔顿小姐倒是刚刚骑马回来。

戈林子爵 （自言自语）嗨！总算没有白等。

詹姆斯 卡弗沙姆伯爵在书房等了罗伯特爵士好一会儿了。我告诉他你在这里。

戈林子爵 谢谢你。请你告诉他我走了好吗?

詹姆斯 （鞠躬）遵命,老爷。

〔仆人下。

戈林子爵 的确,我连着三天不见我老爸都巴不得呢。这对当儿子的真是天大的快活。老天在上,他可别来啊,父亲们是见不得也听不得的。家里生活没有父亲的干预是最起码的基础。母亲却完全不一样。母亲是可亲

Mothers are darlings. (*Throws himself down into a chair, picks up a paper and begins to read it.*)

  Enter LORD CAVERSHAM.

  LORD CAVERSHAM: Well, sir, what are you doing here? Wasting your time as usual, I suppose?

  LORD GORING (*throws down paper and rises*): My dear father, when one pays a visit it is for the purpose of wasting other people's time, not one's own.

  LORD CAVERSHAM: Have you been thinking over what I spoke to you about last night?

  LORD GORING: I have been thinking about nothing else.

  LORD CAVERSHAM: Engaged to be married yet?

  LORD GORING (*genially*): Not yet; but I hope to be before lunch-time.

  LORD CAVERSHAM (*caustically*): You can have till dinner-time if it would be of any convenience to you.

  LORD GORING: Thanks awfully, but I think I'd sooner be engaged before lunch.

  LORD CAVERSHAM: Humph! Never know when you are serious or not.

  LORD GORING: Neither do I, father.

  A pause.

  LORD CAVERSHAM: I suppose you have read *The Times* this morning?

  LORD GORING (*airily*): *The Times*? Certainly not. I only read *The Morning Post*. All that one should know about modern life is where the Duchesses are; anything else is quite demoralising.

  LORD CAVERSHAM: Do you mean to say you have not read *The Times* leading article on Robert Chiltern's career?

第 四 幕

可爱的。(猛地坐在椅子里,拿起报纸阅读。)

〔卡弗沙姆伯爵上。

卡弗沙姆伯爵　嗨,先生,你在这里干什么?我看你又是和平常一样在浪费时间吧?

戈林子爵　(扔下报纸站起来)我亲爱的老爸,一个人访问别人就是为了浪费别人的时间,而不是浪费自己的时间。

卡弗沙姆伯爵　昨天晚上我跟你说的事你往心里去了吗?

戈林子爵　我心里就没有想过别的事,只想你说的事了。

卡弗沙姆伯爵　把婚姻大事订下来了吗?

戈林子爵　(亲切地)还没有;不过我希望午饭以前就订下来。

卡弗沙姆伯爵　(挖苦地)如果对你还算方便的话,你晚饭前订下来就算早的了。

戈林子爵　多谢了,不过我想不到午饭前就准能订下这门亲事。

卡弗沙姆伯爵　哼!从来弄不懂你是认真的还是打哈哈。

戈林子爵　我也弄不清楚,老爸。

〔冷场。

卡弗沙姆伯爵　你看过今天早上的《泰晤士报》了吗?

戈林子爵　(快活地)《泰晤士报》?当然没有。我只看《早邮报》。你要是想了解现代生活,那你只要弄清公爵夫人们的去向就行了;别的事情不过是些伤风败俗的勾当。

卡弗沙姆伯爵　这么说你还没有看到《泰晤士报》上关于罗伯特·奇尔顿生涯的主要文章吗?

LORD GORING: Good heavens! No. What does it say?

LORD CAVERSHAM: What should it say, sir? Everything complimentary, of course. Chiltern's speech last night on this Argentine Canal scheme was one of the finest pieces of oratory ever delivered in the House since Canning.

LORD GORING: Ah! Never heard of Canning. Never wanted to. And did... did Chiltern uphold the scheme?

LORD CAVERSHAM: Uphold it, sir? How little you know him! Why, he denounced it roundly, and the whole system of modern political finance. This speech is the turning-point in his career, as *The Times* points out. You should read this article, sir. (*Opens The Times.*) 'Sir Robert Chiltern... most rising of our young statesmen... Brilliant orator... Unblemished career... Well-known integrity of character... Represents what is best in English public life... Noble contrast to the lax morality so common among foreign politicians.' They will never say that of you, sir.

LORD GORING: I sincerely hope not, father. However, I am delighted at what you tell me about Robert, thoroughly delighted. It shows he has got pluck.

LORD CAVERSHAM: He has got more than pluck, sir, he has got genius.

LORD GORING: Ah! I prefer pluck. It is not so common, nowadays, as genius is.

LORD CAVERSHAM: I wish you would go into Parliament.

LORD GORING: My dear father, only people who look dull ever get into the House of Commons, and only peo-

第 四 幕

戈林子爵　天哪！没有。文章都说了些什么？

卡弗沙姆伯爵　还会说什么，先生？当然都是赞美的话了。奇尔顿关于阿根廷运河计划的讲话，是自从坎宁①以后在议院里发表的最漂亮的讲演。

戈林子爵　啊！从来没有听说过坎宁是谁，也从来不想知道。不过……奇尔顿支持那项计划了吗？

卡弗沙姆伯爵　支持那个计划吗，先生？你对他了解得太少喽！哈，他把那个计划彻底否决了，并否定了现代政治经济的整个体系。正如《泰晤士报》指出的，这个讲话是他生涯的转折点。你应该看看这篇文章，先生。（打开《泰晤士报》）"罗伯特·奇尔顿爵士……我们青年政治家的新星……杰出的演说家……光明磊落的生涯……众所周知的完美性格……代表了英国公众生活的最佳形象……其高贵品德同外国政治家中屡见不鲜的道德堕落形成了鲜明对照。"他们永远不会为你说这些话的，先生。

戈林子爵　我巴不得他们不理睬我，老爸。不管怎样，我还是很高兴你告诉我这些关于罗伯特的消息，非常高兴。这说明他有勇气了。

卡弗沙姆伯爵　他何止有勇气，他有的是天才。

戈林子爵　啊！我说是勇气。当今之日，天才到处都是，勇气却不多见。

卡弗沙姆伯爵　我希望你有朝一日能进议会。

戈林子爵　我亲爱的老爸，只有看上去枯燥无味的人才进下

---

① 坎宁（George Canning，1770—1827），英国外交大臣（1807—1809，1822—1827），1827年出任首相。托利党人，主张独立自主政策，脱离神圣同盟，支持希腊的独立战争。

ple who are dull ever succeed there.

LORD CAVERSHAM: Why don't you try to do something useful in life?

LORD GORING: I am far too young.

LORD CAVERSHAM (*testily*): I hate this affectation of youth, sir. It is a great deal too prevalent nowadays.

LORD GORING: Youth isn't an affectation. Youth is an art.

LORD CAVERSHAM: Why don't you propose to that pretty Miss Chiltern?

LORD GORING: I am of a very nervous disposition, especially in the morning.

LORD CAVERSHAM: I don't suppose there is the smallest chance of her accepting you.

LORD GORING: I don't know how the betting stands today.

LORD CAVERSHAM: If she did accept you she would be the prettiest fool in England.

LORD GORING: That is just what I should like to marry. A thoroughly sensible wife would reduce me to a condition of absolute idiocy in less than six months.

LORD CAVERSHAM: You don't deserve her, sir.

LORD GORING: My dear father, if we men married the women we deserved, we should have a very bad time of it.

Enter MABEL CHILTERN.

MABEL CHILTERN: Oh!... How do you do, Lord Caversham? I hope Lady Caversham is quite well?

LORD CAVERSHAM: Lady Caversham is as usual, as usual.

LORD GORING: Good-morning, Miss Mabel!

MABEL CHILTERN (*taking no notice at all of* LORD

议院,而且只有真正枯燥无味的人才在那里呆得下去。

卡弗沙姆伯爵　你为什么不在生活里找点有用的事情干呢？

戈林子爵　我太年轻了。

卡弗沙姆伯爵　（暴躁地）我就看不上这种假装青春的行为,先生。今天这都成了流行病了。

戈林子爵　青春是装不出来的。青春是一门艺术。

卡弗沙姆伯爵　你为什么不去向可爱的奇尔顿小姐求婚？

戈林子爵　我生来爱紧张,尤其在上午。

卡弗沙姆伯爵　要我看人家就根本不会接受你的求婚。

戈林子爵　我倒要看今天的赌怎么打了。

卡弗沙姆伯爵　如果她真的接受你的求婚,那她就是全英国最可爱的傻瓜了。

戈林子爵　我还就想娶个傻瓜做老婆呢。真要娶个精明透顶的老婆,不出六个月,她就会把我彻底调教成一个白痴的。

卡弗沙姆伯爵　你配不上她啊,先生。

戈林子爵　我亲爱的老爸,如果我们男人娶了我们配得上的女人,那我们的日子可就过不安生了。

〔梅布尔·奇尔顿上。

梅布尔·奇尔顿　啊！……你好吗,卡弗沙姆伯爵？卡弗沙姆夫人也很好吧？

卡弗沙姆伯爵　卡弗沙姆夫人就那么回事,就那么回事。

戈林子爵　早上好,梅布尔小姐！

梅布尔·奇尔顿　（故意不理睬戈林子爵,专门跟卡弗沙姆伯爵

GORING, *and addressing herself exclusively to* LORD CAVERSHAM): And Lady Caversham's bonnets... are they at all better?

LORD CAVERSHAM: They have had a serious relapse, I am sorry to say.

LORD GORING: Good-morning, Miss Mabel.

MABEL CHILTERN (*to* LORD CAVERSHAM): I hope an operation will not be necessary.

LORD CAVERSHAM (*smiling at her pertness*): If it is, we shall have to give Lady Caversham a narcotic. Otherwise she would never consent to have a feather touched.

LORD GORING (*with increased emphasis*): Good-morning, Miss Mabel!

MABEL CHILTERN (*turning round with feigned surprise*): Oh, are you here? Of course you understand that after your breaking your appointment I am never going to speak to you again.

LORD GORING: Oh, please don't say such a thing. You are the one person in London I really like to have to listen to me.

MABEL CHILTERN: Lord Goring. I never believe a single word that either you or I say to each other.

LORD CAVERSHAM: You are quite right, my dear, quite right as far as he is concerned, I mean.

MABEL CHILTERN: Do you think you could possibly make your son behave a little better occasionally? Just as a change.

LORD CAVERSHAM: I regret to say, Miss Chiltern, that I have no influence at all over my son. I wish I had. If I had, I know what I would make him do.

MABEL CHILTERN: I am afraid that he has one of those terribly weak natures that are not susceptible to in-

第 四 幕

说话)卡弗沙姆夫人的帽子呢……她的帽子好多了吗?

卡弗沙姆伯爵　说来遗憾,她的帽子全瘫痪了。

戈林子爵　早上好,梅布尔小姐。

梅布尔·奇尔顿　(对着卡弗沙姆伯爵)总不至于需要动一次手术吧。

卡弗沙姆伯爵　(对她的俏皮话报以微笑)如果需要手术,那我们得先给卡弗沙姆夫人进行麻醉。否则她永远不会让人动一动它们。

戈林子爵　(加强了口气)早上好,梅布尔小姐!

梅布尔·奇尔顿　(假装吃惊地转过身来)噢,你也在这里吗?当然你心里明白,你失约以后我就再也不会跟你讲话了。

戈林子爵　噢,快别这样说话。你可是伦敦城里唯一喜欢听我讲话的人。

梅布尔·奇尔顿　戈林子爵,我从来不相信你我彼此说过的话。

卡弗沙姆伯爵　你说得对,我亲爱的,我的意思是说他就是你说的那种德性。

梅布尔·奇尔顿　你认为你能让你的儿子偶尔表现得好一点吗?哪怕是一丁点儿呢。

卡弗沙姆伯爵　奇尔顿小姐,说来遗憾,我根本管不了我的儿子了。我很想管啊。我要是管得了他,我知道怎么调理他。

梅布尔·奇尔顿　恐怕他天生的可怕弱点就是冥顽不化。

205

fluence.

LORD CAVERSHAM: He is very heartless, very heartless.

LORD GORING: It seems to me that I am a little in the way here.

MABEL CHILTERN: It is very good for you to be in the way, and to know what people say of you behind your back.

LORD GORING: I don't at all like knowing what people say of me behind my back. It makes me far too conceited.

LORD CAVERSHAM: After that, my dear, I really must bid you good-morning.

MABEL CHILTERN: Oh! I hope you are not going to leave me all alone with Lord Goring? Especially at such an early hour in the day.

LORD CAVERSHAM: I am afraid I can't take him with me to Downing Street. It is not the Prime Minister's day for seeing the unemployed.

Shakes hands with MABEL CHILTERN, *takes up his hat and stick, and goes out, with a parting glare of indignation at* LORD GORING.

MABEL CHILTERN (*takes up roses and begins to arrange them in a bowl on the table*): People who don't keep their appointments in the Park are horrid.

LORD GORING: Detestable.

MABEL CHILTERN: I am glad you admit it. But I wish you wouldn't look so pleased about it.

LORD GORING: I can't help it. I always look pleased when I am with you.

MABEL CHILTERN (*sadly*): Then I suppose it is my duty to remain with you?

第 四 幕

卡弗沙姆伯爵　他无情无义,顶无情无义了。

戈林子爵　听你们的话音,我在这里有点碍事。

梅布尔·奇尔顿　你在这里再好不过,能知道一下别人在你背后说些什么。

戈林子爵　我压根就不愿意知道别人在我背后说我什么。知道了我就不知道我是天下老几了。

卡弗沙姆伯爵　话就说这里了,我的孩子,我真的必须跟你说再见了。

梅布尔·奇尔顿　哦!你总不能把我和戈林子爵留在一起吧?大早上起来,你更不应该这样做。

卡弗沙姆伯爵　可我恐怕也不能带他去唐宁街。今天不是首相接见失业者的日子。

〔和梅布尔·奇尔顿握手,然后拿起帽子和手杖,狠狠地瞪了戈林子爵一眼,下。

梅布尔·奇尔顿　(拿起玫瑰花,开始往桌子上的瓶子里装)那些不去公园按时赴约的人太可恶。

戈林子爵　可恶极了。

梅布尔·奇尔顿　你承认就好。不过我不希望看见你为这事洋洋得意。

戈林子爵　我管不了自己。只要和你在一起我就忍不住会洋洋得意。

梅布尔·奇尔顿　(悲哀地)这么说跟你呆在一起就是我义不容辞的了?

207

LORD GORING: Of course it is.

MABEL CHILTERN: Well, my duty is a thing I never do, on principle. It always depresses me. So I am afraid I must leave you.

LORD GORING: Please don't, Miss Mabel. I have something very particular to say to you.

MABEL CHILTERN (*rapturously*): Oh! is it a proposal?

LORD GORING (*somewhat taken aback*): Well, yes, it is—I am bound to say it is.

MABEL CHILTERN (*with a sigh of pleasure*): I am so glad. That makes the second to-day.

LORD GORING (*indignantly*): The second to-day? What conceited ass has been impertinent enough to dare to propose to you before I had proposed to you?

MABEL CHILTERN: Tommy Trafford, of course. It is one of Tommy's days for proposing. He always proposes on Tuesdays and Thursdays, during the Season.

LORD GORING: You didn't accept him, I hope?

MABEL CHILTERN: I make it a rule never to accept Tommy. That is why he goes on proposing. Of course, as you didn't turn up this morning, I very nearly said yes. It would have been an excellent lesson both for him and for you if I had. It would have taught you both better manners.

LORD GORING: Oh! bother Tommy Trafford. Tommy is a silly little ass. I love you.

MABEL CHILTERN: I know. And I think you might have mentioned it before. I am sure I have given you heaps of opportunities.

LORD GORING: Mabel, do be serious. Please be serious.

戈林子爵　那还用说。

梅布尔·奇尔顿　按原则讲,我的义不容辞就是永远不干的事情。我总是受不了那一套。所以我还是离开你为好。

戈林子爵　请别走,梅布尔小姐。我有特别重要的事情要和你说。

梅布尔·奇尔顿　(异常兴奋)哦！是要求婚吗？

戈林子爵　(有几分吃惊)噢,是的,正是——我敢肯定说,是这么回事。

梅布尔·奇尔顿　(面露快活之色)我太高兴了。这下得有第二个今天了。

戈林子爵　(气愤地)第二个今天？哪个傲慢的傻瓜这般目中无人,竟敢在我向你求婚之前冒犯你？

梅布尔·奇尔顿　当然是汤米·特拉福德了。今天正好是汤米的求婚日子。在这个社交季节,他总是在星期二和星期四求婚。

戈林子爵　但愿你没有接受他吧？

梅布尔·奇尔顿　我永远不会接受他的求婚是我的规矩。他一直坚持求婚的道理就在这里。当然,由于你今天早上没有赴约,我差一点就接受了。我要是接受了,那么对他对你都是一次很不错的教训。

戈林子爵　哦！讨厌的汤米·特拉福德。汤米是个愚蠢的小傻瓜。我爱你。

梅布尔·奇尔顿　我知道。我认为你应该早一些说明白。我敢说我给你的机会可不少了。

戈林子爵　梅布尔,严肃起来。请严肃起来好吧。

MABEL CHILTERN: Ah! that is the sort of thing a man always says to a girl before he has been married to her. He never says it afterwards.

LORD GORING (*taking hold of her hand*): Mabel, I have told you that I love you. Can't you love me a little in return?

MABEL CHILTERN: You silly Arthur! If you knew anything about... anything, which you don't, you would know that I adore you. Every one in London knows it except you. It is a public scandal the way I adore you. I have been going about for the last six months telling the whole of society that I adore you. I wonder you consent to have anything to say to me. I have no character left at all. At least, I feel so happy that I am quite sure I have no character left at all.

LORD GORING (*catches her in his arms and kisses her. Then there is a pause of bliss*): Dear! Do you know I was awfully afraid of being refused!

MABEL CHILTERN (*looking up at him*): But you never have been refused yet by anybody, have you, Arthur? I can't imagine any one refusing you.

LORD GORING (*after kissing her again*): Of course I'm not nearly good enough for you, Mabel.

MABEL CHILTERN (*nestling close to him*): I am so glad, darling. I was afraid you were.

LORD GORING (*after some hesitation*): And I'm... I'm a little over thirty.

MABEL CHILTERN: Dear, you look weeks younger than that.

LORD GORING (*enthusiastically*): How sweet of you to say so!... And it is only fair to tell you frankly that I am fearfully extravagant.

第 四 幕

梅布尔·奇尔顿　啊！男人在和姑娘结婚前总是对姑娘说这种话。婚后他可就再也不说了。

戈林子爵　（抓住她的手）梅布尔，我跟你说了我爱你。难道你就不能反过来给我点爱吗？

梅布尔·奇尔顿　你这傻子亚瑟呀！你要是早知道一点……你不懂的事，那么你应该明白我是深爱你的。伦敦谁都知道这点，就你不明白。我深爱的方式已经成了公开的丑闻。这六个月来，我在上流社会里见人就说我深深爱上你了。我想你总该有什么话和我说的。我是一点脾气都没有了。好啊，我至少很高兴地知道我是一点脾气都没有了！

戈林子爵　（用双臂拥抱住她，亲吻他。随后是一阵欣喜）亲爱的！你知道我是多么害怕被人拒绝啊！

梅布尔·奇尔顿　（仰脸看着他）可是你从来就没有被人拒绝过，是吧，亚瑟？我想象中谁都不会拒绝你的。

戈林子爵　（又是一阵狂吻）我确确实实配不上你，梅布尔。

梅布尔·奇尔顿　（紧紧依偎着他）我太高兴了，亲爱的。我知道你配得上我。

戈林子爵　（犹豫少许）而且我……我都三十出头了。

梅布尔·奇尔顿　亲爱的，你看上去年轻得多。

戈林子爵　（热情高涨地）你说这话多么让人中听啊！……公平地说，我得坦率地告诉你我说话办事都很放肆。

211

MABEL CHILTERN: But so am I, Arthur. So we're sure to agree. And now I must go and see Gertrude.

LORD GORING: Must you really? (*Kisses her.*)

MABEL CHILTERN: Yes.

LORD GORING: Then do tell her I want to talk to her particularly. I have been waiting here all the morning to see either her or Robert.

MABEL CHILTERN: Do you mean to say you didn't come here expressly to propose to me?

LORD GORING (*triumphantly*): No; that was a flash of genius.

MABEL CHILTERN: Your first.

LORD GORING (*with determination*): My last.

MABEL CHILTERN: I am delighted to hear it. Now don't stir. I'll be back in five minutes. And don't fall into any temptations while I am away.

LORD GORING: Dear Mabel, while you are away, there are none. It makes me horribly dependent on you.

Enter LADY CHILTERN.

LADY CHILTERN: Good-morning, dear! How pretty you are looking!

MABEL CHILTERN: How pale you are looking, Gertrude! It is most becoming!

LADY CHILTERN: Good-morning, Lord Goring!

LORD GORING (*bowing*): Good-morning, Lady Chiltern!

MABEL CHILTERN (*aside to* LORD GORING): I shall be in the conservatory, under the second palm tree on the left.

LORD GORING: Second on the left?

MABEL CHILTERN (*with a look of mock surprise*): Yes; the usual palm tree.

梅布尔·奇尔顿　我也一样,亚瑟。所以我们正好是一对儿啊。现在我必须去见格特鲁德了。

戈林子爵　你真的必须去吗?(亲吻她。)

梅布尔·奇尔顿　真的。

戈林子爵　那请告诉她我要跟她专门谈谈。我在这里等了一早上,就是为了见她或者罗伯特。

梅布尔·奇尔顿　听你话中的意思,你一大早赶到这里来不是为了向我求婚吗?

戈林子爵　(狂喜地)不是;向你求婚是天才的一闪念。

梅布尔·奇尔顿　你的天才是一流的。

戈林子爵　(毫不犹豫地)我的天才是末流的。

梅布尔·奇尔顿　这话我喜欢听。呆着别动。我五分钟就回来。我不在时你可千万别受什么诱惑啊。

戈林子爵　亲爱的梅布尔,你一走了,这里就没有任何诱惑了。

〔奇尔顿夫人上。

奇尔顿夫人　早上好,亲爱的!你今天真漂亮!

梅布尔·奇尔顿　格特鲁德,你看上去可是太憔悴了!简直憔悴透了!

奇尔顿夫人　早上好,戈林子爵!

戈林子爵　(鞠躬)早上好,奇尔顿夫人!

梅布尔·奇尔顿　(向戈林子爵旁白)我要到暖房里,左边的第二棵芭蕉树下。

戈林子爵　第二棵树下?

梅布尔·奇尔顿　(故作惊讶之色)是的,就是往常那棵芭蕉树。

Blows a kiss to him, unobserved by LADY CHILTERN, *and goes out.*

LORD GORING: Lady Chiltern, I have a certain amount of very good news to tell you. Mrs. Cheveley gave me up Robert's letter last night, and I burned it. Robert is safe.

LADY CHILTERN (*sinking on the sofa*): Safe! Oh! I am so glad of that. What a good friend you are to him—to us!

LORD GORING: There is only one person now that could be said to be in any danger.

LADY CHILTERN: Who is that?

LORD GORING (*sitting down beside her*): Yourself.

LADY CHILTERN: I! In danger? What do you mean?

LORD GORING: Danger is too great a word. It is a word I should not have used. But I admit I have something to tell you that may distress you, that terribly distresses me. Yesterday evening you wrote me a very beautiful, womanly letter, asking me for my help. You wrote to me as one of your oldest friends, one of your husband's oldest friends. Mrs. Cheveley stole that letter from my rooms.

LADY CHILTERN: Well, what use is it to her? Why should she not have it?

LORD GORING (*rising*): Lady Chiltern. I will be quite frank with you. Mrs. Cheveley puts a certain construction on that letter and proposes to send it to your husband.

LADY CHILTERN: But what construction could she put on it?... Oh! not that! not that! If I in—in trouble, and wanting your help, trusting you, propose to come to you... that you may advise me... assist me.... Oh! are there women so horrible as that...? And she proposes

〔趁奇尔顿夫人看不见，朝他飞吻，下。

戈林子爵　奇尔顿夫人，我要告诉你一个大好消息。谢弗利太太昨天夜里把罗伯特那封信还给我，我当下就烧了。罗伯特没事了。

奇尔顿夫人　（深深坐进沙发里）没事了！哦！我这下可算放心了。你对他——对我们俩，都是多么好的朋友啊！

戈林子爵　现在就有一个人可以说还在危险之中。

奇尔顿夫人　谁？

戈林子爵　（在她身边坐下）就是你。

奇尔顿夫人　我啊！在危险中？你这话是什么意思？

戈林子爵　危险这个词儿太大了点。我不该用这个词儿。可是我得说我有点事要告诉你，也许会让你苦恼，让你十分苦恼的。昨天晚上你给我写了一封非常漂亮、非常有女人味儿的信，要我帮助你。你给我写信，是把我当成你的老朋友，你丈夫的老朋友才写的。谢弗利太太从我房间把那封信偷走了。

奇尔顿夫人　哦，那封信对她有什么用呢？她为什么要偷它呢？

戈林子爵　（站起）奇尔顿夫人，我还是把话向你说明了吧。谢弗利太太在那信上写了些话，给你丈夫寄出去了。

奇尔顿夫人　可是她能往上面写什么话呢？……喔！不是那个意思！不是那个意思呀！我要是有……有麻烦，需要你的帮助，相信你，打算去找你……找你给我出点主意……帮我一把……喔！真有像她这样坏的女人吗……她是打算寄给我丈夫么？快告诉我发生什么事

to send it to my husband? Tell me what happened. Tell me all that happened.

LORD GORING: Mrs. Cheveley was concealed in a room adjoining my library, without my knowledge. I thought that the person who was waiting in that room to see me was yourself. Robert came in unexpectedly. A chair or something fell in the room. He forced his way in, and he discovered her. We had a terrible scene. I still thought it was you. He left me in anger. At the end of everything Mrs. Cheveley got possession of your letter— she stole it, when or how, I don't know.

LADY CHILTERN: At what hour did this happen?

LORD GORING: At half-past ten. And now I propose that we tell Robert the whole thing at once.

LADY CHILTERN (*looking at him with amazement that is almost terror*): You want me to tell Robert that the woman you expected was not Mrs. Cheveley, but myself? That it was I whom you thought was concealed in a room in your house, at half-past ten o'clock at night? You want me to tell him that?

LORD GORING: I think it is better that he should know the exact truth.

LADY CHILTERN (*rising*): Oh, I couldn't, I couldn't!

LORD GORING: May I do it?

LADY CHILTERN: No.

LORD GORING (*gravely*): You are wrong, Lady Chiltern.

LADY CHILTERN: No. The letter must be intercepted. That is all. But how can I do it? Letters arrive for him every moment of the day. His secretaries open them and hand them to him. I dare not ask the servants to bring me his letters. It would be impossible. Oh! why don't you

了。把发生的事情全都告诉我。

戈林子爵　谢弗利太太藏在我的书房的隔壁屋子里,事先我一点不知道。我本以为在那间屋子等着的是你本人。罗伯特突然来了。那房间的一把椅子还是什么东西倒在了地上。他不听劝阻硬过去看,发现是她。我们大吵了一架。这时我仍然以为是你呢。他气鼓鼓地走了。等该发生的事情全都发生过,谢弗利太太把你的信拿在手里了——她偷去了,什么时候偷的,怎么偷的,我一点不知道。

奇尔顿夫人　这是几点发生的?

戈林子爵　十点半钟。我看我们得马上把这事全告诉罗伯特。

奇尔顿夫人　(十分紧张地看着他)你是要我告诉罗伯特,你等待的那个女人不是谢弗利太太,而是我自己吗?告诉他你以为夜里十点半钟藏在你住宅房间里的是我吗?你要我把这一切都告诉他吗?

戈林子爵　我觉得他知道了真相更好。

奇尔顿夫人　(起立)唉,我办不到,我办不到!

戈林子爵　我告诉他好吗?

奇尔顿夫人　不行。

戈林子爵　(严肃地)你错了,奇尔顿夫人。

奇尔顿夫人　不。这封信一定要截下来。只有这个办法了。可我怎么才能办到呢?信件一天随时都可能来。他的秘书拆封看过才给他过目。我不敢叫仆人把他的信交给我。那是行不通的。哦!你为什么不告诉我该

217

tell me what to do?

LORD GORING: Pray be calm, Lady Chiltern, and answer the questions I am going to put to you. You said his secretaries open his letters.

LADY CHILTERN: Yes.

LORD GORING: Who is with him to-day? Mr. Trafford, isn't it?

LADY CHILTERN: No, Mr. Montford, I think.

LORD GORING: You can trust him?

LADY CHILTERN (*with a gesture of despair*): Oh! how do I know?

LORD GORING: He would do what you asked him, wouldn't he?

LADY CHILTERN: I think so.

LORD GORING: Your letter was on pink paper. He could recognise it without reading it, couldn't he? By the colour?

LADY CHILTERN: I suppose so.

LORD GORING: Is he in the house now?

LADY CHILTERN: Yes.

LORD GORING: Then I will go and see him myself, and tell him that a certain letter, written on pink paper, is to be forwarded to Robert to-day, and that at all costs it must not reach him. (*Goes to the door, and opens it.*) Oh! Robert is coming upstairs with the letter in his hand. It has reached him already.

LADY CHILTERN (*with a cry of pain*): Oh! you have saved his life; what have you done with mine?

Enter SIR ROBERT CHILTERN. *He has the letter in his hand, and is reading it. He comes towards his wife, not noticing* LORD GORING's *presence.*

SIR ROBERT CHILTERN: "I want you. I trust you. I am

怎么办呢？

戈林子爵　请平静，奇尔顿夫人，回答我向你提出的问题。你说他的秘书给他拆信。

奇尔顿夫人　是的。

戈林子爵　谁今天和他在一起？特拉福德先生，是不是？

奇尔顿夫人　不，我想是蒙特福德先生。

戈林子爵　你信得过他吗？

奇尔顿夫人　（做出绝望的样子）哦！我怎么知道呢？

戈林子爵　你要求做的事，他会成全吗？

奇尔顿夫人　我想还行吧。

戈林子爵　你的信是粉色的。他不看你的信就能认出你的信，是吧？一看颜色就知道是你的？

奇尔顿夫人　我相信可以。

戈林子爵　他现在在这里吗？

奇尔顿夫人　在。

戈林子爵　那我这就去亲自见他，告诉他有一封粉色信纸的信今天将寄给罗伯特，但是无论如何不能给他看。（走向门口，打开门）哦！罗伯特手里拿着那封信上楼来了。他已经拿到它了。

奇尔顿夫人　（痛苦地叫了一声）噢！你把他救了；可你把我置身何地了？

〔罗伯特·奇尔顿爵士上。他手里拿着那封信，一边念着。他径直走向妻子，没有看见戈林子爵在场。

罗伯特·奇尔顿爵士　"我需要你。我信任你。我就来找

coming to you. Gertrude."Oh, my love! Is this true? Do you indeed trust me, and want me? If so, it was for me to come to you, not for you to write of coming to me. This letter of yours, Gertrude, makes me feel that nothing that the world may do can hurt me now. You want me, Gertrude.

LORD GORING, *unseen by* SIR ROBERT CHILTERN, *makes an imploring sign to* LADY CHILTERN *to accept the situation and* SIR ROBERT's *error*.

LADY CHILTERN: Yes.

SIR ROBERT CHILTERN: You trust me, Gertrude?

LADY CHILTERN: Yes.

SIR ROBERT CHILTERN: Ah! why did you not add you loved me?

LADY CHILTERN (*taking his hand*): Because I loved you.

LORD GORING *passes into the conservatory*.

SIR ROBERT CHILTERN (*kisses her*): Gertrude, you don't know what I feel. When Montford passed me your letter across the table—he had opened it by mistake, I suppose, without looking at the handwriting on the envelope—and I read it—oh! I did not care what disgrace or punishment was in store for me, I only thought you loved me still.

LADY CHILTERN: There is no disgrace in store for you, nor any public shame. Mrs. Cheveley has handed over to Lord Goring the document that was in her possession, and he has destroyed it.

SIR ROBERT CHILTERN: Are you sure of this, Gertrude?

LADY CHILTERN: Yes; Lord Goring has just told me.

SIR ROBERT CHILTERN: Then I am safe! Oh! what a

你。格特鲁德。"噢,我亲爱的!你真的信任我吗?真的需要我吗?果真如此,那我应该来找你,而不用你给我写信叫我来。你的这封信,格特鲁德,使我感觉到现在世界上任凭什么都没法伤害我了。你需要我,格特鲁德。

〔戈林子爵还没有被罗伯特发现,赶紧向奇尔顿夫人示意接受罗伯特爵士的话,将错就错。

奇尔顿夫人　是的。

罗伯特·奇尔顿爵士　你信任我,格特鲁德?

奇尔顿夫人　是的。

罗伯特·奇尔顿爵士　啊!为什么不加上你爱我的话呢?

奇尔顿夫人　(拉住他的手)因为我爱你。

〔戈林子爵趁机进了暖房。

罗伯特·奇尔顿爵士　(亲吻她)格特鲁德,你不知道我有什么感受。蒙特福德从桌子那边把你的信给我时——我估计他没有辨认手迹就误把信拆开了——我当时就看了——啊!我当时就一点不在乎等待着我的耻辱和惩罚是什么了,我首先想到的是你还爱着我。

奇尔顿夫人　你面前没有什么耻辱了,也没有任何公共丑闻了。谢弗利太太把她掌握的那封信交给了戈林子爵了,戈林子爵已经把它毁掉了。

罗伯特·奇尔顿爵士　你敢保证吗,格特鲁德?

奇尔顿夫人　是的。戈林子爵刚刚告诉我的。

罗伯特·奇尔顿爵士　这么说我安全了!噢!安全是多么

221

wonderful thing to be safe! For two days I have been in terror. I am safe now. How did Arthur destroy my letter? Tell me. -

LADY CHILTERN: He burned it.

SIR ROBERT CHILTERN: I wish I had seen that one sin of my youth burning to ashes. How many men there are in modern life who would like to see their past burning to white ashes before them! Is Arthur still here?

LADY CHILTERN: Yes; he is in the conservatory.

SIR ROBERT CHILTERN: I am so glad now I made that speech last night in the House, so glad. I made it thinking that public disgrace might be the result. But it has not been so.

LADY CHILTERN: Public honour has been the result.

SIR ROBERT CHILTERN: I think so. I fear so, almost. For although I am safe from detection, although every proof against me is destroyed, I suppose, Gertrude... I suppose I should retire from public life? (*He looks anxiously at his wife.*)

LADY CHILTERN (*eagerly*): Oh yes, Robert, you should do that. It is your duty to do that.

SIR ROBERT CHILTERN: It is much to surrender.

LADY CHILTERN: No; it will be much to gain.

SIR ROBERT CHILTERN *walks up and down the room with a troubled expression. Then comes over to his wife, and puts his hand on her shoulder.*

SIR ROBERT CHILTERN: And you would be happy living somewhere alone with me, abroad perhaps, or in the country away from London, away from public life? You would have no regrets?

LADY CHILTERN: Oh! none, Robert.

SIR ROBERT CHILTERN (*sadly*): And your ambition

美妙的事啊！两天来我胆战心惊。我现在没事了。亚瑟是怎么把那封信毁掉的？快告诉我听。

奇尔顿夫人　他把它烧掉了。

罗伯特·奇尔顿爵士　我要是能看见我年轻时犯的罪过烧成灰烬多好啊。在现代生活里，有多少人希望看见他们的过去烧成灰烬啊！亚瑟还在这里吗？

奇尔顿夫人　在，他就在暖房里。

罗伯特·奇尔顿爵士　现在我就更高兴我昨天夜里在议院发表那篇讲话了，非常高兴。我讲演时还想公开的丑闻也许是最终结果了。可是情况并非如此。

奇尔顿夫人　公开的荣誉倒是最终结果了。

罗伯特·奇尔顿爵士　我想是的。恐怕十拿九稳了。不过尽管我不怕人揭老底儿了，尽管所有于我不利的证据都毁掉了，可是格特鲁德……我觉得我应该退出公众生活了。（他焦急地看着他的妻子。）

奇尔顿夫人　（急切地）哦，是的，罗伯特，你应该这样做。这样做是你的责任。

罗伯特·奇尔顿爵士　这下失去的太多了。

奇尔顿夫人　不。是得到的太多了。

〔罗伯特·奇尔顿爵士在屋子里踱来踱去，一脸烦躁不安的表情。然后走到他妻子身边，把手放在她的肩上。

罗伯特·奇尔顿爵士　离开公众生活，到远离伦敦的乡下，或许国外，你愿意跟我在一起幸福地生活吗？你会有什么遗憾吗？

奇尔顿夫人　噢！没有，罗伯特。

罗伯特·奇尔顿爵士　（认真地）你对我寄予的抱负呢？你

for me? You used to be ambitious for me.

LADY CHILTERN: Oh, my ambition! I have none now, but that we two may love each other. It was your ambition that led you astray. Let us not talk about ambition.

LORD GORING *returns from the conservatory, looking very pleased with himself, and with an entirely new buttonhole that some one has made for him.*

SIR ROBERT CHILTERN(*going towards him*): Arthur. I have to thank you for what you have done for me. I don't know how I can repay you. (*Shakes hands with him.*)

LORD GORING: My dear fellow, I'll tell you at once. At the present moment, under the usual palm tree... I mean in the conservatory...

Enter MASON.

MASON: Lord Caversham.

LORD GORING: That admirable father of mine really makes a habit of turning up at the wrong moment. It is very heartless of him, very heartless indeed.

Enter LORD CAVERSHAM. MASON *goes out.*

LORD CAVERSHAM: Good-morning, Lady Chiltern! Warmest congratulations to you, Chiltern, on your brilliant speech last night. I have just left the Prime Minister, and you are to have the vacant seat in the Cabinet.

SIR ROBERT CHILTERN(*with a look of joy and triumph*): A seat in the Cabinet?

LORD CAVERSHAM: Yes; here is the Prime Minister's letter. (*Hands letter.*)

SIR ROBERT CHILTERN(*takes letter and reads it*): A seat in the Cabinet!

LORD CAVERSHAM: Certainly, and you well deserve it

过去对我寄予很大的抱负的。

奇尔顿夫人　喔,我的抱负!我现在什么也没有了,只想我们两个彼此相爱。过去是你的雄心大志让我误入了歧途。我们现在不谈野心了。

〔戈林子爵从暖房返回来,一副欢喜的样子,有人给他别了一朵崭新的扣眼插花。

罗伯特·奇尔顿爵士　(走向他)亚瑟,谢谢你为我所做的事情。我真不知道怎么还你这笔情了。(和他握手。)

戈林子爵　我亲爱的老兄,我马上告诉你怎么还。就在这会儿,在往常那棵芭蕉树下……我是说在暖房里……

〔梅森上。

梅森　卡弗沙姆伯爵到。

戈林子爵　我这位可亲可爱的老爸总是在不该来的时候来。他才真是无情无义,无情无义得很哪。

〔卡弗沙姆伯爵上。梅森下。

卡弗沙姆伯爵　早上好,奇尔顿夫人!热烈祝贺你昨天晚上发表的精彩讲话,奇尔顿。我刚从首相那里来,内阁的那个空位归你了。

罗伯特·奇尔顿爵士　(一副欣喜和得意的样子)内阁里的空位?

卡弗沙姆伯爵　是的;这里是首相的信。(递信。)

罗伯特·奇尔顿爵士　(接过信看)内阁的一个位子!

卡弗沙姆伯爵　一点错没有,你也当之无愧。你在今天的

too. You have got what we want so much in political life nowadays—high character, high moral tone, high principles. (*To* LORD GORING): Everything that you have not got, sir, and never will have.

LORD GORING: I don't like principles, father. I prefer prejudices.

SIR ROBERT CHILTERN *is on the brink of accepting the Prime Minister's offer, when he sees his wife looking at him with her clear, candid eyes. He then realises that it is impossible.*

SIR ROBERT CHILTERN: I cannot accept this offer, Lord Caversham. I have made up my mind to decline it.

LORD CAVERSHAM: Decline it, sir?

SIR ROBERT CHILTERN: My intention is to retire at once from public life.

LORD CAVERSHAM (*angrily*): Decline a seat in the Cabinet, and retire from public life? Never heard such damned nonsense in the whole course of my existence. I beg your pardon, Lady Chiltern. Chiltern, I beg your pardon. (*To* LORD GORING.): Don't grin like that, sir.

LORD GORING: No, father.

LORD CAVERSHAM: Lady Chiltern, you are a sensible woman, the most sensible woman in London, the most sensible woman I know. Will you kindly prevent your husband from making such a... from talking such.... Will you kindly do that, Lady Chiltern?

LADY CHILTERN: I think my husband is right in his determination, Lord Caversham. I approve of it.

LORD CAVERSHAM: You approve of it? Good heavens!

LADY CHILTERN (*taking her husband's hand*): I admire him for it. I admire him immensely for it. I have

政治生活中成了我们所期望的表率——高尚的道德调子,高度的原则。(对戈林子爵)你可是一无所获呀,先生,而且永远也得不到什么。

戈林子爵　我不喜欢原则,老爸。我更喜欢偏见。

〔罗伯特·奇尔顿爵士正打算接受首相的提议,这时看见他的妻子用清澈坦率的目光看着他。随后他马上意识到这是做不得的。

罗伯特·奇尔顿爵士　我不能接受这个位子,卡弗沙姆伯爵。我已决定谢绝它了。

卡弗沙姆伯爵　谢绝,先生?

罗伯特·奇尔顿爵士　我打算马上退出公众生活。

卡弗沙姆伯爵　(气愤地)谢绝内阁的位子,退出公众生活?我活了这么大从来没有听说过这样的浑话。你说说是怎么回事,奇尔顿夫人。奇尔顿,你也说说这是怎么回事。(对戈林子爵)别出怪相,先生。

戈林子爵　没有啊,老爸。

卡弗沙姆伯爵　奇尔顿夫人,你是一个通情达理的女人,是伦敦城最通情达理的女人,我很清楚。请你劝劝你丈夫别这样干好吧……别这样说话……请你劝劝吧,奇尔顿夫人?

奇尔顿夫人　我想我丈夫的决定是对的,卡弗沙姆伯爵。我同意他这样做。

卡弗沙姆伯爵　你同意他的决定?天哪!

奇尔顿夫人　(拉住她丈夫的手)我佩服他这样干。我从心里

never admired him so much before. He is finer than even I thought him. (*To* SIR ROBERT CHILTERN): You will go and write your letter to the Prime Minister now, won't you? Don't hesitate about it, Robert.

SIR ROBERT CHILTERN(*with a touch of bitterness*): I suppose I had better write it at once. Such offers are not repeated. I will ask you to excuse me for a moment, Lord Caversham.

LADY CHILTERN: I may come with you, Robert, may I not?

SIR ROBERT CHILTERN: Yes, Gertrude.

LADY CHILTERN *goes with him*.

LORD CAVERSHAM: What is the matter with this family? Something wrong here, eh? (*Tapping his forehead.*)Idiocy? Hereditary, I suppose. Both of them, too. Wife as well as husband. Very sad. Very sad indeed! And they are not an old family. Can't understand it.

LORD GORING: It is not idiocy, father, I assure you.

LORD CAVERSHAM: What is it then, sir?

LORD GORING (*after some hesitation*): Well, it is what is called nowadays a high moral tone, father. That is all.

LORD CAVERSHAM: Hate these new-fangled names. Same thing as we used to call idiocy fifty years ago. Shan't stay in this house any longer.

LORD GORING(*taking his arm*): Oh! just go in there for a moment, father. Third palm tree to the left, the usual palm tree.

LORD CAVERSHAM: What, sir?

LORD GORING: I beg your pardon, father, I forgot. The conservatory, father, the conservatory—there is some one there I want you to talk to.

佩服他。我从来没有像现在这样佩服他。(对罗伯特·奇尔顿爵士)你这就去给首相写信吧,是吗?别犹豫了,罗伯特。

罗伯特·奇尔顿爵士 (流露出一丝苦色)我看马上写为好。这样的肥缺是耽误不得的。我得请你原谅我一会儿了,卡弗沙姆伯爵。

奇尔顿夫人 我和你一起去好吗,罗伯特?

罗伯特·奇尔顿爵士 很好,格特鲁德。

〔奇尔顿夫人和罗伯特·奇尔顿爵士下。

卡弗沙姆伯爵 这家人是怎么了?这里出什么问题了,呵?(拍拍自己的脑门儿。)愚蠢?我看是家传问题。他们俩都有问题。妻子有,丈夫也有。很可悲呀。的确非常可悲!他们都不是出身世家呀。就是搞不明白。

戈林子爵 老爸,这肯定不是愚蠢所致。

卡弗沙姆伯爵 那会是什么呢,先生?

戈林子爵 (犹豫少许)哦,这就是我们今天所谓的高尚道德调子。不会是别的。

卡弗沙姆伯爵 我就不爱听这些新名词儿。我们五十多年前就叫这种行为是愚蠢。不能再在这家呆下去了。

戈林子爵 (拉住他的胳膊)嗨!请进这里呆一会儿,老爸。左边的第三棵芭蕉树,就是往常的那棵。

卡弗沙姆伯爵 干什么,先生?

戈林子爵 对不起,老爸,我忘记了。暖房里,老爸,暖房——我想让你和那里的一个人谈谈话。

229

LORD CAVERSHAM: What about, sir?

LORD GORING: About me, father.

LORD CAVERSHAM (*grimly*): Not a subject on which much eloquence is possible.

LORD GORING: No, father; but the lady is like me. She doesn't care much for eloquence in others. She thinks it a little loud.

　　　　LORD CAVERSHAM *goes into the conservatory*.

LADY CHILTERN *enters*.

LORD GORING: Lady Chiltern, why are you playing Mrs. Cheveley's cards?

LADY CHILTERN (*startled*): I don't understand you.

LORD GORING: Mrs. Cheveley made an attempt to ruin your husband. Either to drive him from public life, or to make him adopt a dishonourable position. From the latter tragedy you saved him. The former you are now thrusting on him. Why should you do him the wrong Mrs. Cheveley tried to do and failed?

LADY CHILTERN: Lord Goring?

LORD GORING (*pulling himself together for a great effort, and showing the philosopher that underlies the dandy*): Lady Chiltern, allow me. You wrote me a letter last night in which you said you trusted me and wanted my help. Now is the moment when you really want my help, now is the time when you have got to trust me, to trust in my counsel and judgment. You love Robert. Do you want to kill his love for you? What sort of existence will he have if you rob him of the fruits of his ambition, if you take him from the splendour of a great political career, if you close the doors of public life against him, if you condemn him to sterile failure, he who was made for triumph and success? Women are not meant to judge us,

卡弗沙姆伯爵　谈什么,先生?

戈林子爵　谈谈我呀,老爸。

卡弗沙姆伯爵　(严厉地)这可不是一个发挥口才的话题。

戈林子爵　是的,老爸;不过那个小姐喜欢我。她不在乎口才不口才的。她认为好口才有点吵得慌。

〔卡弗沙姆伯爵进了暖房。奇尔顿夫人上。

戈林子爵　奇尔顿夫人,你为什么扮演谢弗利太太的角色呢?

奇尔顿夫人　(惊讶)我不明白你的意思。

戈林子爵　谢弗利太太曾经试图毁掉你的丈夫:或者把他赶出公众生活,或者逼迫他采纳可耻的意见。你让他在后一点上悬崖勒马了。可你现在却逼迫他退出公众生活。谢弗利太太想干而没有干成的错事,你为什么硬逼他做呢?

奇尔顿夫人　戈林子爵?

戈林子爵　(镇静下来,鼓起勇气,拿出纨绔习气下隐藏的哲学家派头)奇尔顿夫人,请允许我多说几句。你昨天晚上给我写了一封信,在信里说你相信我,需要我的帮助。现在是你真正需要我的帮助的时候,现在是你一定要相信我的时候,相信我的忠告和判断。你爱罗伯特。你想扼杀他对你的爱吗?你要是剥夺了他出人头地的果实,剥夺了他政治生涯的光明前程,把他关在公众生活的大门之外,宣告他的无谓失败,而他实际上已经取得了胜利和成功,那么,他的生活还有什么意义呢?女人

but to forgive us when we need forgiveness. Pardon, not punishment, is their mission. Why should you scourge him with rods for a sin done in his youth, before he knew you, before he knew himself? A man's life is of more value than a woman's. It has larger issues, wider scope, greater ambitions. A woman's life revolves in curves of emotions. It is upon lines of intellect that a man's life progresses. Don't make any terrible mistake, Lady Chihern. A woman who can keep a man's love, and love him in return, has done all the world wants of women, or should want of them.

LADY CHILTERN (*troubled and hesitating*): But it is my husband himself who wishes to retire from public life. He feels it is his duty. It was he who first said so.

LORD GORING: Rather than lose your love, Robert would do anything, wreck his whole career, as he is on the brink of doing now. He is making for you a terrible sacrifice. Take my advice, Lady Chiltern, and do not accept a sacrifice so great. If you do, you will live to repent it bitterly. We men and women are not made to accept such sacrifices from each other. We are not worthy of them. Besides, Robert has been punished enough.

LADY CHILTERN: We have both been punished. I set him up too high.

LORD GORING (*with deep feeling in his voice*): Do not for that reason set him down now too low. If he has fallen from his altar, do not thrust him into the mire. Failure to Robert would be the very mire of shame. Power is his passion. He would lose everything, even his power to feel love. Your husband's life is at this moment in your hands, your husband's love is in your hands. Don't mar both for him.

生来不是来审判我们男人的，而是在我们需要原谅的时候原谅我们的。她们的使命是原谅，而不是惩罚。他还没有认识你以前，还没有认识他自己之前，年纪轻轻犯下了罪过，你现在为什么应该跟他算后账？一个男人的生命价值大于一个女人的。男人的生命释放量更大，范围更广，志向更远。女人的生命在感情世界里迂回前行。女人的生命依附在男人生命的智力线上。别再铸成大错了，奇尔顿夫人。一个能留住男人的爱并还以爱的女人，就是为这个世界做了女人应该做的，尽了她们的责任。

奇尔顿夫人　（迷惑和犹豫）可是我丈夫希望退出公众生活的呀。他认为这是他的责任。是他先说的。

戈林子爵　为了不致失去你的爱，他宁愿干任何事情，宁愿毁掉他的整个生涯，就像他现在正处于悬崖边一样。他在为你作出巨大的牺牲。接受我的意见吧，奇尔顿夫人，可别接受如此巨大的牺牲。如若你接受了，你今后的生活会追悔莫及的。我们男人女人生来不是为了彼此接受这样的牺牲的。我们的价值远远超出了这些。再说，罗伯特所受惩罚已经够多了。

奇尔顿夫人　我们俩都已经受了惩罚。我对他的期望太高了。

戈林子爵　（声音里满含深情地）别再为此现在就期望他太低了。如果他已经从他的圣坛上掉下来了，那就别把他往泥坑里推了。对罗伯特来说，失败就可能是羞耻的泥坑。权力才是他的激情。失去权力，他就失去了一切，以至他感受爱的力量。你丈夫的生命这时就掌握在你的手里，你丈夫的爱也在你的手里。千万别给他毁了这两样东西啊。

Enter SIR ROBERT CHILTERN.

SIR ROBERT CHILTERN: Gertrude, here is the draft of my letter. Shall I read it to you?

LADY CHILTERN: Let me see it.

SIR ROBERT *hands her the letter. She reads it, and then, with a gesture of passion, tears it up.*

SIR ROBERT CHILTERN: What are you doing?

LADY CHILTERN: A man's life is of more value than a woman's. It has larger issues, wider scope, greater ambitions. Our lives revolve in curves of emotions. It is upon lines of intellect that a man's life progresses. I have just learnt this, and much else with it, from Lord Goring. And I will not spoil your life for you, nor see you spoil it as a sacrifice to me, a useless sacrifice!

SIR ROBERT CHILTERN: Gertrude! Gertrude!

LADY CHILTERN: You can forget. Men easily forget. And I forgive. That is how women help the world. I see that now.

SIR ROBERT CHILTERN (*deeply overcome by emotion, embraces her*): My wife! my wife! (*To* LORD GORING): Arthur, it seems that I am always to be in your debt.

LORD GORING: Oh dear no. Robert. Your debt is to Lady Chiltern, not to me!

SIR ROBERT CHILTERN: I owe you much. And now tell me what you were going to ask me just now as Lord Caversham came in.

LORD GORING: Robert, you are your sister's guardian, and I want your consent to my marriage with her. That is all.

LADY CHILTERN: Oh, I am so glad! I am so glad! (*Shakes hands with* LORD GORING.)

第 四 幕

〔罗伯特·奇尔顿爵士上。

罗伯特·奇尔顿爵士　格特鲁德，我把信的草稿写好了。我给你念念好吗？

奇尔顿夫人　让我看看。

〔罗伯特·奇尔顿爵士把信给了她。她看过，随后用力把它撕掉了。

罗伯特·奇尔顿爵士　你这是干什么？

奇尔顿夫人　一个男人的生命价值比一个女人的更大。男人的生命释放量更大，范围更广阔，志向更远大。我们女人的生命在感情的曲线里转弯子。依附在男人生命的进程的智力线上。我刚刚听戈林子爵说了这番话，还有许多别的内容。为了你，我不能把你的生命毁了，也不能看着你为我牺牲而毁了你的生命，那是一种无谓的牺牲！

罗伯特·奇尔顿爵士　格特鲁德！格特鲁德！

奇尔顿夫人　你可以忘记。男人容易忘记。而我应该原谅。这正是女人对这个世界的帮助。我现在明白这点了。

罗伯特·奇尔顿爵士　（深深地动了情，把她搂在怀里）我的妻子！我的妻子！（对戈林子爵）亚瑟，看样子我这辈子总是欠你的情了。

戈林子爵　哦，亲爱的，不会，罗伯特。你只欠奇尔顿夫人的，不会欠我的！

罗伯特·奇尔顿爵士　我该你的太多了。现在说说吧，卡弗沙姆伯爵进来之前你正打算跟我说什么来着。

戈林子爵　罗伯特，你是你妹妹的监护人，我想要你同意我和她的婚姻。就是这个。

奇尔顿夫人　哦，我一百个赞成！我一百个赞成！（和戈林子爵握手道贺。）

LORD GORING: Thank you, Lady Chiltern.

SIR ROBERT CHILTERN (*with a troubled look*): My sister to be your wife?

LORD GORING: Yes.

SIR ROBERT CHILTERN (*speaking with great firmness*): Arthur, I am very sorry, but the thing is quite out of the question. I have to think of Mabel's future happiness. And I don't think her happiness would be safe in your hands. And I cannot have her sacrificed!

LORD GORING: Sacrificed!

SIR ROBERT CHILTERN: Yes, utterly sacrificed. Loveless marriages are horrible. But there is one thing worse than an absolutely loveless marriage. A marriage in which there is love, but on one side only; faith, but on one side only; devotion, but on one side only and in which of the two hearts one is sure to be broken.

LORD GORING: But I love Mabel. No other woman has any place in my life.

LADY CHILTERN: Robert, if they love each other, why should they not be married?

SIR ROBERT CHILTERN: Arthur cannot bring Mabel the love that she deserves.

LORD GORING: What reason have you for saying that?

SIR ROBERT CHILTERN (*after a pause*): Do you really require me to tell you?

LORD GORING: Certainly I do.

SIR ROBERT CHILTERN: As you choose. When I called on you yesterday evening I found Mrs. Cheveley concealed in your rooms. It was between ten and eleven o'clock at night. I do not wish to say anything more. Your relations with Mrs. Cheveley have, as I said to you

第 四 幕

戈林子爵　谢谢你,奇尔顿夫人。

罗伯特·奇尔顿爵士　(脸上表情复杂)我的妹妹给你做妻子?

戈林子爵　是的。

罗伯特·奇尔顿爵士　(用了很大决心)阿瑟,我很遗憾,这件事根本不行啊。我得为梅布尔以后的幸福着想。我认为他的幸福掌握在你的手里不保险啊。我可不能眼看着她当牺牲品!

戈林子爵　牺牲品?

罗伯特·奇尔顿爵士　是的,纯粹的牺牲品。没有爱情的婚姻是非常可怕的。可是有的事情比完全没有爱情的婚姻还可怕。那就是婚姻里虽有爱情,却只是单方面的;有忠诚,也只是单方面的;献身虽有,还只是单方面的,两颗心却非有一颗破碎不可。

戈林子爵　可是我爱梅布尔啊。我生活里没有第二个女人。

奇尔顿夫人　罗伯特,如果他们两个彼此相爱,那他们为什么不可以结婚呢?

罗伯特·奇尔顿爵士　亚瑟不能给梅布尔应有的爱情。

戈林子爵　你有什么理由这样讲话?

罗伯特·奇尔顿爵士　(稍停)你真的要我坦率相告吗?

戈林子爵　那还用说。

罗伯特·奇尔顿爵士　愿意就好。我昨天晚上去拜访你,发现谢弗利太太藏在你的房间里。那时已经夜里十点多快十一点了。我不想多说什么了。正像昨天晚上我跟你讲过的,你和谢弗利太太的关系不关我任何事。

237

last night, nothing whatsoever to do with me. I know you were engaged to be married to her once. The fascination she exercised over you then seems to have returned. You spoke to me last night of her as of a woman pure and stainless, a woman whom you respected and honoured. That may be so. But I cannot give my sister's life into your hands. It would be wrong of me. It would be unjust, infamously unjust to her.

  LORD GORING: I have nothing more to say.

  LADY CHILTERN: Robert, it was not Mrs. Cheveley whom Lord Goring expected last night.

  SIR ROBERT CHILTERN: Not Mrs. Cheveley! Who was it then?

  LORD GORING: Lady Chiltern.

  LADY CHILTERN: It was your own wife. Robert, yesterday afternoon Lord Goring told me that if ever I was in trouble I could come to him for help, as he was our oldest and best friend. Later on, after that terrible scene in this room, I wrote to him telling him that I trusted him, that I had need of him, that I was coming to him for help and advice. (SIR ROBERT CHILTERN *takes the letter out of his pocket*.) Yes, that letter. I didn't go to Lord Goring's, after all. I felt that it is from ourselves alone that help can come. Pride made me think that. Mrs. Cheveley went. She stole my letter and sent it anonymously to you this morning, that you should think .... Oh! Robert, I cannot tell you what she wished you to think ....

  SIR ROBERT CHILTERN: What! Had I fallen so low in your eyes that you thought that even for a moment I could have doubted your goodness? Gertrude, Gertrude, you are to me the white image of all good things, and sin can never touch you. Arthur, you can go to Mabel, and

第 四 幕

我知道你和她曾经订下过婚约。她昨天晚上对你表示出来的那种过分的热情,似乎旧情复燃了。你昨天晚上跟我说她是个纯洁而无瑕的女人,一个你尊敬和爱戴的女人。情况也许如此。可是我不能把我妹妹的生活交在你的手里。那样我会犯下大错。那样对她也不公正,可耻地不公正。

戈林子爵　我没有更多话可说。

奇尔顿夫人　罗伯特,戈林子爵昨天晚上等的人不是谢弗利太太。

罗伯特·奇尔顿爵士　不是谢弗利太太!那么是谁呢?

戈林子爵　奇尔顿夫人。

奇尔顿夫人　就是你自己的妻子。罗伯特,昨天下午戈林子爵告诉我,我要是有了麻烦,尽管找他去请求帮助,因为他是我们最老的朋友,最好的朋友。后来,在这间屋子里发生了那可怕的一幕,我给他写信说我信任他,我需要他,我要去找他请求帮助,出个主意。(罗伯特·奇尔顿爵士从口袋里掏出信来。)是的,就是这封信。后来我终于没有去找戈林子爵。我觉得帮助只能来自我们自己。自尊让我想到了这点。谢弗利太太却去了。她偷了我的信,今天早上匿名寄给了你,你还以为……噢!罗伯特,我没法告诉你她希望你怎么想……

罗伯特·奇尔顿爵士　天哪!我在你的眼里竟然这样腌臜,你以为我哪怕一瞬间会想到你的贞洁吗?格特鲁德,格特鲁德,你在我眼里是万物中的一尊洁白形象,什么罪孽都沾染不了你。亚瑟,你可以去见梅布尔了,

239

you have my best wishes! Oh! stop a moment. There is no name at the beginning of this letter. The brilliant Mrs. Cheveley does not seem to have noticed that. There should be a name.

LADY CHILTERN: Let me write yours. It is you I trust and need. You and none else.

LORD GORING: Well, really, Lady Chiltern, I think I should have back my own letter.

LADY CHILTERN (*smiling*): No; you shall have Mabel. (*Takes the letter and writes her husband's name on it.*)

LORD GORING: Well, I hope she hasn't changed her mind. It's nearly twenty minutes since I saw her last.

Enter MABEL CHILTERN *and* LORD CAVERSHAM.

MABEL CHILTERN: Lord Goring, I think your father's conversation much more improving than yours. I am only going to talk to Lord Caversham in the future, and always under the usual palm tree.

LORD GORING: Darling! (*Kisses her.*)

LORD CAVERSHAM (*considerably taken aback*): What does this mean, sir? You don't mean to say that this charming, clever young lady has been so foolish as to accept you?

LORD GORING: Certainly, father! And Chiltern's been wise enough to accept the seat in the Cabinet.

LORD CAVERSHAM: I am very glad to hear that, Chiltern.... I congratulate you, sir. If the country doesn't go to the dogs or the Radicals, we shall have you Prime Minister, some day.

Enter MASON.

MASON: Luncheon is on the table, my Lady! (MASON *goes out.*)

第 四 幕

祝你万事如意！噢！等一会儿。这封信的开头没有名字。精明的谢弗利太太好像没有发现这点。这上面应该有个名字。

奇尔顿夫人　让我把你的名字写上边吧。我信任的是你，需要的是你。只有你，没有别人。

戈林子爵　噢，真的，奇尔顿夫人，我认为我应该把我的信要回来。

奇尔顿夫人　(微笑)不。你有了梅布尔了。(拿过信，写上她丈夫的名字。)

戈林子爵　嗨，但愿她没有改变主意啊。我已经快二十分钟没有看见她了。

〔梅布尔·奇尔顿和卡弗沙姆伯爵上。

梅布尔·奇尔顿　戈林子爵，我认为你父亲的谈话远比你的让人受益。以后我只跟卡弗沙姆伯爵谈话就成了，就一直在那棵老芭蕉树下。

戈林子爵　亲爱的！(吻她。)

卡弗沙姆伯爵　(大吃一惊)这叫怎么回事，先生？你这种举动难道真的是说，这个可爱聪明的小姑娘傻得不能再傻，糊糊涂涂地就接受了你的求婚吗？

戈林子爵　就是这么回事，老爸！而且奇尔顿很明智地接受了内阁的那个空位。

卡弗沙姆伯爵　这消息让人特别高兴，奇尔顿……我祝贺你，先生。如果这个国家没有垮台或者落入激进派手中，那我们总有一天要选你当首相。

〔梅森上。

梅森　午餐已上餐桌，夫人！(梅森下。)

241

MABEL CHILTERN: You'll stop to luncheon, Lord Caversham, won't you?

LORD CAVERSHAM: With pleasure, and I'll drive you down to Downing Street afterwards, Chiltern. You have a great future before you, a great future. Wish I could say the same for you, sir. (*To* LORD GORING): But your career will have to be entirely domestic.

LORD GORING: Yes, father, I prefer it domestic.

LORD CAVERSHAM: And If you don't make this young lady an ideal husband, I'll cut you off with a shilling.

MABEL CHILTERN: An ideal husband! Oh, I don't think I should like that. It sounds like something in the next world.

LORD CAVERSHAM: What do you want him to be then, dear?

MABEL CHILTERN: He can be what he chooses. All I want is to be...to be...oh! a real wife to him.

LORD CAVERSHAM: Upon my word, there is a good deal of common sense in that, Lady Chiltern.

They all go out except SIR ROBERT CHILTERN. *He sinks into a chair, wrapt in thought. After a little time* LADY CHILTERN *returns to look for him.*

LADY CHILTERN (*leaning over the back of the chair*): Aren't you coming in, Robert?

SIR ROBERT CHILTERN (*taking her hand*): Gertrude, is it love you feel for me, or is it pity merely?

LADY CHILTERN (*kisses him*): It is love, Robert. Love, and only love. For both of us a new life is beginning.

CURTAIN

第 四 幕

梅布尔·奇尔顿　你留下来用午餐好吧,卡弗沙姆伯爵?

卡弗沙姆伯爵　好啊好啊,然后我用马车把你送到唐宁街,奇尔顿。你的前途无量,前途无量啊。(对戈林子爵)但愿我也能跟你说这样的话,先生。可是你的生涯以后就全窝在家里了。

戈林子爵　是的,老爸,我更愿意窝在家里。

卡弗沙姆伯爵　如果你不给这位年轻姑娘做一个理想丈夫,那我就剥夺了你的继承权。

梅布尔·奇尔顿　一个理想的丈夫!哦,我可不喜欢理想丈夫。那听起来像是另一个世界的东西。

卡弗沙姆伯爵　那你想让他成为什么丈夫,亲爱的?

梅布尔·奇尔顿　他喜欢成为什么随他去好了。我想要的只是……成为……噢!成为一个他名副其实的妻子。

卡弗沙姆伯爵　我的天,这话里说的全是常识呢,奇尔顿夫人。

〔他们全都离去,只有罗伯特·奇尔顿未动。随后他深坐进椅子里,陷入深思。过一会儿,奇尔顿夫人回来看他。

奇尔顿夫人　(倚在椅子背上)你不去用餐吗,罗伯特?

罗伯特·奇尔顿爵士　(拉住她的手)格特鲁德,你这样对我是出于爱还只是同情?

奇尔顿夫人　(吻他)是爱,罗伯特。爱,只有爱。因为我们两个人的新生活开始了。

幕　落

名著名译英汉对照读本

《哈姆莱特》
〔英〕莎士比亚 著　朱生豪 译

《黑暗的心》
〔英〕康拉德 著　黄雨石 译

《简·爱》
〔英〕夏洛特·勃朗特 著　吴钧燮 译

《凯撒和克莉奥佩特拉》
〔英〕萧伯纳 著　杨宪益 译

《理想丈夫》
〔英〕王尔德 著　文心 译

《马克·吐温短篇小说选》
〔美〕马克·吐温 著　叶冬心 译

《名利场》
〔英〕萨克雷 著　杨必 译

《欧·亨利短篇小说选》
〔美〕欧·亨利 著　王永年 译

《一间自己的房间》
〔英〕弗吉尼亚·吴尔夫 著　贾辉丰 译

《伊坦·弗洛美》
〔美〕伊迪丝·华顿 著　吕叔湘 译

A Series of Fine Translation of Classics

HAMLET
William Shakespeare

HEART OF DARKNESS
Joseph Conrad

JANE EYRE
Charlotte Brontë

CAESAR AND CLEOPATRA
Benard Shaw

AN IDEAL HUSBAND
Oscar Wilde

SELECTED SHORT STORIES OF MARK TWAIN
Mark Twain

VANITY FAIR
William Thackeray

SELECTED SHORT STORIES OF O. HENRY
O. Henry

A ROOM OF ONE'S OWN
Virginia Woolf

ETHAN FROME
Edith Wharton